Beyond the Desktop

Computers and People Series

Edited by

B.R. GAINES and A. MONK

Monographs

Communicating with Microcomputers. An introduction to the technology of man–computer communication, *Ian H. Witten* 1980
The Computer in Experimental Psychology, *R. Bird* 1981
Principles of Computer Speech, *I.H. Witten* 1982
Cognitive Psychology of Planning, *J-M. Hoc* 1988
Formal Methods for Interactive Systems, *A. Dix* 1991
Human Reliability Analysis: Context and Control, *E. Hollnagel* 1993

Edited Works

Computing Skills and the User Interface, *M.J. Coombs and J.L. Alty (eds)* 1981
Fuzzy Reasoning and Its Applications, *E.H. Mamdani and B.R. Gaines (eds)* 1981
Intelligent Tutoring Systems, *D. Sleeman and J.S. Brown (eds)* 1982 (1986 paperback)
Designing for Human–Computer Communication, *M.E. Sime and M.J. Coombs (eds)* 1983
The Psychology of Computer Use, *T.R.G. Green, S.J. Payne and G.C. van der Veer (eds)* 1983
Fundamentals of Human–Computer Interaction, *A. Monk (ed)* 1984, 1985
Working with Computers: Theory versus Outcome, *G.C. van der Veer, T.R.G. Green, J-M. Hoc and D. Murray (eds)* 1988
Cognitive Engineering in Complex Dynamic Worlds, *E. Hollnagel, G. Mancini and D.D. Woods (eds)* 1988
Computers and Conversation, *P. Luff, N. Gilbert and D. Frohlich (eds)* 1990
Adaptive User Interfaces, *D. Browne, P. Totterdell and M. Norman (eds)* 1990
Human–Computer Interaction and Complex Systems, *G.R.S. Weir and J.L. Alty (eds)* 1991
Computer-supported Cooperative Work and Groupware, *Saul Greenberg (ed)* 1991
The Separable User Interface, *E.A. Edmonds (ed)* 1992
Requirements Engineering: Social and Technical Issues, *M. Jirotka and J.A. Goguen (eds)* 1994
Perspectives on HCI: Diverse Approaches, *AF Monk and GN Gilbert (eds)* 1995
Information Superhighways: Multimedia Users and Futures, *SJ Emmott (ed)* 1995
Structure-based Editors and Environments, *G Szwillus and L Neal (eds)* 1996
Beyond the Desktop: Designing and Using Interaction Devices, *C Baber* 1997

Practical Texts

Effective Color Displays: Theory and Practice, *D. Travis* 1991
Understanding Interfaces: A Handbook of Human-Computer Dialogue, *M.W. Lansdale and T.R. Ormerod* 1994

EACE Publications
(Consulting Editors: *Y. WAERN and J-M. HOC*)

Cognitive Ergonomics, *P. Falzon (ed)* 1990
Psychology of Programming, *J-M. Hoc, T.R.G. Green, R. Samurcay and D. Gilmore (eds)* 1990

Beyond the Desktop

Designing and Using Interaction Devices

Christopher Baber

Lecturer in Industrial Ergonomics
School of Manufacturing and Mechanical Engineering
University of Birmingham

ACADEMIC PRESS
Harcourt Brace & Company, Publishers
San Diego   London   Boston
New York   Sydney   Tokyo   Toronto

Academic Press, Inc.
525 B Street, Suite 1900, San Diego, California 92101–4495, USA

Academic Press Limited
24–28 Oval Road, London NW1 7DX, UK

ISBN 0–12–069550–2

Library of Congress Cataloging-in-Publication Data

A catalogue record for this book is available from the British Library

Typeset by J&L Composition Ltd, Filey, North Yorkshire
Printed in Great Britain by the University Press, Cambridge

97 98 99 0 01 02 EB 9 8 7 6 5 4 3 2 1

Table of Contents

Preface xi

1. Introduction 1
    1.1   Introduction.. 1
    1.2   Interaction devices not input devices 2
    1.3   Developments in human–computer interaction................ 4
    1.4   Ways of seeing interaction devices.. 6
    1.5   On the use of tools 8
    1.6   Towards a theory of tool use.. 10
    1.7   The task–artifact cycle.. 13
    1.8   Conclusions... 16
    1.9   Key points for practitioners 16
    1.10   Key points for researchers 17
    1.11   Chapter overviews.. 17

Part I   Interaction Devices

2. Keyboards.. 25
    2.1   Introduction.. 25
    2.2   Alternatives to QWERTY 31
    2.3   Standards for keyboard design 35
    2.4   Other forms of keys... 37
    2.5   Other types of keyboard... 40
    2.6   Conclusions... 43
    2.7   Key points for practitioners 45
    2.8   Key points for researchers 46

3. Pointing devices... 47
    3.1   Introduction.. 47
    3.2   Indirect pointing devices 47
    3.3   Direct pointing devices.. 53
    3.4   Virtual controls.. 56
    3.5   Device comparisons 57
    3.6   Conclusions... 62
    3.7   Key points for practitioners 63
    3.8   Key points for researchers 63

4. Alternative interaction devices... 64
   4.1   Introduction.. 64
   4.2   Interaction devices for portable computers..................... 65
   4.3   Gesture at the human–computer interface....................... 66
   4.4   Beyond pointing devices... 68
   4.5   Pen-based computing... 72
   4.6   Speech-based computing... 77
   4.7   Conclusions.. 81
   4.8   Key points for practitioners.. 82
   4.9   Key points for researchers... 82

5. Classifying devices.. 83
   5.1   Introduction.. 83
   5.2   Defining generic actions.. 83
   5.3   Generic actions and widget-level design......................... 91
   5.4   Operational characteristics of interaction devices........ 92
   5.5   Performance-shaping factors.. 94
   5.6   Conclusions.. 103
   5.7   Key points for practitioners.. 104
   5.8   Key points for researchers... 104

Part II   Using Interaction Devices

6. Modeling device use... 107
   6.1   Introduction.. 107
   6.2   Modeling in HCI research.. 108
   6.3   Three-state device description... 109
   6.4   The keystroke level model.. 114
   6.5   Network models... 120
   6.6   Cognitive models.. 126
   6.7   Predicting human error... 132
   6.8   Conclusions.. 134
   6.9   Key points for practitioners.. 135
   6.10   Key points for researchers... 135

7. Typing.. 136
   7.1   Introduction.. 136
   7.2   Basic elements of typing skills.. 137
   7.3   The timing of typing.. 138
   7.4   Typing considered as skilled behavior............................. 141
   7.5   Psychomotor skills and chord keyboards......................... 149
   7.6   Typing with limited keypads.. 149
   7.7   Conclusions.. 151
   7.8   Key points for practitioners.. 151
   7.9   Key points for researchers... 152

8. Writing and drawing 153
  8.1 Introduction 153
  8.2 Using writing instruments 154
  8.3 Planning and handwriting 158
  8.4 Planning and drawing 161
  8.5 Writing with pen-based computer systems 163
  8.6 Drawing with pen-based computer systems 164
  8.7 Computer-aided design 165
  8.8 Conclusions 168
  8.9 Key points for practitioners 169
  8.10 Key points for researchers 169

9. Pointing 170
  9.1 Introduction 170
  9.2 Direct manipulation 171
  9.3 Pointing 173
  9.4 Users' knowledge 175
  9.5 Pointing as a psychomotor skill 177
  9.6 Psychomotor skills research 183
  9.7 Interaction devices and psychomotor skills 188
  9.8 Conclusions 195
  9.9 Key points for practitioners 196
  9.10 Key points for researchers 196

10. Speaking 197
  10.1 Introduction 197
  10.2 Speech as sound 197
  10.3 Levels of control in speech production 200
  10.4 Dialogue 201
  10.5 Rules for interaction? 202
  10.6 Errors and speech recognition systems 206
  10.7 Conclusions 209
  10.8 Key points for practitioners 210
  10.9 Key points for researchers 211

Part 3 Further Topics

11. Devices for restricted environments 215
  11.1 Introduction 215
  11.2 Restrictions of movement 216
  11.3 The effects of environmental factors on performance ... 220
  11.4 Psychological restrictions 228
  11.5 Discussion 230
  11.6 Key points for practitioners 231
  11.7 Key points for researchers 231

12. Physical aspects of interaction device use 232
    12.1   Introduction... 232
    12.2   Musculoskeletal problems and office work.................... 233
    12.3   Work-related upper limb disorder 235
    12.4   Surveys of computer operators..................................... 235
    12.5   Keyboard-related problems... 240
    12.6   Mouse-related problems 243
    12.7   Problems associated with other devices........................ 245
    12.8   Conclusions.. 247
    12.9   Key points for practitioners 248
    12.10 Key points for researchers... 248

13. Interaction devices at work 249
    13.1   Introduction... 249
    13.2   Sociotechnical systems 256
    13.3   Organizational computing.. 260
    13.4   Conclusions.. 263
    13.5   Key points for practitioners 263
    13.6   Key points for researchers... 264

14. Multimodal human-computer interaction 265
    14.1   Introduction... 265
    14.2   Combining tasks... 266
    14.3   Combining speech with other activities........................ 268
    14.4   Multiple resource theory 271
    14.5   Conclusions.. 275
    14.6   Key points for practitioners 276
    14.7   Key points for researchers... 277

References 279

Index 305

"Strictly speaking, nothing is a tool unless during actual use. The essence of a tool, therefore, lies in something outside the tool itself. It is not in the head of the hammer, nor in the handle, nor in the combination of the two that the essence of mechanical characteristics exists, but in the recognition of its unity and in the forces directed through it in virtue of this recognition."

[Samuel Butler]

"One cannot understand a technology without having a functional understanding of how it is used. Furthermore, that understanding must incorporate a holistic view of the network of technologies and activities into which it fits, rather than treating the technological devices in isolation."

[Winograd and Flores]

For Sara and Megan

Preface

During the course of its development the computer has shrunk from the size of a bungalow to something which can be carried in a briefcase. While the most common manifestation of the computer is a machine which sits on the desk of your office at home or at work, it is clear that the technology is moving beyond this design and towards computers which are not only portable but can also be used in a range of settings which were previously beyond normal operating environments. As the nature of computers changes, so too does the nature of human interaction with them. Thus, as computers move beyond the desktop, they will encounter new environments and will require new forms of interaction.

In this book, interaction is considered to be essentially a physical process, e.g., hitting keys on a typewriter, speaking a command, moving a cursor, pointing in virtual space; each of these activities requires some physical expression in order to be performed. This view sits rather uncomfortably with the tradition of human–computer interaction research which is essentially grounded in cognitive psychology. However, in order to perform the physical activity, one must plan and prepare actions. In this book, it is argued that the design of the various devices which people use in their interaction with computers shape, constrain and otherwise influence this planning and preparation of action. Just as the field of human–computer interaction has witnessed a revolution in display design, so it is witnessing a revolution in the design of devices that people can use to enter data, draw pictures and otherwise interact with computers. This book is an attempt to define the state of this revolution. However, my concern is not merely with describing these devices; this can be performed in a chapter or two and is bound to become outdated in a short space of time. Rather, I am concerned with how people use contemporary devices, such as keyboards and mice, and how they will use the developing devices, such as speech and handwriting recognition systems. If we can gain an insight into the activities that people perform and the goals they are attempting to achieve when using computers, then we can move closer to the goal of 'human computing'.

A number of people have commented on drafts of this book during the course of its writing, and I am especially grateful to Neville Stanton, Jan

Noyes, Brian Mellor, Roger Gimson and Graham Johnson for their advice on what to change and their encouragement to proceed. Three anonymous referees commented helpfully on an early version of the manuscript, and I thank them for their marathon efforts. I would also like to thank Bob Harrison for the photographs in the book.

Birmingham
April, 1996

CHAPTER 1

Introduction

Abstract

Human–computer interaction (HCI) research should consider interaction devices (rather than input devices). The implications of this statement are threefold: (i) by considering input devices, physical activity is reduced to the end-product of cognition, i.e., "input" implies entering information. On the other hand, interaction is conventionally used to mean a dynamic process of communication; (ii) the contrast of interaction devices with input devices leads to the proposal that user activity with interaction devices ought to be considered as tool use; (iii) the use of tools implies goal-directed, purposeful behavior, which is grounded in work practice. Thus, rather than being the objects which one uses to perform the *real* job of using a computer, interaction devices are brought center stage as the tools through which HCI is mediated.

1.1 Introduction

Computer technology has developed at a breathtaking pace, no sooner has an item of technology become established than it is obsolete and replaced by faster or smarter items. Yet there are limits to the power and ability of computer systems. One of the limits which no amount of technological fixing can overcome is that of the human who is using the computer. No doubt the reader is familiar with the notion that humans are, computationally speaking, very limited information processors. People have a tendency to forget or to confuse information, or to exhibit other forms of "bias" in their reasoning (Evans, 1989). People can also make mistakes and commit "human error". However, human error needs to be seen in the wider context in which an action is performed or not performed (Reason, 1990). This wider context contains the work domain, the knowledge, skills and abilities of the individual and the technology which the individual uses.

For many years, ergonomics (or human factors) has been attending to the problems of designing technology for human use. Much of the earlier work sought to define the appropriate design of controls, and this work has reached a stage where it can be communicated in the form of guidelines (for example, Sanders and McCormick, 1992). While there are recognized guidelines for traditional controls there are fewer guidelines for computer-based controls. For instance, while it is possible to find guidelines pertaining to the placement and size of control knobs, there is little guidance on where to place a trackball or how it should be used to interact with software packages. In the absence of ready-to-hand human factors guidelines, design decisions may be based on other factors, such as available desk space (Baber, 1995). Furthermore, a great deal of thought and effort has been devoted to the design of visually displayed information, but less attention to the physical devices by which people can act upon that information (Buxton, 1986), i.e., while HCI can boast a number of books on display design (Brown, 1988; Wagner, 1988; Galitz, 1989; Foley et al., 1990), it has produced few books specifically on the subject of the devices which are used to control computers. It is proposed that, in order to develop human factors guidelines for the design of such devices, it is necessary to understand how people use them.

1.2 Interaction devices not input devices

Let us dispense with the term "input" device as an anachronism from a time when people only input data into computers. Rather let us think in terms of devices which allow people to interact with computers in a far richer manner. The discipline of human–computer interaction requires a shift in the way it views these devices, from devices as objects to devices in use. This requires researchers to consider interaction devices in their own right; now that interaction devices have grown legion, there is every reason to see their design and development as warranting special attention. The development of all manner of ingenious devices, from handwriting recognition to monitoring the electrical activity of the user's brain, requires an understanding of how people will use these devices and how one can optimize design for human use.

The argument presented so far might appear to call for a separation of controls from displays in computer systems. However, this is not what is intended; the aim is merely to put equal emphasis on the design and use of interaction devices as on other aspects of HCI. It is hoped that this book will not only help users and designers to identify common problems in device use, but also to suggest potential solutions in the design and modification of interaction devices for human use.

Given the wide range of interaction devices on the market, and the impetus for computers to be usable, consumers are prepared to shop around for computer technology, and yet people still seem happy to accept whatever interaction device comes packaged with their computer, usually the QWERTY keyboard and the mouse. Given the relative age of these devices, one might be forgiven for asking whether the computer industry has reached the zenith of interaction device design? In an industry with as notorious a pace of change as computing, one might have expected to see rapid developments of interaction devices; after all, when the mouse first appeared in the late 1960s (English et al., 1967), writers had already been discussing the use of lightpens (Sutherland, 1963), touchscreens (Johnson, 1967) and speech recognition (Devoe, 1967). Either the QWERTY keyboard and mouse combination represents the definitive form of interaction device, or other factors have influenced the choice of device.

With the rise in public concern over work-related upper-limb disorder and injury in computer-related work, people are becoming aware that using interaction devices may have an adverse effect on their well-being and health. Not only can this adverse affect take the form of physical stress and strain arising from overloading of particular muscle groupings, but can also relate to psychological stress and frustration, and to the impairment of performance.

One might assume that, given the infinite resourcefulness of humans, these are minor irritants which can be overcome. Humans can adapt to the demands made by the devices. In some cases, the adaptation may be a simple matter of slowing down performance, in other cases it might arise from the adoption of a potentially harmful posture, or from the over-use of particular muscle grouping which, given prolonged activity, could lead to musculoskeletal strain. It should also be clear that the peculiar demands made on users can lead to frustration, and that they can interfere with the fast, accurate performance of a particular task. For instance, in a hospital, the image from an ultrasound-scanner was being manipulated using cross-hairs and cursor which were used to select part of the scan for enlargement. The cursor was controlled by a joystick, much to the frustration of the midwife, who kept overshooting the point of interest. Eventually, the joystick was replaced by a trackball. The overshoot persisted.

This example, in which one interaction device was replaced by another, illustrates one response to these problems: to identify a specific symptom and attempt to treat that. One might ask why a trackball was chosen. The principal reason is space. The interaction device is used on a piece of equipment mounted on a trolley, and there is a limited amount of space for the device to be positioned. However, the interaction device (whether joystick or trackball) is positioned behind the screen, to the left of the trolley. Given a right-handed midwife, operating the interaction device implies a reach across the screen, thus blocking the image, or an operation from behind the screen. In either case, there is a chance of overshooting the object of interest. The consequence of this design was a piece of equipment which was fitted onto a trolley, had a screen with reasonably high resolution, but was frustrating to use and which led to lengthy periods of cursor manipulation. One could suggest a number of alternatives to this design, e.g., a lightpen or a touchscreen would not require the use of a separate device. The point of this example is that the principal difficulty lay in the match between interaction device and user requirements.

A number of writers have suggested that our current range of interaction devices limit people to a handful of actions, often to be performed in serial and often only using one hand (Buxton, 1986; Shneiderman, 1992; Jacob et al., 1993). There has been much effort to produce devices which are multifunctional, with little consideration given to how people will use them. A good example of this is a design for a 64-button mouse, i.e., a combined mouse and QWERTY keyboard. When new designs are proposed they often focus on specific aspects of device use rather than the full range of activity. However, as Whitefield (1986) points out, it is unlikely that we will manage to develop a single device which is suitable for all of the many different functions for which people use interaction devices.

1.3 Developments in human–computer interaction

In the late 1940s, "forecasters" were predicting (with their usual unerring accuracy), that by the end of the twentieth century, the computing requirements of the United States would be met by six computers; in 1990, there were an estimated 100 million personal computers in the industrialized world (Palfreyman and Swade, 1991). Rapid technological advances in computing since the 1960s have been made on a number of fronts.

Developments in hardware have led to the growth of new markets, with computers being introduced to users who were previously termed "naive", i.e., people unschooled in the complexities of computing. Not only are computers being increasingly used by people with limited knowledge of how computers work (which should not be viewed as a particular problem: after all, how many car drivers can explain in detail the mysteries of the four-stroke cycle?), but also by people with limited skill in what remains the principal means of communicating with the computer, i.e., typing (Smith, 1980). This has led to the goal of designing computers which can be easy to understand and to use. The last decade has seen a rapid development of the concept of the WIMP interface (Windows, Icons, Menus, Pointing device) as a means of enabling an ever greater number of people to use computers.

Early computers permitted only a very limited sequence of actions to be performed in order to input data. Often the "user" of the computer was not the person who wanted the data processed. One had to complete a set of cards, which were punched to produce a machine-readable code. The cards were passed on to the computing department, where they were fed into a computer, and the data processed. After processing, the results were passed back to the user. Being locked out of the main processing stage meant that the user had to wait until receiving the results before deciding whether the data and its analysis were correct.

Often any errors made during the preparation of the cards were not spotted until the processing had been completed; when things went wrong, there was little that the computer operator could do, and even less opportunity for the person who submitted the cards for processing. In the era of punched cards, the data were entered in batches and limited commands could be given concerning the manner in which the processing was to be performed. As the processing was discrete, it was possible to make interruptions at certain points. The computer gave minimal display of its status, operators often sought additional cues, such as the changes in sounds emitted by the machine. Rarely was this information communicated to the initiator of the processing. Thus, the computer did not permit direct interaction; for the user, contact was through an intermediary, for the operator contact was limited to certain points in the processing. With the advent of personal computers in the 1960s, however, the contact between user and computer began to become more direct: individuals could not only enter their own data, but also manipulate these data while they used the computer. This has produced many changes in the ways in which we think about and use computers, not the least of which is the demand for "real-time" interaction, with computers responding immediately to users' commands.

1.3.1 Implications for research and development

The developments in human–computer interaction outlined above can be seen to have several implications for research and development. By designing to capitalize upon humans' "natural" ways of performing tasks, it will be possible to produce computers which are highly efficient and easy to use. In order to define "natural" ways of performing tasks, it is necessary to turn to the human sciences. However, questions that engineers and designers would ask of the human sciences have not been answered (Underwood, 1980), because they require a change in the subject matter of these sciences (Tatham, 1992). Furthermore, advances in computer intelligence have led to an interest in producing a form of interaction, which will flow as smoothly as conversation between people (of course, it is a moot point as to whether human conversation can be described as "smooth"). Finally, computer capabilities have advanced rapidly, usually technology-driven, but people still have difficulty with computers. Thus, HCI is faced with a human bottleneck which it needs to overcome in order to develop further.

1.4   Ways of seeing interaction devices

One can propose several perspectives on the study of interaction devices. From the perspective of software engineering, an interaction device might be used to enter variables into the software, i.e., the device is viewed primarily as a means of "editing" code in real time. For a cognitive psychologist, an interaction device might be a transducer, which allows a user's goal to be translated into some change in the state of the computer, i.e., HCI involves first and foremost cognitive activity, which then leads to physical action using an interaction device. For an ergonomist, an interaction device might be an object which requires specific physical activities to operate and which requires users to adopt a specific posture during operation. Each perspective can be said to address a particular aspect of interaction devices, but none of these perspectives provide a complete picture of how people use interaction devices.

There are several approaches to the research of interaction devices. Each approach emphasizes a different agenda. Researchers can compare the relative performance of devices on a set of tasks under controlled, experimental conditions. The results of such studies, and the problems associated with this approach, feature in Chapters 2, 3 and 4. An alternative approach involves the development of a means of classifying interaction devices, in terms of either device characteristics or usage. This approach is considered in Chapter 5. It is also possible to consider device use in terms of user performance, and several predictive models have been developed to this end. These are discussed in Chapter 6.

The way in which interaction devices are designed and studied is influenced by the ways in which researchers and practitioners see these devices, i.e., the way in which the devices are described, the way in which the performance of the devices is calibrated, measured and compared. If there are limitations in the design and use of interaction devices, it might be possible to trace these problems to the ways in which interaction devices are seen by the HCI community.

The design of the majority of personal computers suggests that HCI is tied to the idea of a computer situated in a workstation, with a single user who is interacting with a single application using, if not a single interaction device, then at least only two interaction devices. HCI research has developed, both in scope and in knowledge, over the past decade, to such an extent that there are numerous multi-person, multi-site applications. However, there is still a tendency to consider much of HCI as the study of one person doing one thing to one computer. Kelley (1984) observes that the concept of a "workstation" appears to owe a debt to the term "workbench". Both concepts imply a location at which work is performed, and that this work is characterized by repetitive activity, performed from the seated position. From this point of view, computer workstations are bound to involve a seated "operator", working in one place. Indeed, the HCI community seems to be governed by the "desktop metaphor" which takes the notion of workstation as given, and uses the idea of the surface of a desk as a principle for design. Naturally, we have moved beyond the literal interpretation of this metaphor but its continued usage ought to be seen as a potential problem.

Should HCI move away from the desktop metaphor? Certainly the rise in portable computing technology, from laptops to notepads to palmtops, suggests that the face of computing is changing dramatically, and the ever-increasing role of computers in all manner of domains, from automobiles to helicopters to intensive care units, means that we need to refine the way in which people interact with computers. Attempts to cram a number of interaction devices onto one computer, in the quest for multimodal HCI, further suggests a move away from the "workstation". Negroponte (1989) has proposed that, in the near future, computers will effectively exist as "a society of objects which compute" (p. 110). By this he means that most of the artifacts of our homes, vehicles and workplaces will possess computing capabilities. He does, however, venture a description of the "computer" as a hand-held device, about the size of a magazine and made of flexible material with a very high resolution display. The user would interact with this device using a stylus, although Negroponte (1989) also discusses the pros and cons of speech-based interaction with computers. Negroponte's ideas have, of course, been taken further by the ongoing work at MIT's "MediaLab", where societies of objects which compute are being developed for use in all manner of applications. Much of this work appears to be in an embryonic form at present. However, one of the implications of this work for the future computing systems is simply the removal of interaction devices. The interaction between user and computer becomes less a direct link between an intelligent human and a dumb computer than an alliance of two intelligent entities, with the computer receiving and handling information from other computers. While the work could clearly reduce the need for people to interact with computers for data-entry and other "house-keeping" tasks, the need for devices to allow direct, uncomplicated interaction between people and computers will become more important, not less important.

In a recent position paper outlining a research agenda for interaction devices, Jacob et al. (1993) argue that research will be directed towards the classification of existing interaction devices and the development of "novel" devices; they cite the following as possibilities: speech, eye tracking, gesture recognition, virtual interaction devices, monitoring of user attitude and state, and direct contact with objects. In addition to this, they propose an extension of the range of activities, such as 3D pointing and manipulation of multidimensional data, and work towards increasing the range of the potential users of computers. One can add a human-factors requirement to this list: a need to understand how people use interaction devices (both cognitively and physically), in order to develop and improve devices. One way in which this issue can be approached is through consideration of the use of tools.

1.5 On the use of tools

One of the principal themes of this book is that interaction devices have a significant impact on what people do with computers, in that they represent the tools through which interaction is conducted. Tools often have a dual meaning for humans, depending on the relationship between tools and people. On the one hand, they exist as objects which can be defined and recognized. On the other hand, they exist in relation to their use by humans, i.e., not as the objects which are acted upon but as objects which mediate activity. This latter point can be illustrated by considering the use of a hammer. We can focus on concrete manifestations of the concept of a hammer as an object, but the activity of hammering requires us to focus on the object to be hammered. Indeed, we need not use a hammer for hammering, but can use a piece of wood or a shoe. This suggests some "knowledge" of the activity which can exist independently of the tool. While there might be a range of hammers which can be used by a skilled craft worker, it is probable that many of these have specific uses, and the worker will select a hammer for a job on the basis of its weight and balance. Thus, even in the definition of a tool, a skilled craft worker will consider the role of that tool in the performance of a specific activity.

When we watch a blacksmith hammering a piece of metal into a C-scroll, for instance, we are struck by the rhythm of the action. The smith leans over the anvil, one foot slightly in front of the other, knees bent, and swings the hammer from shoulder height. When not striking the metal, the smith continues hammering the anvil. The purpose of this action is to check the balance of the hammer in the smith's hand. Furthermore, the style of hammering will vary in terms of the type of metal being worked and the final design being made, e.g., in terms of the pace and force of striking the metal, the ratio of blows on the metal to those on the anvil etc. Therefore, in order to understand either the selection of the most appropriate tool, or the optimal design of a tool, it is necessary to consider the tool in its relation to work activity.

Following this we might next ask, should one consider the work activity of a skilled or novice person in this context? Retaining our example of blacksmiths, novice smiths might stand upright and clear of the metal they are forming. This means that they have further to move the hammer (leading to greater fatigue), that the hammer strike will occur below maximal force with less precision (requiring more effort to shape the metal and so leading to more fatigue), that the coordination and grip of the hammer will be difficult to control (leading to a great deal of play in its handling, and to less accuracy in striking the metal). From this perspective, one might wish to design a hammer which is lighter, in order to make movement less tiring, which has a different center of gravity and a larger head to maximize the force that is employed. However, this would be a very different design to that suited to the skilled blacksmith. One could argue that the simplest solution to the problem would be to ensure that the novice blacksmith was properly trained in the use of the tools. However, when considering HCI, the current fashion seems to be to minimize training by making products "usable". In this respect, training might not be an option.

It is possible to apply the points made in the preceding discussion to the design and study of interaction devices. A tool-use metaphor will view HCI in terms of the use of a tool to achieve goals. While some writers have questioned the utility of the metaphor (Kammersgard, 1990), it has been growing in popularity in recent years, not least as a result of the "Kittel House Manifesto" of Carroll (1991). The application of the tool-use metaphor in this book is as follows. The physical appearance of an interaction device can lead to users' interpreting a device in terms of permissible actions. This implies that human–computer interaction is task-specific, with tools serving to mediate human activity. The interaction occurs in "real time", with performance being shaped by several types of feedback, ranging from kinesthetic information relating to limb movement, to information presented to the user which requires some form of translation and interpretation. From the argument presented thus far, my focus is on the motor aspect of human activity. As Shaffer (1993) notes, cognitive psychology often has limited use for physical activity; at an extreme position, physical activity is seen simply as the end-product of cognitive processes. However, a great deal of the time and effort involved in interacting with computers involves the user engaging in physical activity. Furthermore, this activity can be considered to arise from, and influence, cognitive activity. This means that to see it simply as the end-product of cognitive activity could lead to the omission of significant aspects of behavior. Thus, a theory of tool use in HCI would require a combination of physical and cognitive behavior. In order to expand upon these ideas, the following section outlines the basis for a theory of tool use, with reference to the use of interaction devices.

1.6   Towards a theory of tool use

In order to consider interaction devices, one needs to think of the interaction between people and computers not simply in terms of information processing but in terms of action. This allows us to ask what a theory of tool use ought to contain.

Physical actions are performed with a purpose and a goal in mind. This notion can be seen as the basis for the influential work of Miller et al. (1960), specifically in terms of their proposal that activity is planned before it commences, and then monitored and evaluated during its course. This may strike the reader as self-evident, but as a growing number of writers have pointed out in recent years (e.g., Suchman, 1987; Lave, 1988; Hoc, 1988), there is a tendency for cognitive psychology to marginalize the issues of goal and purpose in human action, or at least to subsume these under the general heading of knowledge use or information processing. The problem for the information processing approach is that it has difficulty in dealing with the fluidity of human activity, and with the recursions, twists and loops which link plans to action (Hayes-Roth and Hayes-Roth, 1979). As Lave (1988) points out, the type of cognitive activity that people perform in everyday tasks (and we ought to include work activity under this heading), will involve not simply the processing of information but also responses to other people and to the environment and setting of the activity.

If we are to have a theory of tool use it should be able to deal with the intertwining of cognitive and physical activity within specific work domains (see Chapter 13). It is necessary to include work domains in a discussion of HCI for the simple reasons that work settings tend to dictate, or at least have a strong bearing upon, the goals of computer users. Furthermore, the problems people report when using computers are not simply a response to the computer itself but arise from a computer being used for a particular work activity in a specific work domain.

The approach proposed here can be considered in terms of a tradition in cognitive psychology stemming from the work of Miller et al. (1960), and from Neisser's (1976) call for the introduction of "ecological validity" into psychological research, to contemporary discussions of everyday cognition (Lave, 1988; Rogoff and Lave, 1988), coupled with the wealth of research on the nature of skilled performance (Holding, 1989; Ericsson and Smith, 1991). Within this paradigm, action can be defined as purposeful, goal-directed behavior. Frese and Sabini (1985) argue that work will involve an individual pursuing a defined goal, and will generally require a plan of action which is either defined by the individual or provided by the organization in which the individual works.

Miller et al. (1960) argue that any action needs a plan to guide it, and that the plan will draw upon a person's current level of knowledge about the environment in which they are acting and their recall of previous, similar actions. This requires a feedback mechanism which can match the current system state against a desired state. In Miller et al. (1960), the feedback mechanism operated through the stages shown in Figure 1.1. One could expand the stages beyond the level of higher-order goals, to consider the impact of social, cultural and organizational constraints and requirements on human behavior, but for the purposes of the present discussion we will maintain a three-level hierarchy (of goal, plan, action). A notion of hierarchical coordination and control is central to a number of psychomotor skills theories which will be considered in subsequent chapters to account for such tasks as typing, speaking, drawing, writing and "pointing" in HCI.

Cognitive psychologists often divide knowledge into two broad categories: declarative and procedural knowledge (Anderson, 1990). Declarative knowledge can be defined as that aspect of knowledge which can be put into words (or some other code, such as a mathematical equation) and which can be learned from text or verbal instruction. Procedural knowledge, on the other hand, can be defined as that aspect of knowledge which involves performance of a task, such as changing gear in a car. This type of knowledge is often difficult to put into words and is generally acquired through practice of the particular task. There will be some separation in people's knowledge of how to perform a specific task and how to use a specific device. For instance, while I might be a proficient user of a mouse to move a cursor, I might need to spend some time learning how to perform the same task with a trackball. Studies reported by Allard and Starkes (1991) illustrate the relationship between performance on a video-game and users' experience in using a particular interaction device. The results of these studies suggest that it is necessary to know both the required control activity and the consequences of performing actions with a particular device; when faced with a new interaction device the player needs to learn a new set of actions rather than relearn the required activity. This implies that it is possible to split knowing and doing a skill into independent sources of information, i.e., that skilled performance is characterized not simply by

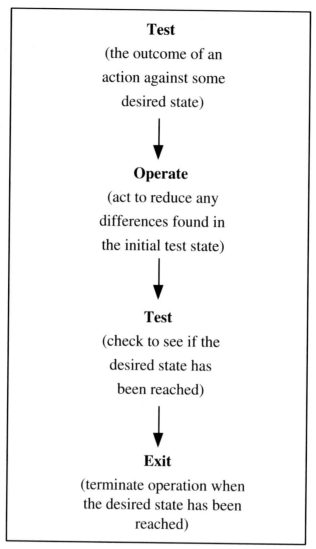

Test

(the outcome of an
action against some
desired state)

Operate

(act to reduce any
differences found in
the initial test state)

Test

(check to see if the
desired state has
been reached)

Exit

(terminate operation when
the desired state has been
reached)

Figure 1.1   Stages in TOTE description of performance

an ability to use a particular interaction device, but by an ability to use it appropriately for a given range of tasks.

People mediate their activity by tool use. This notion stems from the work of Vygotsky (1978), who argued that tools are the means by which people master nature. As discussed above, it is felt that contemporary HCI tends to view interaction devices as objects rather than in terms of how they mediate human action. In order to perform a task, a person will select a tool. This need not be a tool specifically designed for the performance of that task, so much as an object deemed appropriate for the performance of that task in that context. Interestingly enough, a characteristic of skilled tool use appears to be the selection of appropriate tools prior to task performance. Indeed, selection and changing of tools seems to mark the boundaries between sets of activities in task performance for skilled craftspeople (Baber et al., 1995). Not only will task objectives influence tool selection, but also tool design will influence task performance. For instance, the way in which a handle is designed will impact on the way in which it is held, which in turn influences the range of actions which can be performed using that tool.

In summary, it is important to consider interaction devices in use by people, rather than as engineered objects, to define the context in which interaction devices are used, and to consider how interaction devices are used for specific tasks by specific people. Focusing on the processes of activity, it is possible to hypothesize certain contextual factors which will influence performance. This relationship is illustrated by Figure 1.2.

The activities in Figure 1.2 are described in terms of a flow from top to bottom. However, each of the activities also feeds back to the previous activity. This allows activity to be checked and to influence subsequent task objectives. The term "praxis" in the second column is taken to mean "work practices" (Bannon and Bødker, 1991), i.e., ways of working which are socially constructed and which, consequently, are shared by groups of people and vary across organizations. Thus, there are a number of factors which can be identified which will have an influence on how activity is performed. In the following section, the relationship between device design and user performance will be considered in terms of the notion of task–artifact cycle.

1.7   The task–artifact cycle

The notion of a "task–artifact cycle" has been proposed by Carroll et al. (1991) to explain the relationship between an artifact's design and its use. This is illustrated by Figure 1.3, and suggests that not only will the design of an artifact be influenced by user requirements, but that user requirements can be shaped by the design of the artifact. For instance, while a piece of software may permit users to write business letters, the provision of additional features in word-processing packages will strongly influence how the letter-writing task is approached (e.g., by the use of proforma layouts and standard paragraphs), which might produce different tasks to those encountered when writing letters on, say, a typewriter.

Each artifact contains within its design a "theory" of human action. In other words, an artifact will be designed to be the way that it is in order to

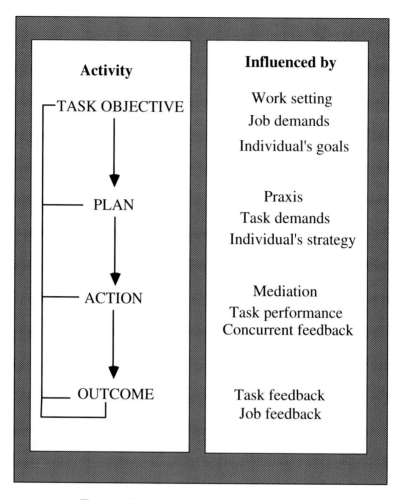

Figure 1.2 The influence of context on activity

support a specific range of human activities. However, manufacture is concerned with solving the problems of actually making the artifact. This means that some of the engineering and manufacturing solutions may take precedence over user requirements. Therefore, artifacts embody "partial" theories of human action. The actions which the artifact supports will not necessarily be those which would have been included in a detailed specification of user requirements, but will involve the user adapting to the product. A consequence of this view is that artifacts are manufactured for human adaptation. The design of an artifact will permit certain ranges of action, perhaps by limiting the way in which the artifact can be held and manipulated. The design of the artifact invites, and requires, people to conceptualize its use in order to plan their actions and set goals.

The notion of mediation would suggest that the design of the artifact will suggest certain ways of using the device (possibly in addition to those envisaged by the designer). For instance, when using a word-processing package, the ability to use predefined layouts means that one need not spend time in preparing the layout of a document, but could simply type into a selected layout. This latter point is illustrated by Figure 1.3 and could be seen as a potentially beneficial, albeit serendipitous, aspect of design.

It has been proposed that artifacts embody theories of human action. In order to explore this notion, consider the design of the humble mouse. What theory of human action can mice be said to contain? The answer would appear to be that their "theory" comprises at least six parts:

- It is easier to select an object than to remember a command.
- Selection requires both moving a cursor to an object and signalling that this is the required object.
- Human action should mirror cursor movement.
- Pointing to an object should be a manual activity.
- The device should fit in the hand.
- The device should be operated in close proximity to the computer on which the cursor is moving.

One could argue that the over-riding concern of mice is not the selection of objects but the movement of a cursor, and one could ask whether the cursor, rather than the objects, should be the focus of user activity.

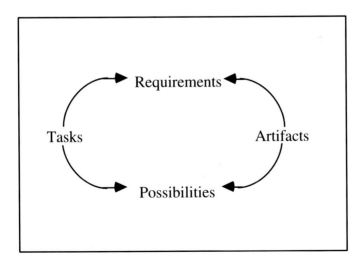

Figure 1.3 The task–artifact cycle (reproduced with permission from Carroll et al., 1991, *Designing Interaction: Psychology at the Human–Computer Interface*, Cambridge University Press)

1.8 Conclusions

It has been proposed that HCI researchers and practitioners tend to think of interaction devices as technical artifacts designed to perform specific functions. That is, interaction devices are often viewed as objects, which can be engineered to fit certain specifications and whose performance can be calibrated in some gross fashion. The very term "input device" suggests that the functions are not considered in detail. It is as if the devices which users physically manipulate in their interactions with computers are simply added on to working software. Consequently, it is argued that this perspective fails to consider the type of human activity supported, and required, by these devices. This has led to a situation in which the standard workstation houses a VDU, a keyboard and a mouse.

The notion of workstation is rapidly becoming outdated and research and development efforts around the world are being directed towards developing products which move beyond the desktop metaphor. With the rise of portable computers and with the expansion of computer technology into all walks of life, it is unlikely that the standard workstation will suit all of the demands placed upon computers. However, as computers move off the desk and into other domains, the devices which people use to interact with computers will also need to change.

It is argued that the design of interaction devices should be considered in terms of their use, and that the tool-use metaphor provides a framework for the approach. However, it is further proposed that the use of interaction devices will be shaped and influenced by a host of contextual factors, not least of which will be the users' goals in performing a task with the devices. These goals will be influenced by the work domain in which they are being performed, and be tempered by environmental factors. In this book I seek to explore how interaction devices have been designed and studied to date, before considering the use of interaction devices and the implications for future design and development.

1.9 Key points for practitioners

In each chapter in the book there will be bullet point summaries or brief discussions which relate the themes of the chapter to either practice or research.

- What tasks will be performed using interaction devices?
- What are the motives for choosing one device over others?
- Do users experience problems in using the devices provided?

- What factors influence the ease of use of the devices?
- What knowledge, skills and abilities are required of the users in order to operate the devices?
- Can user performance be improved?

1.10 Key points for researchers

This chapter contains four concepts for organizing ways of seeing interaction devices:

- Consider devices for interaction rather than simply for input.
- Consider the use of interaction devices in terms of tool use.
- Consider the manner in which interaction devices mediate user performance.
- Consider the context in which interaction devices are to be used.

There has been, for some time, a drive to the development of multi-purpose interaction devices which can be manufactured at low cost and high volume and which can be shipped for use on all types of computer. It is not clear that this trend will be sustainable, especially with the shifts in computer use. Consequently, there is an increasing need to consider bespoke interaction devices for specific products. The underlying perspective of the ideas presented in this chapter and throughout the book can be termed "user-centered design" (Norman and Draper, 1984). To a certain extent the arguments presented in this chapter have defined and delimited this perspective in terms of the design of interaction devices. If one wants to reduce the argument in the chapter to a single slogan, one could say that the aim of the book is to support the design of interaction devices for human use.

1.11 Chapter overviews

In this section a brief precis is given of each chapter to allow readers to determine the relevance of that chapter to their requirements. This book is divided into three Parts: Interaction Devices; Using Interaction Devices; and Advanced Topics.

Part I: Interacton devices

Part I not only provides an overview of the range of interaction devices which are currently available but also reviews previous HCI research. This research has taken the broad approaches of device comparisons and device classification.

Chapter 2:   Keyboards

This chapter contains a review of the design and development of the QWERTY keyboard, and a discussion of some alternative alphanumeric keyboard arrangements and layouts. Following discussion of alphanumeric keyboards, attention is turned to the design of other forms of interaction devices based on the use of keys.

Chapter 3:   Pointing devices

In this chapter, the current range of interaction devices which can be used for cursor manipulation and control are considered. The studies in which comparisons have been made between devices are reviewed, and it is proposed that efforts should be made to relate devices to tasks.

Chapter 4:   Alternative interaction devices

This chapter reviews interaction devices which have been proposed as alternatives to conventional devices, such as speech, gesture and hand-writing recognition.

Chapter 5:   Classifying devices

Various approaches which have been proposed for classifying interaction devices are presented. The aim of such classification is to produce a taxonomy which can inform device design and selection. The chapter also introduces the ergonomic concepts of compatibility and perfor-mance-shaping factors as approaches to the consideration of device operation.

Part II: Using interaction devices

The second part considers the ways in which interaction devices are used, focusing on five broad classes of activity: typing, writing, drawing, pointing and speaking. Each activity is considered in terms of skilled activity, and attention is given to the ways in which activities are sequenced by the individual and constrained by the limitations of the individual, the demands of a task and the design of a device. The part begins with a discussion of how user activity can be modeled.

Chapter 6:   Modeling device use

There are several approaches which aim to model the performance of devices when they are used for simple tasks. The definition of model used in this chapter is that of a description of behavior which can allow predictions to be made. Generally, this will take the form of predicted total task performance times. This chapter reviews these approaches and asks whether they describe what their proponents claim.

Chapter 7:   Typing

In this chapter, the wealth of research on the human skills involved in typing is reviewed. It will describe attempts to define models of "typists", and discuss the implications of these models for keyboard design. In addition to typing on alphanumeric keyboards, the chapter will also consider the use of numeric and chord keyboards.

Chapter 8:   Writing and drawing

The study of how people manipulate pens and other writing instruments has been developing rapidly in recent years. In this chapter, contemporary psychomotor theories of writing and drawing are considered. The interaction between pen type, physical actions of the user and what is drawn or written are discussed. The implications for the design of pen-based computing systems and CAD are discussed.

Chapter 9:   Pointing

In this chapter, the activity involved in using interaction devices to select objects is discussed. Following a review of the application of Fitt's law to HCI research, attention is turned to alternative theories of skilled motor activity. The implications of these theories for the design and use of pointing devices are considered.

Chapter 10:   Speaking

The metaphor of dialogue has permeated HCI research so deeply that it is often easy to forget the differences between speaking to other people and speaking to a computer. In this chapter, the way in which speech is produced is considered in order to understand why speech recognizers are prone to error and how speech-based systems can be designed to support human use.

Part III: Further topics

While the first two parts tend to focus on the relationship between an individual user and an interaction device in terms of user performance, Part III contains three chapters which advance beyond this relationship. Although performance is an issue, it should not be the sole focus of research into interaction devices; of equal importance are the problems arising from poor design or inappropriate use of device. Furthermore, the importance of the work domain is implicit in much of the other discussion in the book and is developed in this section. Finally, the issue of combining several interaction devices into multimodal systems is considered.

Chapter 11:   Devices for restricted environments

There are many situations in which the use of an interaction device can become problematic; these situations can typically be defined by the reduction in human physical ability, through levels of workload, or through levels of environmental stress, or through reduced physical capabilities. In this chapter, the effects of such problems on device use are considered.

Chapter 12:   Physical aspects of interaction device use

In this chapter, the growing number of reports of injuries arising from the use of computer workstations is discussed. Consideration is given to the risks which are presented by use of other interaction devices.

Chapter 13: Interaction devices at work

In this chapter, we consider the relationship between organizational and work demands and the praxis of interaction device use. This provides a social context for considering many of the issues discussed in previous chapters.

Chapter 14: Multimodal HCI

There have been several attempts to introduce computers which can be operated using more than one modality. In this chapter, these multimodal systems are considered.

Part I
Interaction Devices

Chapter 2   Keyboards
Chapter 3   Pointing devices
Chapter 4   Alternative interaction devices
Chapter 5   Classifying devices

CHAPTER 2

Keyboards

Abstract

In this chapter, consideration is given to the keyboard. It is instructive to ask how the most common layout of keys came about, and to consider the human factors problems associated with this layout. Some of the solutions which have been proposed to deal with these problems are discussed, before noting that it is now accepted internationally. Other aspects of keyboard design are considered, together with some alternative forms of keyboard.

2.1 Introduction

The first interaction device to be considered in this book is the keyboard. It is fitting that the keyboard should be given pole position because it was the first device which people used for interacting with computers and because it is the device which accompanies all personal computers; it is difficult to imagine a computer without a keyboard, even today with the wealth of alternative devices which can be ported to personal computers.

2.1.1 The invention of the typewriter

Before discussing the ergonomics of computer keyboards, it will be useful to digress to consider the invention of the typewriter, as the antecedent of the computer keyboard. Readers might assume that the typewriter was invented towards the end of the nineteenth century. However, there were designs for typewriters which predate this period. The basic rationale, in the earlier designs, was that a machine could be built for applying type to paper, and that the type could be moved by striking keys. In 1711, James Ranson discussed a design for a machine "with small keys like those on . . . harpsichords." (Tepper, 1993). Thus, the analogy upon which these early designs was based was the twin keyboard of the harpsichord, and users of the machines were assumed to produce type in much the same way as they would play a harpsichord. The problem was less one of visualizing the machine than of achieving an adequate, working model.

It was in 1868 that Scholes and his colleagues, Glidden and Soulé, patented a typewriter, although other workers were also developing similar products at this time. This machine was designed primarily as an aid in the fight against ticket forgery on railways; by having a portable machine which could be used to print ticket numbers, it would be possible to reduce the possibility of people forging handwritten tickets. Interestingly enough, the first model built by Scholes et al. had two rows of keys, arranged alphabetically N–Z and A–M (Beeching, 1974). However, while the early notions of producing type with harpsichord keyboards imply the use of all ten fingers to operate the machine, Scholes et al.'s design was based on the assumption that people would use two fingers, i.e., the index fingers of each hand.

In 1878, Scholes et al. applied for a patent on a three-row keyboard. The layout of this design was similar to what is now the standard layout, and is often referred to by the acronym formed from the first six letters of its top line (see Figure 2.1), i.e., "QWERTY". The resulting typewriter was then marketed by Remington. However, it was not until ten years after the sale of the first typewriter that ten-finger typing was made popular; in a competition held in 1888, in Cincinnati, the "world's fastest typist" beat a contender by using ten fingers and memorizing the design of the keyboard.

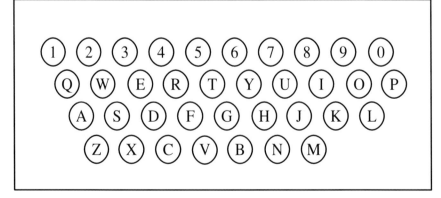

Figure 2.1 The QWERTY layout

2.1.2   On the origins of QWERTY

As Noyes (1983), in an authoritative history of the now standard QWERTY keyboard, noted, there are many rumors concerning the origin of the layout of keys on this keyboard, but little evidence of "the" reason. Hackmeister (1979), somewhat tongue-in-cheek, pointed out that the top row of the keyboard contains all the letters in the word "typewriter", thus combining demonstration with advertising. A number of writers have proposed that the QWERTY layout came into being as a means to prevent jamming of the bars which held the type face. The common assumption is that this aim was achieved by either slowing typing speed or by distributing commonly paired letter combinations as far apart as possible (Shneiderman, 1992). This claim has been reported so often that it has been accepted as a truism. However, if one pauses to reflect on the substance of this claim, it is possible to spot some flaws in its logic.

The early models were designed, manufactured and marketed on the assumption that they would be operated by two fingers (recall that it was not until some ten years after the product was first launched that the idea of "ten-finger typing" became popular). This suggests that the initial design accepted that typing would be "hunt and peck" (Gentner and Norman, 1984). It seems strange to design a layout to slow users when the use of the machine was already quite slow; this is a problem when one considers that Scholes claimed that typing could be performed quickly, and that the typewriter would allow people to produce text as quickly as handwriting. Furthermore, if one notes the initial application for which the machine was designed (producing tickets), it is difficult to imagine achieving remarkable typing rates for such small combinations of letters as would be necessary for rail tickets. The second problem concerns the distribution of the keys. Griffith (1949) showed that the QWERTY layout actually requires people to use a slightly larger number of closely positioned pairs of keys than a random layout.

The point of this discussion is simply this: it is quite feasible that the QWERTY layout arose by chance. In other words, the interface between user and machine was a consequence of the engineering of the machine. It was not designed to either aid or abet users. Indeed, there are grounds for proposing that the layout of keys on a QWERTY keyboard was simply copied from the layout of type stored in trays in a hot-metal print shop (Phillips, 1968); after all, Scholes and his colleagues worked as printers. While this is an attractive solution to the problem of discerning the origins of QWERTY, it is not entirely plausible because of the wide variety in design of type-trays. If one considers the efforts of producing keyboards for typesetting machines through the decades preceding the work of Scholes, then one might assume that the layout arose from rearranging the letters of the alphabet. Indeed, Griffith (1949) suggests that it is possible to move from an alphabetic layout to the QWERTY layout by two transformations of the layout. This does not, of course, imply that the transformations were made by Scholes, nor that the resulting design can be considered good ergonomics.

Thus, a machine was designed to the following specification: produce legible ticket numbers by striking type against an ink-impregnated ribbon onto paper. The principal engineering requirement was to produce a lever system which was sufficiently robust to allow the machine to be transported, and which positioned typed characters in a specific space. The levers would be moved by keys, and the layout for keys was probably unimportant (this is apparent when one considers that the later, alternative typewriter designs also used lever systems, but placed the keys in different orders). It is possible that the QWERTY layout was not designed as an interface to the type-writer, but was attached to a sound, mechanical product: in other words, the user interface for the QWERTY keyboard was a by-product of the typewriter.

The typewriter then became a victim of its ingenious mechnical design. This point can be illustrated using the task–artifact cycle (see Chapter 1). A machine which could produce type, ostensibly for numbering tickets, was invented. The entrepreneurs who marketed the machine described its ability to produce letters and numbers, and the range of possible applications expanded. As longer sequences of characters were produced, there developed a need to increase the rate at which keys were pressed. This led to the development of ten-finger "touch-typing", which replaced the two-finger typing for which the keyboard was designed.

Undoubtedly, a prime reason for the success of QWERTY must have been the marketing of the typewriter by Remington. One can propose four other factors, which are as relevant to HCI today as they are to the history of the keyboard. One of the banes of human factors research is that people often learn to cope with poorly designed technology. This does not make the technology any better from a human factors perspective, but can serve to disguise some of the problems inherent in the design. This point will be illustrated with reference to QWERTY in the following sections. A second factor relates to the work domain in which the technology will be used; the typewriter had a significant impact on the way in which work was performed and the people who performed that work. Consequently, there was a strong incentive to learn to "cope" in order to protect one's job.

The next two factors relate to the marketing of the product. It is often the case that marketing "sells" the functions a product offers, rather than the interface. Thus, the marketing of QWERTY would have focused on the benefits offered by the technology. Finally, the benefits would only have been achieved through appropriate training, and the training of competent typists became big business at this time. Thus, an initial design (which, as is illustrated below, can be said to fail on many human factors requirements) is marketed to potentially revolutionize office work. In order for the revolution to succeed, people need to adapt to the technology (rather than have the technology designed for them), and the mechanism via which people adapt is training.

2.1.3 Problems with QWERTY

The QWERTY layout was not specifically designed for ten-finger typing. Consequently, one should ask whether the familiar, not to say standard, layout of keys on keyboards can be considered well designed. The easiest way to address this question is to consider whether using the QWERTY layout presents specific problems to users.

The first extensive investigation of the QWERTY layout was carried out by Dvorak and his colleagues in the 1940s. Dvorak (1943), in a comparison of 250 keyboard layouts, declared the QWERTY keyboard to be one of the worst possible. There are a number of physical problems associated with the QWERTY layout (see Chapter 12). The most obvious problem relates to the fact that the layout causes the left hand to work harder than the right (see Figure 2.2) despite the fact that some 90% of the population are right handed. Not only does the left hand work harder than the right, but Ward (1936) reports a study which found that of a sample of 3000 words, some 2700 were typed exclusively with the left hand, e.g., "was", "were".

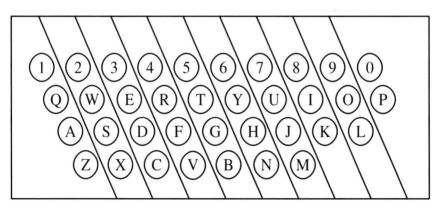

Figure 2.2   Finger positions when using QWERTY

When considering the movement between rows, only 32% of typing is performed on the "home" (centre) row. This means that the majority of typing activity involves movement to and from this "home" row, and that frequently used sequences of letters require a great deal of row hopping. For instance, Griffith (1949) proposed that 68% of typing requires reaching from the home row, and 48% of motions to reposition fingers laterally between keystrokes are one handed. Some authors have suggested that this latter problem represents a benefit of the QWERTY layout, in that it requires the user to engage in constant motion, which, in turn, provides additional feedback to the user (Cakir et al., 1980; Noyes, 1983). A final problem concerns the slope of the keys, from left to right. If there is an excessive load on the typists' left hand, it will obscure the next letter to be typed, at least in hunt and peck operation (Noyes, 1983).

The case against the QWERTY layout can be summarized by the following statements:

- It tends to overload the left hand. However, the loading will depend on what is being typed. Finally, considering the force required to depress keys on computer keyboards, rather than typewriters, the issue of over-loading may be something of a "red herring";
- It tends to require "excessive" movement between rows. Some authors have suggested that this is advantageous, in preference to restricted movement around specific keys;
- The slope of the keyboard may lead to the typists' left hands obscuring some of the letters, thus interfering with visual search. This raises the question of not only how the keyboard is used but also who is using it, i.e., touch-typists vs. hunt-and-peck typists.

2.1.4 The triumph of QWERTY

The average typing speed, for touch typists, which can be obtained when using the QWERTY layout is 60–90 words per minute. It is a moot point as to whether these speeds are achieved by the untrained typist. This raises interesting questions about the requirements that different user groups might have from a keyboard. However, to remain with typists of average ability using a QWERTY layout, Kinkade (1975) has suggested that this range of speed represents near optimum performance, concluding that a fictitious "improved" layout would only improve performance by some 8%. Thus, despite the problems one can see little definitive evidence for dispensing with the QWERTY layout of keys, at least as far as typing speed is concerned.

From Kinkade's (1975) proposals, QWERTY would appear to be operated at or near its maximum capacity. From a human factors perspective, the question remains as to which component in the human–keyboard system is operating at near capacity. If it is the human, then one might anticipate that efforts to prolong maximum capacity could lead to physical problems (see Chapter 12). If it is the keyboard, then there may be ways of redesigning the keyboard. Finally, the discussion has tended to focus on touch typing, rather than on the slower speeds which might be obtained from untrained typists. Perhaps, somewhat paradoxically, striving for designs to improve typing speed might lead to an increase in work-related upper-limb disorders, with more people being able to work at maximum capacity. Thus, while it might not always be possible to modify designs to increase typing speed, it is still sensible to consider ways of reducing physical problems.

Suffice it to say that, despite the problems, the QWERTY layout has become enshrined in many standards, e.g., ISO 4169 (1979), BS 5959 (1980), ISO 9241 (in draft). Thus, one can only agree with Pheasant (1988) when he wryly notes that the QWERTY layout is the "unergonomic layout which most ergonomists recommend" (p. 242).

2.2 Alternatives to QWERTY

There have been a number of developments in keyboard design since the launch of the QWERTY keyboard, many of which reached a peak between the 1930s and 1950s and which are now being explored by manufacturers, primarily in response to fears about work-related upper-limb disorder. In this section, two classes of alternative design are considered: alternative layouts of keys, and alternative designs of the keyboard.

2.2.1 Alternative layouts

In a number of studies, researchers have attempted to distribute the keys on the keyboard in terms of the frequency with which pairs of letters are typed. The aim is to produce a design which maximizes the alternation of hands during typing, in order to distribute the load on hands more evenly. While there have been many designs based on these proposals, the most widely cited was proposed by Dvorak (1943), as is shown in Figure 2.3. Indeed, the Dvorak simplified keyboard (in which the numbers are ordered sequentially) has been accepted as an alternative to QWERTY.

Figure 2.3   The Dvorak keyboard layout

There are large claims made for the Dvorak layout. Russell (1986) suggests that the Dvorak layout dramatically reduces finger travel and thus reduces the possibility of fatigue. Other writers have claimed improvements in typing speed, training time and user preference, in addition to reductions in fatigue (Dunn, 1971; McCauley and Parkinson, 1971).

Unfortunately, there are few published studies comparing Dvorak with QWERTY layouts, and often such studies are flawed by the fact that trained typists are used. In other words, the studies tend to be unfairly biased against Dvorak by using people who have a high degree of experience with the QWERTY layout, while being unfamiliar with the Dvorak layout. This would result in performance with the QWERTY being at the level of touch typing, while that with the Dvorak could still be improving from hunt and peck as the users find their way around the keyboard. Some people have suggested large performance advantage can be gained from Dvorak, due to the distribution of workload and the use of alternating hands. When results are reported they often follow those of Alden et al. (1972) who found little difference in performance between QWERTY and Dvorak, after a short period of practice with the Dvorak. This is interesting in that it would appear to contradict one of the main reasons why people do not wish to invest in Dvorak, or similar keyboards, viz. retraining costs (the other main reason being the cost of replacing equipment). Martin (1972) suggests that the Dvorak layout failed to become a commercial success for a variety of reasons, but proposed a repackaged version for use in the 1970s (i.e., the alphametric keyboard), although this was not a success.

The main problems pertaining to typing appear to be less to do with the layout of the keys than with the rate of keying and the posture a typist adopts (see Chapter 12). Thus, other approaches to redesigning keyboards have focused on changing the typists' posture. Before we consider these, we will briefly turn our attention to the alphabetic layout.

The alphabetic layout is most commonly used on devices for children. The assumption appears to be that it is easy to learn. If this is true, then one might anticipate some performance advantages of the alphabetic layout over the QWERTY. The studies which have been performed to compare these layouts tend to come out in favor of QWERTY (Barmack and Sinaiko, 1966; Hirsch, 1970; Michaels, 1971; Norman and Fisher, 1982). Card et al. (1980), using the keystroke level model (see Chapter 5), predict that typing speed for a QWERTY layout is around 72 words per minute (wpm), but that for the alphabetic layout is around 67 wpm (a difference of 8 wpm). However, in one of these studies, the alphabetic layout was shown to be superior to an entirely random layout (Norman and Fisher, 1982).

One of the differences between the layouts is the implication that users of the alphabetic keyboard must first recall the position of the letter in the alphabet and then search the keyboard in the right place to find it. If people are visually searching for letters, then, by definition, they are not touch typing. Given the familiarity that people have with QWERTY, the studies may be somewhat biased against the alphabetic keyboard and one might expect differences in performance time. If we take occasional users of keyboards, we may well be able to indicate some benefits for the alphabetic design. Marmaras and Lyritzis (1990), for instance, found that users of a public information system performed better with a diagonally sloping alphabetic keyboard than a (Greek-character) QWERTY (although this study could be criticized because the participants were only requested to type a single, short phrase). Bodensher (1970) also found superior performance with an alphabetic layout over a QWERTY (although this study could be criticized because in the alphabetic layout, Bodensher also rearranged numeric and function keys).

2.2.2 Alternative designs

In recent years a veritable proliferation of keyboards have been designed which are quite different to conventional keyboards. Klockenberg (1926) and Kroemer (1972) had proposed dividing a keyboard into two halves, so that the typists hands could be kept in a more natural position, i.e., to reduce problems arising from ulnar abduction (see Chapter 12). A number of studies have shown that such layouts markedly reduce abduction of the hands and minimize the resulting strain on shoulder/arm muscles (Zipp et al., 1983; Nakaseko et al., 1985). Grandjean (1987) suggests that the angle between the two halves should be 25°, with the distance between the "G"

Figure 2.4 A split keyboard design

and "H" keys being 950 mm, and that the halves should have a lateral slope of 10°. Figure 2.4 illustrates one of the commercially available versions of the split keyboard concept.

In addition to splitting the keyboard, there have been attempts to move from flat, horizontal rows of keys to a more "natural" shape. Malt (1977) placed the keys in arcs which were supposed to follow the shape made by the fingertips when the hand is held above a keyboard. The layouts of keys was based on a detailed analysis of the frequency with which digrams, i.e., pairs of letters, occur in the English language. Unfortunately, there is little published research comparing the Maltron with other keyboard designs. Floyd (1979) found no difference in typing speed between Maltron and QWERTY layouts. This study used only six typists, and exists only in the form of a student project report. However, a keyboard which combines the split keyboard, discussed above, with a sculpted design similar to the Maltron, has been produced by Kinesis in the US. Gerard et al. (1994) have demonstrated that use of the Kinesis keyboard can lead to a reduction in musculoskeletal loading during typing. A similar conclusion was drawn by Hargreaves et al. (1992) on their research into a split design. This research is discussed in Chapter 12.

2.3   Standards for keyboard design

There are a number of standards which have been drawn up to define the optimum design of a keyboard. As noted above, these standards tend to focus on the QWERTY layout, and to assume a linear design of keys. The standards contain proposals that the keyboard should be separate from the computer (to allow repositioning), adjustable in tilt, and of a matt finish (to minimize reflection). In addition, there are specific guidelines on key design and operation which relate to the human factors literature.

2.3.1   Key size

Published surveys of the physical dimensions of the human hand, such as Garrett (1971) and Pheasant (1988), would lead us to propose that a range of key width of 12–15 mm would accommodate the majority of male and female keyboard users. A forthcoming International Standards Organisation standard, ISO 9241 suggests that the width of the strike surface for keys bearing alphanumerics should be 12–15 mm, and that the surface should have a minimum area of 110 mm^2. On the keyboard shown in Figure 2.5, the key dimensions are 12 mm × 14 mm, giving a surface area of 168 mm^2.

Figure 2.5   A QWERTY keyboard

2.3.2 Key travel

Deininger (1960) found little difference in keying performance for keys with displacement ranging from 0.8 to 4.8 mm. ISO 9241 suggests that key displacement should be 1.5–6 mm. These would appear to cover the range considered by Deininger (1960). The question of what would happen if the keys did not travel or provide other form of feedback is considered below.

2.3.3 Force required to depress keys

Force requirements are defined using the SI unit of newtons. Chapanis and Kinkade (1972) propose a minimum force of 0.14 N. ISO 9241 suggests that the limits of force required will lie between 0.25 N and 1 N, ideally 0.5–0.8 N.

2.3.4 Feedback from keypressing

When you press a key, you receive several different sorts of feedback: the movement of the finger from one key to another (kinesthetic feedback), the feel of the key moving (tactile feedback), the click of the key as it is depressed (auditory feedback), and the appearance of text on the VDU (visual feedback). How important are these different forms of feedback?

Brunner and Richardson (1984) found that the preferred, and most effective, form of feedback regarding key movement combines a high initial increase in resistance on depress, with resistance disappearing with switch closure, and increasing with overshoot. This is the type of feedback recommended by ISO 9241. Interestingly, with this design there was little difference in typing speed between providing and not providing auditory feedback, and slightly fewer insertion errors *without* auditory feedback. Thus, one can propose that tactile feedback is far more important than auditory feedback.

For keyboards on touchscreens and touch tablets, it is necessary to consider whether or not tactile feedback can be added to the design. Roe et al. (1984) compared feedback for membrane keypads, i.e., no key travel, and found that some form of feedback indicating that a key has been pressed is essential. They suggested that embossing the keys, i.e., giving keys a raised rim, was not effective, but that providing either a raised metal dome over each key or auditory feedback was useful, and they argued that a combination of raised dome and auditory feedback was best. Nevertheless, Loeb (1983) shows that membrane keyboards usually yield worse performance in comparison with QWERTY keyboards, even with practice. Thus, one should aim to provide tactile feedback as a priority, before considering the other types of feedback.

2.4   Other forms of keys

The QWERTY layout and alternative layouts and designs have been discussed above. The keyboard on which I am typing this book is shown in Figure 2.5. Notice that not only does the keyboard contain the letters of the alphabet, it also contains several other "keypads", notably a set of function keys, a set of cursor keys and a set of number keys.

2.4.1   Function keys

Many commercially available keyboards are provided with a row of keys at the top of the keyboard. Some of the keys are labeled (using a detachable strip), while others are not. Some of the keys have a definition which has gained widespread acceptance, such as F1 for "help", although this is by no means universal; if I press F1 on the keyboard shown in Figure 2.5, I "undo" the previous action, which illustrates that the operation of these keys relates to their role in the software package being used and the conventions which are followed by the manufacturer. In some packages, the definition of the function keys is presented on the screen, often this is because their definition changes in different parts of the software.

Function key design can be justified by the arguments that they reduce transaction time (by having a single key to perform a commonly used function, rather than typing the command or selecting a menu item), and that they reduce learning time (by having important functions presented in an easily accessible fashion). However, both of these claims can be countered by noting the memory load involved in remembering and finding the appropriate key, especially when they are not labeled. Add to this the physical requirement to keep the number of function keys within the width of the keyboard, and one will appreciate that the number of function keys which can be used needs to be kept within, say between 15 and 20. It is possible to follow accepted human factors practice to improve function key design. First, aim to position the function keys according to function, e.g., on the keyboard in Figure 2.5, the "editing" functions are grouped on the left-hand side of the keyboard. Second, aim for consistent layout of the keys. For instance, ensure that the "help" key is always in the same place; people have an irritating tendency not to read labels, but to use other forms of memory to find keys, such as "spatial memory", e.g., I "know" that pressing the F1 key of this keyboard will "undo" a command and do not have to look for the key. However, if I apply this "knowledge" to another arrangement of function keys, I may well achieve a different outcome, e.g., F1 on another keyboard might select "help".

2.4.2   Numeric keys

In Figure 2.5, there are two sets of keys for numbers: one positioned on the "main" QWERTY keyboard, and a numeric keypad to the right of the keyboard. While it is not clear why one needs to duplicate a set of ten keys (perhaps because of the assumed distinction between entering numbers when word processing and when performing numerical transactions, such as populating a spreadsheet), this section will focus on the design of the keypad.

Basically, there are two layouts which have been used for numeric key-pads. In one, the top row consists of the numbers 1–2–3, and is used on the keypads of telephones, and in the other the top row consists of the numbers 7–8–9, and is used on the keypads of calculators and computers. The 7–8–9 layout was adopted as a British Standard in 1963 (BS 1909). Deininger (1960) suggested that performance using a numeric keypad would be acceptable using a 1–2–3, i.e., 3 row + 0 layout as on a telephone, or a 1–2–3–4–5, i.e., a 2 row. However, telephones tend to use the three-row + 0 layout (presumably for reasons of physical space). Although the 7–8–9 layout was standardized (in the UK at least), the research tends to suggest that the 1–2–3 layout yields a slight performance advantage (Lutz and Chapanis, 1955; Conrad and Hull, 1968). In the Conrad and Hull (1968) study, layouts were compared and there was little difference in keying speed and a small (i.e., non-significant) difference in the number of errors (6.4% for the 1–2–3 layout vs. 8.2% for the 7–8–9 layout).

Siebel (1972) proposes that performance will probably be more likely to be affected by cognitive factors, such as familiarity with the key design and with the information to be entered. This makes sense when we consider some of the components which constitute the activity of entering sequences of numbers, in which people can be shown to plan sequences of keypressing movements (see Chapter 7). Finally, Conrad and Hull (1968) did find differences in keying speed when the two layouts were used alternately across trials. It would seem that switching from one layout could be problematic. While there appears to be evidence in favor of the 1–2–3 layout (Chapanis, 1988; Straub and Granaas, 1993), ISO 9241 permits both layouts.

2.4.3   Cursor keys

There have been some studies comparing different configurations of cursor keys. Shneiderman (1992) gives a good overview of this research. The choice of cursor key layout often seems constrained by factors such as the space available on the keyboard and the ingenuity of the designer. There are probably around half a dozen different layouts which can be found on commercially available keyboards. However, the layouts which seem to be the most popular are shown in Figure 2.6. Broadly speaking, the cursor key layouts which yield the best performance are those which preserve the spatial compatibility between key layout and cursor movement (Emmons, 1984); in other words, arrangements in which the position of the keys corresponds to direction of cursor movement tend to yield faster performance than keys which are arranged in another manner. Thus, in Figure 2.6, layouts a and b will be superior to c. One would presume that the choice of c over the other arrangements would arise from placing space requirements above human factors requirements.

When considering the use of cursor keys for moving the cursor, it is apparent that their utility declines as the distance to move the cursor increases. From Figure 2.7, one can see that cursor keys appear to be appropriate for moving the cursor a small distance and that, as the distance to move increases beyond 2 cm, other interaction devices will yield faster performance.

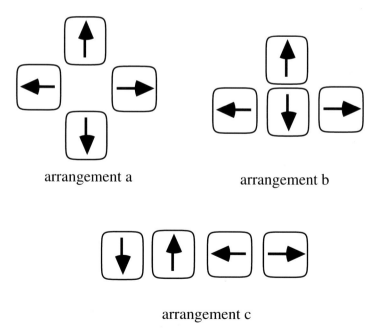

arrangement a   arrangement b

arrangement c

Figure 2.6 Examples of cursor key layouts

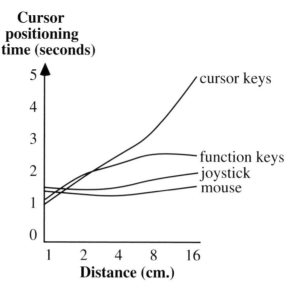

Figure 2.7 Cursor positioning speed × distance (reproduced with permission from Card et al., 1978, *Ergonomics* **21**, 601–613, Taylor & Francis)

2.5   Other types of keyboard

The discussion has focused on the design of keyboards for entering text, but there are several other types of keyboard which are commonly used in HCI. In this section, two of these keyboards will be considered: function and chord keyboards.

2.5.1   Function keyboards

Function keyboards comprise a number of labeled keys, each representing a specific function. To a certain extent, this represents an extension of the concept of function keys discussed above. Lam and Greenstein (1984) demonstrated that people using function keyboards for an air traffic control task produced fewer keying errors and faster command entry times than people using a QWERTY layout and typing in command words. This difference should not strike one as particularly surprising; with the function keyboard, we are reducing the number of key presses required to enter a command to a single keypress. However, while the potential performance advantages to be gained from grouping several keypresses into a single keypress is attractive, this must be weighed against the visual search demands imposed by a function keyboard, especially when the number of keys increases.

There appear to be two popular solutions to this problem of visual search. In one solution, the keys are coded and grouped according to function (Emmons and Hirsch, 1982). This could be said to represent the human factors solution to the problem, in which principles of functional grouping are followed. In the second solution, one could alter the labeling of the keys. In this condition (also known as concept keyboards), the keys can be relabeled in different modes (generally because the keys are presented using a touch tablet and can be relabeled in response to software commands). This could be said to represent a software engineering solution to the problem, with fewer keys displayed to the user but the labels on the keys altering as one progresses through the program. A potential problem with the latter approach would relate to the confusion which might arise if users cannot find the key they expect to find, coupled with the frustration associated with searching the several layers of key labels to find a specific key. However, it strikes me that this approach has much to offer, providing the issue of moding is carefully considered and the options presented to users allow them to perform appropriate operations in that mode, i.e., where the operations match user expectations.

2.5.2 Chord keyboards

There are a number of "short-cuts" which can be called by performing simple chords on a QWERTY keyboard. Many readers will be familiar with the <Ctrl–Alt–Del> combination for rebooting a computer. Using the keyboard in Figure 2.4, it is possible to call many of the menu commands by pressing two-key combinations, such as <[🍎]–C> to issue the "copy" command from the Edit menu, or <[🍎]–S> to issue the save command from the File menu. If one considers the shapes made by one's hands in pressing these key combinations, then one can appreciate the concept which underlies chord keyboards. Oborne (1988) points out that some chord keyboards are designed for two-handed operation, whereas others are designed for one-handed operation. Enfield (1978), describes a chord keyboard which allows text entry. A schematic of this keyboard is shown in Figure 2.8. Each finger has a specified resting point in order to allow formation of chords.

There have been several studies aimed at establishing whether chord keyboards are preferable to conventional keyboards. One might anticipate similar results to those found when comparing QWERTY keyboards with function keyboards, in that a single user action will correspond to a sequence of keypresses. However, this overlooks the fact that the "single" action requires users to shape their hands into specific gestures, with each gesture being assigned a different meaning. Thus, there could be potential problems in terms of remembering and executing the gestures. Ratz and

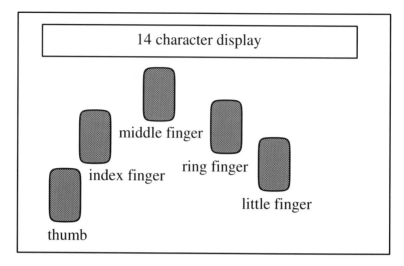

Figure 2.8   Microwriter keying positions

Ritchie (1961) and Siebel (1962) asked people to respond to lights using chords. There were 31 possible combinations, and the error rate varied by 400% between "best" and "worst" performance, but optimal performance was obtained by pairing one light to one key, i.e., simple, one-finger reaction rather than chords.

Conrad and Longman (1965) studied the use of different types of key-board by postal workers in a sorting office for a period of four weeks. The chord keyboard was learnt faster than the typewriter (12.5 vs. 20.5 days) and produced faster operation. Bowen and Guinness (1965), looking at semi-automatic mail sorting, compared 12-chord vs. 24-chord vs. type-writer. They found that more items were sorted using the chord keyboards than the typewriter, and that the 12-chord keyboard was superior to the 24-chord keyboard. This latter finding might be because the finger patterns were easier to either perform or remember using the 12-chord keyboard (McCormick, 1976). In both studies, data entry was performed using short, random combinations of numbers/letters, i.e., zip or postal codes, it would be interesting to discover whether the advantage of the chord keyboard would exist for meaningful text.

Greenstein and Muto (1988) and Siebel (1962) argue that some chords are difficult both to learn and to execute. In Figure 2.9, the chords used to enter my surname are indicated; the letter shapes are superimposed using blackened keys. While the shapes can be relatively easy to copy, I found them difficult to retain for any period of time and found myself constantly referring to the instruction manual. There seems to be a lack of correspondence between the gesture one makes and the letter which is formed, although in Figure 2.9 it is possible to discern why certain chords are

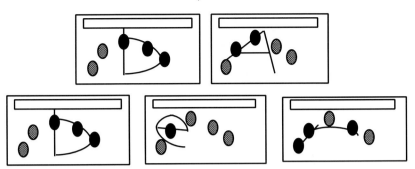

Figure 2.9 Finger positions for typing the author's name on a Microwriter

used to form certain letters. Given this potential problem, the next question is what sort of errors do people make when using chord keyboards. Figure 2.10 gives an idea of the relative distribution of errors when using a Microwriter chord keyboard. The main problems seem to arise from use of inappropriate gestures, either in terms of using the wrong key or omitting a character. Thus, forming the gestures seems problematic. We shall consider the issues of using gestures in HCI in Chapter 4.

2.6 Conclusions

There has long been a debate over the human factors problems associated with the QWERTY keyboard layout and conventional keyboard design. A

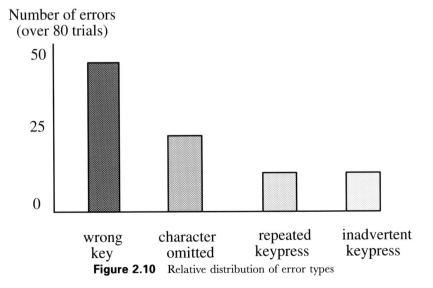

Figure 2.10 Relative distribution of error types

number of researchers have sought to develop alternative layouts and designs, and a sample of these has been reviewed in this chapter. However, attempts to alter the layout of the keyboard, e.g., using Dvorak or alphabetic layouts, do not appear to offer substantial benefits to performance; particularly as there is an ever-increasing tendency for keyboard users to receive little or no formal training (in the UK at least), which makes the design for fast typing speeds difficult to justify. Further, the recommended force required for key displacement is very small, which gives arguments based on finger loading more academic than practical value. However, the conventional horizontal arrangement of keys can lead to problems (a point developed in Chapter 12), and endorses the efforts made in designing keyboards which allow users to adopt a more natural posture. From the published research, the split keyboard appears to offer a number of physical benefits to users. Some readers might be worried about the various costs involved in a switch from conventional design to these split keyboards, particularly in terms of cost and reductions in productivity. The first issue can be considered in terms of a cost:benefit analysis associated with outlay on split keyboards against the increase in claims for work-related upper-limb problems. The second issue is slightly harder to address; in most of the studies comparing performance on the different designs, performance on the conventional design is superior. However, this does not necessarily mean that the conventional design inevitably produces superior performance. In the majority of the studies, the participants are highly experienced in the use of conventional keyboards, so that the design of the study would appear to be unduly biased with little attempt made to balance level of experience. Thus, there is a need for a properly conducted longitudinal study into the interaction between keyboard design, physical load and typing performance. Finally, it is not clear that typing speed is as big an issue as one might think; partly because people who use keyboards with computers tend not to receive formal training in typing skills (although they are trained to use the software packages), partly because current legislation requires people to have regular, short breaks in typing activity, and partly because the role of typing in HCI is gradually diminishing in favor of other forms of interaction.

The human factors issues of numeric keypads have proved to be quite a thorny area, principally because the various standards bodies around the world are happy to accept both designs. Research tends to suggest that the 1–2–3 arrangement is easier to use than the 7–8–9 arrangement. One is tempted to follow the lead of Chapanis (1988) and argue that a standard for numeric keypad layout, based on sound human factors evidence, ought to employ the 1–2–3 layout. However, this would effectively "outlaw" all computer keyboards and calculators. It is, however, worth noting that as far as reasonably practicable, designs ought to use the 1–2–3 layout in preference to the 7–8–9 layout.

In the chapter some of the benefits of using function keyboards were discussed, with the proviso that human factors guidance of functional grouping of keys or mode indication (on concept keyboards) ought to be followed. It was proposed that, given a command set of acceptable size, the function keyboard can outperform typed command entry, for the simple reason that one is substituting a single keypress for a sequence of keypresses.

There are a number of human factors issues associated with the use of chord keyboards. Research suggests that, if used appropriately, they can yield superior performance to conventional keyboards. To a certain extent, the research conducted requires entry of simple codes, so that use of chord keyboards might only require the substitution of one action with a typed string. If the chord keyboard were used to enter longer strings, then one would anticipate problems of recalling the appropriate chord shape and execution of chord sequences. Certainly the distribution of errors reported suggests that the execution of chord sequences can be prone to slips and mistakes.

2.7   Key points for practitioners

- Consider the possible uses of the keyboard in an application: will a keyboard be the most appropriate device?
- Consider the possibility of using alternative layouts.
- Consider the opportunity to use alternative designs.
- Where possible, use the 1–2–3 layout for numeric keypads.
- Ensure cursor keys layout matches user expectations.
- Ensure key size, displacement, and force requirement meet standards.
- Ensure provision of appropriate feedback for key pressing.
- Consider vocabulary size (and possible modifications): will function keyboards be the best solution?
- Consider functional grouping of keys.
- Ensure appropriate labeling.
- Indicate mode for concept keyboards.
- Consider task and data entry requirements – will chord keyboards be the best solution?
- Consider formation of chords and provision of either training or mnemonics.

2.8 Key points for researchers

- Conduct longitudinal studies to compare keyboard designs for ease of learning and typing performance.
- Consider relationship between keyboard layout and typing skills.
- Consider design of keyboards for small spaces, e.g., one-handed operation or chord keyboard or alternative designs.
- Consider psychomotor skills used in chording.

CHAPTER 3

Pointing devices

Abstract

In this chapter, pointing devices are reviewed and compared. It is noted that there is a general lack of agreement as to what constitutes the best device. This lack of agreement arises from lack of adequate control in empirical comparisons and from the relationship between devices and tasks.

3.1 Introduction

It has only been in the last decade that users of personal computers have had an option as to how they could perform object selection and manipulation activities. In the past, the predominant means of interacting with the computer was through a keyboard, requiring users to remember and type commands. However, there are many problems associated with command language interfaces (Shneiderman, 1992). These problems have been addressed by substituting one interaction style for another: pointing for command languages. With the success of the graphical user interface comes the recognition that pointing devices are as permanent an attachment to our computers as keyboards. It is customary to distinguish indirect from direct pointing devices, and this distinction will be followed in the first sections.

3.2 Indirect pointing devices

Indirect pointing devices employ a secondary device, positioned away from the screen, to manipulate a cursor, e.g., joysticks, trackball, mice and tablets.

3.2.1 Joysticks

The joystick has a long history, often functioning as a device to allow a person to manipulate an object in space, the movement and direction of the object corresponding to that of the joystick. The object can be a representation on a display screen or can be a physical artifact, e.g., an aircraft. While the operation of the joystick is conceptually the same in both cases, the manner in which it will be operated will depend upon the user's perspective, e.g., using a joystick to control an aircraft in which one is sitting will differ to using the same joystick to control an image of the aircraft on a display screen. Joysticks tend to share the same appearance, i.e., a short lever mounted in a base (see Figure 3.1), but each type of joystick possess different operational characteristics (see Table 3.1). There is some evidence that controls which employ pressure as kinesthetic feedback, i.e., the isometric joystick, yield superior performance to moving controls (Gibbs, 1954; North and Lomnicki, 1961). Further, Briggs et al. (1957) demonstrate that a spring-loaded joystick, providing both displacement and kinesthetic feedback, produces the most effective performance. While joysticks are not fashionabe for personal computers, there appears to be a trend for their introduction onto portable computers. Rutledge and Selker (1990) report a small, rate-controlled joystick is incorporated into a keyboard. The pointing-stick is located between the G and H keys on a conventional QWERTY keyboard, where it is assumed not to interfere with typing. Results of evaluations of this device are interesting, in that

Figure 3.1 Example of a joystick

Table 3.1 Operational characteristics of joysticks

Joystick type	Operational characteristics
Displacement	Lever moves proportionally in direction of force supplied by user, and remains in end-position.
Spring-loaded	Lever moves proportionally in direction of force supplied by user, and returns to center position when released.
Isometric	Lever does not move. Rather, strain gauges sense the force and direction of pressure on the lever, and then translate these data into cursor movement.
Switch-activated	Lever moves proportionally in direction of force supplied by user. However, there are only eight positions which can be detected, i.e., north, north–east, south–east, south, south–west, west, and north–west.
Rate-controlled	Cursor moves incrementally in direction of force supplied by user, relative to magnitude of force, i.e., as force increase so the cursor appears to accelerate across the screen.

they show a clear superiority of the joystick over a mouse for combined pointing and keyboard tasks (presumably due to the reductions in time to move from keyboard to pointing device), but significantly longer performance times when performing multiple pointing activities, i.e., when the mouse user can keep hold of the mouse for a series of actions.

There have been few empirical comparisons between joysticks and other devices. The earlier studies found joysticks to be more accurate than either mice or lightpens (Ritchie and Turner, 1975), and of equal accuracy to a trackball (Mehr and Mehr, 1972). Subsequent studies found joysticks to be less accurate than mice (Card et al., 1978; Epps, 1986), touchscreens and lightpens (Albert, 1982). Of course, it is not clear whether these advantages relate to all types of joystick, or types used in the studies.

3.2.2 Trackballs

The trackball consists of a ball mounted in a socket (Figure 3.2); the movement of the ball against sensors in the socket corresponds to movement of the cursor on the screen. The direction and velocity of the cursor mimics the movement of the trackball in its socket. The trackball is primarily a cursor-positioning device. An additional button is required to

Figure 3.2 A trackball

allow the user to select and manipulate objects, although the activity of controlling the trackball and manipulating the button can be problematic.

One might anticipate differences in performance when comparing trackballs with other interaction devices. If one compares the operation of the trackball with that of a displacement joystick, one will notice that the trackball provides for additional activities. Whereas the displacement joystick allows the user to move a cursor at a constant rate across the screen, the trackball can be spun in its socket, thus allowing the cursor to cover large areas of the screen in relatively short periods of time. However, if one then compares the trackball against an isometric joystick one will see that both devices allow movement of the cursor without change in the location of the device, or if one compares the trackball against a rate-controlled joystick, one will see that both devices have the ability to "accelerate" a cursor, either by spinning the ball or by increasing the force on the stick. Thus, one cannot say that trackballs are better or worse than joysticks, without specifying the type of joystick used in the comparison.

The principal determinant of these findings is the task that is performed: if the trackball is used simply to move the cursor, then it may have speed advantages over other devices, whereas if it is used for a form of object manipulation, the task of moving the ball and pressing a button can be difficult.

Let us summarize the research findings. Several authors propose that trackballs are relatively easy to learn (Jackson, 1982), although there has been no research on how people learn to use such devices. As with the studies of joysticks, some studies have found in favor of the trackball (Mehr and Mehr, 1972; Albert, 1982; Ball et al., 1980; Ritchie and Turner, 1975), although the current state of research suggests that trackballs are outperformed by mice (Haller et al., 1984; Thomas and Milan, 1987; Murata, 1991; MacKenzie et al., 1991).

3.2.3　Mice

The earliest version of the mouse was developed in the mid-1960s. In this version two wheels, positioned at right angles to each other, were used to convey the x–y movement of the mouse to the computer, in order to drive the cursor on the screen. This initial design has been modified to produce the mechanical mouse of today (see Figure 3.3). The wheels have been replaced by a ball mounted against a number of sensors which can detect movement around 360°.

Mice are cheap, robust devices which can be used to perform a variety of windows management tasks and operations. The mechanical mouse is by far the most common form of pointing device on the market at the present. The movement of the mouse across the surface is translated into movement of the cursor across a computer screen. The mouse, like the trackball, allows cursor manipulation and requires a button, or several buttons, to allow object manipulation.

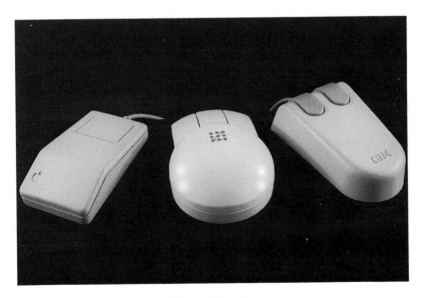

Figure 3.3　Mice

Mice can communicate with the computer in a number of ways, depending on their design. "Bus mice" communicate to the computer via a specific mouse port, whereas "serial mice" communicate via the RS232 port. The main difference between these types lies in the manner in which movement is recorded. In a serial mouse, movement in the X and Y planes are recorded on two counters (with additional counters for button depression), while a bus mouse passes electrical signals directly to the computer to be interpreted by a specific card. As well as differentiating mice in terms of their communicating protocols, it is possible to distinguish mice on the basis of position sensing, e.g., compare a mechanical mouse, described above, with an optical mouse, which senses movement by the reflection of light from a reflective mouse-mat. Finally, while the majority of mice communicate with the computer via leads, there are some mice which use either infrared or ultrasound to transmit data without the use of trailing leads.

There has been some debate as to the relative value of increasing the number of buttons on mice. For single-button mice, it is sometimes necessary to "double click" the button and the inter-button timing seems problematic for novice users. For multi-button mice, there may well be problems in terms of remembering the definition of each button (Sherr, 1988). Price and Cordova (1983) propose that using two or three buttons will be faster and more accurate than using a single button, although the advantages shown by their data are slight. The argument is that single-button mice require the user to learn "double clicks" for object selection.

Research comparing the mouse with other devices tends to show that pointing performance with a mouse is faster and more accurate than performance with other indirect pointing devices (Card et al., 1978; English et al., 1967; MacKenzie et al., 1991), but is inferior to direct pointing devices (Haller et al., 1984; Karat et al., 1984; Ritchie and Turner, 1975; Thomas and Milan, 1987).

3.2.4 Tablets

Tablets comprise a touch-sensitive area, separate from the computer screen, which can return either the location or movement of an object placed on the tablet; typically, the objects can be finger or hand, stylus or pen, or puck. When the location of the object is defined by the position of pressure from finger or pen, the device is also known as a touch pad.

Typically, the position of pressure is captured in one of two ways. In a resistive tablet, two separated resistive sheets are brought together at the point of pressure. Alternatively, in the magnetic tablet, the pen stylus detects changes in a magnetic field on the pad. There are, of course, other technologies, many of which share characteristics with touch screens (see below).

In some applications, a hand-held puck can be moved around the tablet. The puck has the look and feel of a mouse, although the number of buttons can range from a single button to around twenty buttons on the puck. Alternatively, a stylus can be used. The stylus used with magnetic tablets is similar in appearance to a pen, although it is connected to the host computer via a lead and it has a small coil in its tip rather than a pen nib. The stylus used on a resistive tablet, however, can take many forms and does not need to be attached to the host computer. As it is held like a pen, the stylus can be useful for tasks requiring fine motor coordination, such as freehand drawing. Research suggests that people can use a stylus as efficiently as they can a mouse, for a range of office based tasks (Mack and Lang, 1989; Potter et al., 1989). Mack and Montaniz (1991) found the mouse to be slightly faster and more accurate than a stylus, although this difference was reduced when the screen was tilted to enable easier inter-action using the stylus. The touch tablet allows users to use their fingers to move a cursor around the screen. In some recent developments, the tablet is positioned on a portable computer as a replacement for a trackball. Finally, as discussed in Chapter 2, it is also possible for a touch tablet to be used as a keyboard. The advantage of this is that the tablet can be reprogrammed to present different arrangements. However, a problem with touchpad key-boards is the lack of tactile feedback.

3.3   Direct pointing devices

This section contains discussion of the two main forms of direct pointing device, i.e., those which do not require the use of an additional device for object selection, the touchscreen and the lightpen.

3.3.1   Touchscreens

Touchscreens allow people to interact with computers by touching the screen with their finger. The basic concept of operation is that the user can "point" directly at an object on the screen, and by touching it, select the object (see Figure 3.4). Alternatively, recent research has focused on "lift off to select" strategies. In these applications, the selection of an object occurs when users lift their fingers off the screen. While this might appear counter intuitive, it offers the benefit of allowing objects to be dragged around the screen while the finger is in contact with them.

Figure 3.4 Using a touchscreen

There are several forms of technology which support this activity, and some of the most common are shown in Table 3.2.

Schulze et al. (1983) found that the touchscreen types could be classified in terms of accuracy, with the infrared and capacitive overlay devices producing the highest accuracy, followed by cross-wire and surface-acoustic devices, and with conductive overlay devices having the lowest accuracy. However, the authors did not perform any statistical validation of their

Table 3.2 Operational characteristics of touchscreens

Touchscreen type	Operational characteristics
Infrared beam	The user's finger interrupts beams of light which crisscross the screen. The center of the interruption is the position of the touch.
Capacitive overlay	Pressure from the user's finger acts on an overlay, causing a change in the capacitance of the overlay. The point of pressure is the position of the touch.
Resistive overlay	As with capacitive, but change in resistance.
Acoustic wave	The user's finger disturbs a field of acoustic waves covering the surface of the screen. The location of the disturbance corresponds to the object touched.

results nor did they give details of the device parameters. From Table 3.2, it should be apparent that the area of touch can be defined in different ways. Many touchscreens define the touch area in terms of several pixels (although recent advances in touch technology allow a single pixel to be returned, thus giving higher resolution). This has implications for the resolution of the screen and for the definition of objects. Of more importance to the human factors researcher is the problem which arises when the touch area is raised off the screen. This can give rise to parallax.

Parallax is the phenomenon when the user's line of sight is off center to the line of touch, i.e., when the user attempts to touch an object but hits just above or below it. This problem tends to be associated with specific types of touchscreen technology, most notoriously infrared technology, and tends to limit the accuracy of the device. Parallax problems can be simply dealt with by either repositioning the screen so that the direction of touch is in line with the line of sight, e.g., by tilting the screen upwards, or by enlarging the objects to be touched and asking users to aim for the center of the object. Gaernter and Holzhausen (1980) recommend that the object to be touched should be at least 20 mm^2. Both "solutions" introduce their own problems, in terms of limiting the number of objects which could be displayed or in terms of environmental problems, such as glare from overhead lighting.

Usher (1983) reports a significant advantage of touch screen over a function keyboard, in terms of both learning and performance. He also found that the touchscreen was preferred by the majority of participants in the study. The general consensus of the literature tends to be that touchscreens offer a fast but not particularly accurate means of object selection (Albert, 1982; Ball et al., 1980; Dillon et al., 1990; Karat et al., 1984; Ritchie and Turner, 1975; Thomas and Milan, 1987). Sears and Shneiderman (1991) found that stabilizing the touchscreen improved selection accuracy.

3.3.2   Light pens

This form of interaction device comprises a pen-like device, attached to a computer by a lead, which can be used to touch objects. Actually, the light pen is designed to detect bursts of light from the cathode ray tube, which are then used to determine the point of touching. Light pens also include a button which can be used to indicate that a touch has been made. As the pens respond to light from the CRT, they can be made very accurate and can function at the pixel level.

To a great extent, the operation of lightpens will not be dissimilar to the use of styli with touchpads. In the past few years, the pen has undergone something of a revolution in HCI. Rather than simply allowing pointing at objects on the screen, it can be used to enter text and graphics. These developments will be discussed in detail in Chapter 4.

3.4   Virtual controls

There are several applications which provide users with virtual controls on the screen. An example is presented in Figure 3.5. In using these virtual controls, the user must use a pointing device to position a cursor on the control and then use the pointing device to manipulate the control, e.g., by dragging the bars on the slider or by dragging the control knob.

In an extension to this concept, Newman (1990) proposes a virtual device called a "light handle". Imagine a window on the screen, which contains a mesh of invisible lines, paired with a numerical display. When the user moves a cursor in a clockwise motion, the movement is detected and the value in the numerical display increases (if the movement is anticlockwise, the value will decrease). The rate of change in the numerical display will depend upon the location of the cursor in the horizontal plane (with the right-hand side of the window causing slower change), and the accuracy of

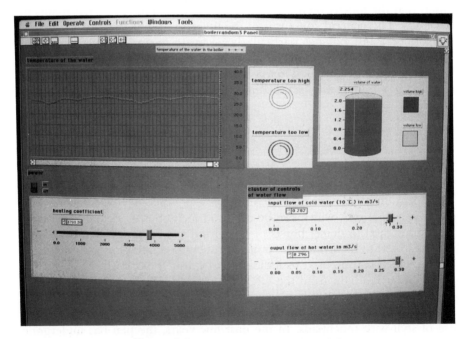

Figure 3.5   A panel of "virtual controls"

the change can be manipulated by moving the cursor vertically on the right-hand side of the window. Thus, the virtual display can be considered analogous to a series of potentiometers fixed in space, but can provide a variety of input activities to control changes in numerical information using one generic action, i.e., moving the cursor.

3.5 Device comparisons

There have been a number of empirical comparisons of interaction devices. Typically these studies focus on the variables of performance speed, accuracy, and user preference. From the preceding discussion, it can be proposed that a measure of "task-fit" could be as important as gross measures such as speed and accuracy. Further, devices differ on a number of dimensions. This implies that studies will have a propensity to find in favor of the device which is most appropriate for the performance of a specific task under specific conditions, rather than to allow the definition of the fastest or most accurate device *per se*.

Table 3.3 contains a selection of standard HCI measures for the evaluation of interaction devices. The measures are broadly categorized into time, task, accuracy and subjective measures.

Having identified a set of possible measures, the following sections will review some of the more commonly used measures and consider the data and conclusions derived from these measures. The measures used will be speed, accuracy and user preference.

3.5.1 Speed

There are two main activities involving interaction devices in which speed is an issue: cursor movement and data entry. While one might feel that the speed at which a cursor can be moved is not an important issue in the use of interaction devices, it can be proposed that devices which lead to long performance times will be disliked. There is a consistent finding in the literature that cursor keys are the slowest, and least popular, form of cursor movement. However, it is possible that cursor keys will be the fastest form of cursor movement for closely spaced objects (see Figure 2.6). Thus, one must be careful of blanket statements concerning interaction device performance, without making reference to task requirements. This is particularly true when it comes to performance times. Moving a cursor is a task which is rarely performed for its own sake: usually cursor movement is associated

Table 3.3   Measures for research

Time-based measures

- time to complete total task
- time to complete each task unit
- proportion of total time spent on each unit task
- time spent dealing with errors
- time spent consulting assistance

Task-based measures

- proportion of total task completed
- ratio of successful:unsuccessful actions
- number of commands used/not used
- frequency with which user is "lost"
- frequency with which task flow is interrupted
- frequency of "regressive"[1] actions
- frequency of repetitions
- frequency of "failed"[2] actions
- number of misinterpretations of system feedback[3]

Accuracy measures

- frequency of errors
- frequency of different types of error

Subjective measures

- proportion of users expressing favorable comments
- number of "good" features reported
- number of users expressing a preference for the system
- frequency of expressions of frustration, anger etc.

[1] A regressive action will be one which takes the user back to a previous system state.
[2] A failed action will be one which does not result in the fulfillment of the user's goals (regardless of whether or not the goals could be deemed correct).
[3] Users could either not understand system prompts or incorrectly interpret the feedback presented to them.

with either selecting an object, or moving the cursor to a specific place on the screen, or moving an object, or drawing.

Given a small number of objects to select and act upon, the function keyboard (in which each key is labeled with the name of an object) represents a fast technique (Goodwin, 1975). However, there is clearly a problem of desk-space; as the number of objects increases, so too will the number of keys needed.

Providing the objects of a display are of a sufficient size and spacing, a touch-screen is the fastest interaction device for object selection and the one which users tend to prefer (Haller et al., 1984; Thomas and Milan, 1987; Usher, 1983). The principal reason for this speed advantage is probably that the touchscreen does not require the use of a cursor; the user simply positions a finger on the desired object. In effect the user's finger acts as a cursor, but the main issue seems to be that touchscreens do not require the additional task of cursor manipulation. Rather than having to monitor the position of the cursor relative to the object, the user touches the object.

From a review of computer interaction devices in general, Milner (1988) notes that, "empirical support for the ubiquitous mouse input device is poor in the literature." However, it is truer to say that mice, generally, are outperformed by direct pointing devices, but tend to outperfom other indirect pointing devices. MacKenzie et al. (1991) show mice to be superior to trackballs in terms of both pointing at, and dragging, objects. In order to drag something across the screen, one must both "grab" the mouse (also holding down a button, which effectively renders the object on the screen as a cursor) and move the mouse (as one would move the cursor). The position of the button on the mouse allows this operation to be performed relatively easily; one can press the button with the index finger while retaining control of the mouse through the thumb and ring finger. For the trackball, control is through the fingers (usually the first two), which means button pressing might have to be performed with the thumb, throwing the hand off balance and rendering the task difficult. These points are discussed further in Chapter 9.

While there is minimal consensus in the literature, there are two conclusions which appear to be valid when discussing performance speed with pointing devices. First, speed would be task dependent, with some tasks using some devices facilitating fast performance.

Second, direct pointing devices *tend* to be faster than indirect pointing devices for object selection. In terms of speed, Carey (1985) orders pointing devices in three groups. In the first group are the direct pointing devices, e.g., touchscreen and lightpen. The second group comprises the tablet and mouse. The third group comprises the trackball, displacement joystick and isometric joystick.

3.5.2 Accuracy

As is shown in Table 3.3, studies tend to focus on errors as a measure of accuracy, often using a fairly coarse-grained analysis. There are some studies which use a more detailed definition of error, e.g., Whitefield et al. (1983), in a study of target acquisition using pointing devices, related error to target location.

While it was possible to approximately group pointing devices in terms of speed of performance, there is far less consensus as to their relative accuracy. The principal problem is that accuracy is highly dependent on both task characteristics, such as target size and position, and device characteristics. For instance, there are some important differences between the operational characteristics of different joysticks which can have a bearing on performance. Further, there does not appear to be a simple relationship between performance speed and accuracy. This might arise from experimental designs which emphasize speed at the expense of accuracy, or might be due to other factors. For instance, while the touchscreen and lightpen are generally found to support fast object selection, their accuracy has been found to be lower than that of other devices (although other research counters this finding, suggesting that poor performance may be technology, or application, dependent).

There are two principal types of error one could anticipate with the use of interaction devices: the first concerns object selection, the second concerns cursor control and positioning. The first error type relates to the design and layout of displayed information, and would result in operators selecting the wrong object. This could be exacerbated by objects having a similar appearance, although attempting to produce distinct objects, say to indicate files, may be impossible. Usually discrimination is performed on the basis of additional labeling or coding of objects. The second type of error relates to the actual control of the interaction device. Some forms of touchscreen technology are prone to problems of parallax (although this usually applies only to older, infrared models or to products at the lower end of the price range). Mice and trackballs, on the other hand, can be prone to target overshoot, especially in unskilled users.

3.5.3   User preference

In studies where users are asked to express a preference for a particular device, the results follow a similar trend to that of performance speed. The touchscreen has been preferred in several studies (Albert, 1982; Haller et al., 1984; Stammers and Bird, 1980; Whitefield et al., 1983). However, Murata (1991) reports that indirect pointing devices were preferred to a touchscreen because they were assumed to reduce fatigue in the upper arm, and in Karat et al. (1984) a keyboard was preferred for typing and menu selection tasks. The lightpen has also received a favorable response from users (Albert, 1982; Goodwin, 1975).

Following the direct pointing devices come the touchpad, trackball and mouse (Albert, 1982; Whitefield et al., 1983; Haller et al., 1984; Karat et al., 1984). The joystick tends to elicit a wide range of opinion, from most preferred (Murata, 1991) to least preferred (Albert, 1982).

As one might expect, there appears to be a relationship between preference for a device and the task which is to be performed. Given the fact that touchscreens were preferred even in studies in which the touchscreen had relatively low accuracy, one might conclude that people prefer devices which permit fast interaction over those with high accuracy. However, it is equally probable that reported preference was dependent on the perceived demands of the experiment.

In a slightly different vein, it is interesting to note that users often have some difficulty in accurately assessing performance time. For instance, in one of her studies Wolf (1992) asked participants to rate using a keyboard, or one of two tablets (one screen mounted and transparent, the other desk mounted). While 58% of the participants were able to correctly identify that their performance was fastest using the screen mounted tablet, 18% stated that they were fastest with the keyboard (the remaining 24% opted for the desk mounted tablet). However, none of the participants achieved faster performance with the keyboard than the tablets. This suggests that people base their perceptions of relative performance time on more than just objective performance times. For instance, statements of subjective preference might simply reflect participants' impressions of how well they performed the experimental task required of them and might vary quite dramatically if the preferences were elicited in a work environment. It is well established that individuals often perform rating and ranking tasks using quite idiosyncratic criteria (Oppenheim, 1992). For this reason alone, one should be a little wary of studies which use subjective preference as the primary measure of comparison between devices, especially if the participants are notably different from the type of people for whom one is designing a new computer system, e.g., undergraduate students versus air traffic controllers.

3.5.4 Summary of device comparisons

Comparison of interaction devices is not a simple matter. There are many variables which can have a bearing on the outcome of an empirical comparison and not all of the published research has effectively controlled the effects of these variables. Thus, if a study finds that performance with one device is faster than another this does not necessarily mean that the device will always be faster. The main determinants of performance appear to be type of task, e.g., pointing or dragging, the characteristics of the target, e.g., size and position of icons, the direction of movement, e.g., horizontal or vertical, and the characteristics of the device. These factors, coupled with characteristics of the user, e.g., training and experience, mean that performance will be affected by a complex relationship between a number of variables. Furthermore, the fit between device and task means that some devices will be especially suited to some types of task, e.g., if the task involves selecting a relatively large icon on a screen, one might opt for a touchscreen, whereas if the task involves selecting and moving relatively small icons, one might opt for a mouse. Following this indication of the influence of additional variables, Figure 3.6 provides a summary of current

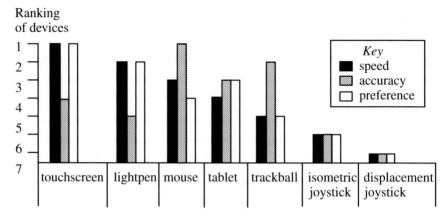

Figure 3.6   Summary of comparisons

research comparing interaction devices. The scale on the *y*-axis is intended to reflect ranking (with 1 = best to 7 = worst) and the bars are coded for speed, accuracy and preference.

3.6 Conclusions

This chapter has presented a review of the human factors literature pertaining to the use of interaction devices. The main conclusion from the review is that studies tend to be adversely affected by the choice of task; devices seem better suited to some tasks than others. If the tasks are redesigned to present a "level playing field", then it is possible to create tasks which are too artificial to translate onto real applications. Furthermore, the variation in operation of the devices (even devices bearing the same name, e.g., joysticks), can make experimental design problematic, i.e., how can all the variables be effectively controlled? For these reasons, it is probable that "head-to-head" comparisons of devices will not provide answers to the question of which device is "best". However, recent trends in research suggest that a different approach is now in favor; device comparisons are tending to focus not on whether one device is "better" than another, but on how the use of the devices vary. From this, it is possible to develop an understanding of how people use different devices to perform tasks, which can then inform design decisions concerning the type of device required.

3.7 Key points for practitioners

- *Choosing a device*: The main point to arise from the discussion is that you are unlikely to find a multi-purpose interaction device which can be used for all the tasks in the application that you are designing. This means that it is important to consider the requirements of the tasks to be performed.
- *Device comparisons*: Different devices serve different purposes. Thus, in many experimental comparisons the task is (perhaps unwittingly) weighted in favor of one device over the other. When using data from device comparisons, examine a number of different studies and try to look for aspects of the tasks which could have had a bearing on the results.
- *The importance of context*: Device performance will be influenced not simply by the design of the device but also by the requirements of the task and the abilities of the user.

3.8 Key points for researchers

- Joysticks are a much maligned interaction device and can offer a number of benefits, especially on portable computers.
- It would be interesting to see what happens when joysticks are used in 3D computer displays, after all they work well in aircraft.
- Trackballs are often used in high-stress/high-workload domains, and yet there seems to be little human factors evidence to show such devices are most appropriate in these domains.
- Despite efforts to redesign mice, they appear to be resilient to change. It would be interesting to discover what characteristics are most valuable, and what characteristics can be added or modified.
- While researchers have been studying how people use mice, there has been very little work on the psychomotor skills involved in using touchscreens. If this area could be investigated, it might be possible to decide whether touch to select or lift to select is the most useful strategy, why some people appear to be more susceptible to parallax than others, etc.
- The notion of the "light handle" seems very attractive and it would be interesting to consider whether other forms of interaction could be supported by such a "virtual device", e.g., would it be possible to develop a menu system which relied on the physical location of user actions to signify different commands?
- Researchers should introduce different contextual variables into their research, and should move into the operational domain of the devices they are studying.

CHAPTER 4

Alternative interaction devices

Abstract

While the keyboard and mouse hold sway in the arena of personal computers, there have been a number of interesting developments of interaction devices which aim to support more "natural" HCI or which can be used when the keyboard/mouse combination is inappropriate. The most commonly cited of these developments are pen-based computing and speech recognition. The human factors issues associated with these devices, along with other forms of interaction device, are considered in this chapter.

4.1 Introduction

In recent years, there has been a growth in the development and marketing of alternative interaction devices ranging from novel ways to move cursors to multifunctional devices intended to be used for text entry and cursor positioning. As the range of applications for computers increases beyond the desktop, so do the demands made on interaction devices; users want to move objects in three dimensions, they want to use computers while on the move, they want to be able to combine several interaction devices into one computer. However, if an aim in developing new interaction devices is to produce more "natural" HCI, then it is necessary to consider the relationship between activity required to use the devices and the other manifestations of that activity. For instance, speaking to a computer is demonstrably different to speaking to a person (Baber, 1993), and writing on a screen is different to writing on paper (Frankish et al., 1995).

4.2   Interaction devices for portable computers

In recent years, one of the challenges for designers of interaction devices
has been the integration of pointing devices into portable computers. One
could simply supply a separate mouse for the computer, but this seems to
miss the point of portability, i.e., where portability means liberation from a
desktop. In Chapter 3, research was discussed which placed a rate-
controlled joystick between keys on a keyboard. An alternative form of
joystick consists of a button which can be tilted and moved in response to
pressure. Loricchio (1992) reports that such a device can yield superior
performance to mouse or cursor keys, but that users tended to prefer the
mouse. This was primarily because the flat button was felt to be too
sensitive, presumably requiring more effort by the users to monitor cursor
movement. In what can be considered a variation on the flat button theme,
Gill et al. (1993) report a device in which one of the keys on the keyboard
acts as a displacement joystick, i.e., fully depressing the key allows contact
with pressure transducers which translate key motion to cursor motion.

A number of manufacturers have experimented with the integration of a
trackball onto a portable computer. While the trackball might appear to be
a sensible solution to integrating pointing devices, it is not without its
drawbacks. A potential problem with the use of trackballs or joystick
devices (using sticks or keys) is the requirement for a means of indicating
a selection, usually with a key or a button. This may lead to a requirement
for two-handed operation on portable computers, because the relative size,
sensitivity and location of the keyboard-integrated devices makes it difficult
to use fingers on one hand to control the device and press a button.

Some manufacturers have moved towards the use of small touch tablets
on the keyboard. The touch tablet could be used for both pointing and
selecting, i.e., selection being performed by tapping the touch tablet.
Alternatively, the touch tablet could require a button for selection. This
has a bearing on the way in which selection is performed. With the
trackball, the user could reach for the button while retaining finger contact
with the trackball (this would appear to be the intention behind the design),
thus leading to problems of slippage. With the touchpad, the user could lift
the finger off the pad, without disruption to cursor position, in order to
press the button. Loricchio (1993) has compared a trackball with a roll bar
for cursor manipulation on a portable computer. The roll bar is located
below the space bar and can be rolled up and down, and slide from left to
right as a means of moving the cursor. Performance was better with the
trackball, and participants preferred the trackball over the roll bar.

4.3   Gesture at the human–computer interface

There was a documentary on British television a few years ago which featured a remarkable musical instrument called the theremin. In order to play the theremin, the musician passed her hands through beams of light and the height of the hand and its position relative to the instrument corresponded to different tones. More recently, the French synthesizer player, Jean-Michel Jarre, has been using an instrument based on a similar concept in his concerts. The implication of such an instrument for HCI is twofold; it ought to be possible to create a device which operates by detecting the motion of hands in space, and, from a more extreme perspective, it ought to be possible to use different gestures to signify different objects, intentions, commands, etc.

With the exception of the hand shapes used to control a chord keyboard, the physical actions that have concerned us so far can be described as simple, in that they do not normally have any semantic content associated with the gesture itself. However, in human communication we have a wide repertoire of movements which can have some semantic content (Morris, 1994). Further, in human communication people use a number of postural and gestural cues to indicate intention, such as using gestures for emphasis, e.g., using one's hands to mark an important point, coordinating turns by gestures, e.g., by pointing to someone to speak next, using gestures as a form of feedback, e.g., nodding, indicating attitude by posture, e.g., by leaning towards the speaker. Koons et al. (1993) classify gestures which could be used in HCI into four categories. Symbolic gestures convey some linguistic meaning, e.g., in signing. Iconic gestures are used to describe specific properties of an object, such as how wide it is. Deictic gestures are used to point to some object in the environment (called "position gestures" by Fairchild, 1992). Pantomimic gestures involving "acting" the use of a tool or object. For instance, if a user moves his hands in space "as if holding a mouse", the movement can be captured and used to control cursor movement.

From this classification, one can see that gestures already exist in contemporary HCI. The use of chords as a form of gesture was considered in Chapter 2, and the use of devices for pointing have been discussed. Hand et al. (1994) make the useful distinction between 2D and 3D gesture in HCI. They argue that 2D gestures are performed using keyboards or pointing devices, and that 3D gestures involve movements of the hand in space. In the following discussion, these terms have been combined into the broad headings of signaling and signing.

4.3.1 Signaling

There are gestures which can be used as a means of signaling, in addition to pointing. Eberts (1994) discusses a system being developed by NTT in Japan, which analyzes a video-image of the user's face to extract cues, such as nodding or shaking the head. However, there might be problems based on the definition of signals in different cultures (Morris, 1994). For instance, in the UK a nod of the head means "yes", whereas there are other cultures in which nodding means "no", e.g., Greek). Furthermore, there will be many facial expressions which have little or no direct relevance to the task in hand. The very ambiguity of human signals might be ground for sticking with the tried and tested interaction devices which permit discrete, unambiguous signals to be transmitted from user to computer.

As with many topics of interest to HCI, pointing only becomes problematic when it "breaks down". An example of the "breakdown" of pointing occurs when people use a remote control handset to focus an image from a 35 mm slide projector: do they point the control at the projector (which, of course, the handset controls), or do they point the handset at the projected image they wish to focus? When people try to focus an image, they are manipulating the object of interest rather than the control device. Perhaps allowing them to focus the projected image by pointing at it would overcome such problems. Extending this proposal slightly, perhaps allowing people to point to objects on displays would simplify selection. We have already met one instantiation of this proposal in Chapter 3; the touch-screen, in all its guises, allows the users to point to and touch an object. Suppose we would like to perform pointing at a distance of a meter or two from the screen, could this be made possible?

Bolt (1980, 1984) reports a system called "put that there", which allows one to point to objects on a screen when the user is positioned some distance from the screen. The system employs position sensing of the person's wrist, relative to a device in a fixed location in the room. In other words, although the person will point at the screen, the screen has no capability of sensing the gesture. Rather the relative location and attitude of the wrist is calculated and translated into cursor positioning. One could imagine developments of this approach which employs screens with active sensing qualities. However, the basic human factors principle of pointing with the hand remains. An important question for such systems will be how accurately can the hand gesture be paired with cursor positioning or object selection? While this could be viewed as a problem, one could imagine a number of ways in which jitter and instability could be removed from the system, e.g., through filtering or sampling of the signals.

4.3.2 Signing

When considering signing in HCI, the most popular form of interaction device is the DataGlove or Z-Glove (Eglowstein, 1990; Herndon et al., 1994; Sturman and Zelter, 1994; Zimmerman et al., 1987). Variations on the design of these gloves allow the user to make signs to which the computer can respond, by varying the position and orientation of the hand. Gloves can be used to manipulate representations of objects by reaching and grasping them. Providing the gloves with some means of force sensing can allow users to "perceive" the physical characteristics of the objects.

An excellent example of using the hands to signal to a computer is provided by a video game. One manufacturer of computer games supplies a device which can interpret a "vocabulary" of about three hand shapes to indicate chops, slaps or punches of different speeds. Users move their hand across the device in the appropriate shape and at the appropriate speed. The implication of this product is that gestures will be most appropriate for relatively small vocabularies. However, it is possible to define a vocabulary of hand shapes (Hand et al., 1994). Taking this to a logical conclusion, computers could respond to sign language. Murakami and Taguchi (1991), for instance, used a neural net to recognize the characters of the Japanese Kana Manual alphabet. A glove was worn by the user, who then formed signs to the computer. Performance, for a skilled signer, was impressive, at around 98%.

There are, however, problems with current glove designs. For instance, it is not always possible to define individual fingers with precision (Rijpkema and Girard, 1991). Furthermore, the design of the gloves make casual use difficult (McAvinney, 1990).

4.4 Beyond pointing devices

The desire to expand both the range of applications and the range of potential users of interaction devices leads to consideration of performing pointing tasks without the use of hands, e.g., either due to physical disability or due to a need to keep hands on another control, say controls in an aircraft. For instance, one could monitor head movements and translate these into cursor movement (Spitz and Drumm, 1991; Hamman et al., 1991; Heuvelmans et al., 1990). Alternatively, one could control cursor movement by the tongue (Schmidt and Zang, 1992; Fortune et al., 1991). While head or tongue movement could be used as a means of moving a cursor, it is necessary to incorporate some other means of indicating that a selection is to be made. For a number of years, devices have been developed which can be used to select objects using the action of sucking or blowing (Haley, 1991).

One might decide that the use of the head would not be possible, e.g., due to environmental problems, such as vibration, or due to technical problems. If the user is seated, then one could use a foot-operated device, placed on the floor, which can be used to move a cursor (Pearson and Weiser, 1988). With limited practice, people can achieve acceptable levels of performance when using foot-operated devices, or "moles", for pointing and more complex cursor positioning tasks (Anderson et al., 1993).

The eyes are the principal means by which we acquire information from our environment. From this one could assume that where the eyes are directed will be the focus of our attention, although this assumption is not strictly true. Consequently, it might be possible to track eye movement and gaze fixation as a means of either cursor positioning or display control. Several recent papers have reported the application of eye movement for cursor control, some use dwell time to indicate selection, some incorporate other gestures using the eye, such as blinking, to indicate selection. There are problems with the approach, most notably that referred to as the "Midas touch" of eye tracking, i.e., in which every fixation of the eye can lead to objects being selected (Jacob, 1990). This is especially problematic when one considers the number of fixations people might make in a second.

From the simple assumption that fixation equals focus of attention, one might be forgiven for thinking that seeing is a simple matter of allowing visual information to enter our eyes and that it is an activity which is uniform across different situations. However, it is well known that there are a number of different types of seeing which relate to different levels of processing. Perception of visual information begins at the level of basic attributes, such as shape and color (Grossberg, 1987). Certain stimuli, by their novelty or their movement, seem to attract visual attention. Richardson-Simon et al. (1988) demonstrate that such basic attributes are recognized much faster than their corresponding words. This is presumably because the use of words requires some form of translation between the perceived stimulus and the appropriate word. In some situations, people may need to sample information from several sources, e.g., between watching the road and checking the instrument panel when driving. This form of visual search is primarily influenced by task demands and by the attention-switching strategy that the individual chooses to adopt. Finally, there is a form of looking which does not seem to focus on visual information, a sort of gazing into space, especially when one is bored or is thinking deeply.

From this classification of ways of seeing, one can begin to see potential problems for eye movement systems. The systems will be most appropriate for applications which can be used with defined task strategies, but performance can be subject to fixation due to the design of objects on the screen. This would be problematic if a specific object, due to its conspicuity, caught the user's attention, leading to unwanted cursor movement. One might feel that allowing the displayed image to alter in response to gaze would be a good idea. Cognitive psychologists would disagree, for the simple reason that dynamically changing the display in response to gaze shifts would lead to disorientation and confusion, and could affect performance, by limiting additional information cues.

4.4.1 The neural interface

In a recent movie, Clint Eastwood has to steal a Soviet fighter aircraft. He is chased by other aircraft and a "dogfight" ensues. The weapons system operates by variations in electro-encephalographic (EEG) readings. In order to operate the weapons, our hero has to think . . . in Russian. While such a scenario may strike readers as far-fetched, there is currently research into the potential of using neural activity, via EEG, to operate computers. For instance, recent commercial work has been using biofeedback to allow users to effect changes in, for instance, direction of cursor movement (Knapp and Lusted, 1992; Pfurtscheller, 1992).

4.4.2 The haptic interface

In Chapter 9, modifications to conventional mice are discussed. The general aim of the modification is to improve pointing performance. One such modification is the use of vibro-tactile feedback to the user, such that the mouse vibrates as the cursor approaches an object on the screen. Haptic information processing involves the coordination of sensory inputs from receptors in the skin, the action of muscles and tendons and the movements around joints. One could imagine interaction devices which provide continuous haptic information to the user during device use. To a certain extent, many devices already provide forms of haptic information (indeed, Buxton, 1990a, categorizes all interaction devices which require physical activity on the part of the user, as haptic).

Haptic information is gained from many interaction devices, e.g., the feeling of keys being depressed to their snap point, the sensation of the trackball rolling against the fingers, the feeling of the mouse moving across its mat and the changing position of the forearm and hand with the mouse movement, the feeling of the screen surface when one touches an object on a touchscreen.

To sidetrack a little, Witelson (1974) and McFarland et al. (1989) asked people to feel shapes and then to either identify the shape from a visual array or to select the shape from a palpated array. For performance on the tasks by right-handed males, the general conclusions drawn from the results of the studies is that performance is superior when participants used their left hand. Nilsson et al. (1980) found that this result was not found with shapes which had easily traceable figures. This suggests that the performance difference may arise from different levels of perceptual demand. Furthermore, there is some evidence that sensory input from receptors in muscles and joints of the fingers may interact with the incoming information from the tactile receptors in the finger tips (Lederman, 1983). Lederman and Klatzky (1993) have been researching the behavior of people during haptic exploration; typically people are given objects to feel and are asked to say what the objects are. The fact that many of the objects can be recognized with ease suggests that there is a level of information processing which can access verbal labels from haptic information. Furthermore, there seems to be a set of activities which are dominant in this type of task: contour following; lateral motion, i.e., rubbing the surface of the object; pressure; unsupported holding; enclosure. In some cases, people may also attempt to test the function or range of motion of the objects.

It is possible to allow haptic exploration of objects presented to computer users. One way in which this could be achieved would be to use a data glove as the means of providing feedback to the user. In this way, it would be possible to move beyond the notion of objects as representations on the screen, to a notion of objects as physical entities with physical properties which can be explored haptically. One could present a "virtual", manipulable object to the user, which could be molded, shaped and deformed as if it were made of modeling clay (Kameyama and Ohtomi, 1993).

4.4.3 Interaction devices as clothing

In this section, attention is given to a range of applications which I prefer to characterize by the term interaction devices as clothing. Naturally, this encompasses some of the recent developments in virtual reality, but before getting too carried away, let us consider a mundane example. In the digital watch, and its derivatives, we have what can be considered the essence of miniaturization, where, in the near future, computer technology can be shrunk to fit onto an item of clothing. To date, features such as calculators, pagers and televisions have been fitted to watches. The principal human factors problems that such developments raise relate to the quality of the display, and to the physical size of the controls, e.g., some watches require the use of a stylus to press buttons which can make interaction slow and frustrating.

There have been a number of attempts to produce wearable keyboards, e.g., gauntlet-like artifacts which are worn on the user's forearm and operated using the other hand. In an extension of this concept, Masaaki and Yasuhito (1994) report a device comprising accelerometers which are worn at the base of each finger and which detect finger movement. The device can be used for data entry (by allowing chord to be formed by the hand).

In a number of flying suits, there are small pads attached to the front of the trouser leg just above the knee, which can be used to jot down notes when the pilot is seated. It does not take too great a leap of the imagination to see these pads as pen-based interfaces to a small computer, capable of storing volumes of data (so that the pilot does not have to keep erasing the pad, and can keep a full record of notes during the mission), and performing limited processing of the information written on to the pad.

Another example comes from the use of radio microphones for speech recognition equipment (Usher, 1993). Hollingum and Cassford (1987), for instance, demonstrate the use of such a system on an automobile inspection task in a factory.

The above examples illustrate the potential for interaction devices which can be worn on part of the body (the use of gloves for capturing gesture and movement has been considered above). However, the notion of interaction devices as clothing can be taken to its logical extreme by considering sensing of full body movement. Bolt (1984) discusses the use of human movement as input to animation packages. This can be achieved by simply placing photosensitive markers on body joints, filming a sequence of movement and using the position of the markers to drive an animation. To take the analogy further, Schiportst et al. (1994) describe a system comprising six transmitters which are fitted onto the body and which can be used to drive a computer image of a person in 3D space. I have not mentioned work at MITs Media Lab for reasons discussed in Chapter 1.

4.5 Pen-based computing

The lay observer of the computer world might be forgiven for thinking that all interaction devices are soon to be replaced by pen-based computer systems, so ubiquitous has the advertising been for products based on this technology. Recall that one of the goals for developing the typewriter was to produce readable script at a rate faster than handwriting. This would suggest that pen-based computing is unlikely to yield any significant speed advantages in terms of entering large amounts of text into a system, especially when one considers the additional overhead of processing times. Pen-based computing systems will not be used in preference to keyboards because of reduced transaction times, but for other reasons.

The first reason for adopting pen-based computing is the removal of the keyboard, which means that the technology can be made to fit onto small devices. While I would accept that keyboards can also be fitted onto small "personal organizer" products, I would question the overall usability of such small keyboards. The second reason is the fact that pens can be used for a variety of generic tasks, beyond text entry; specifically, they can be used for operations which are performed with pointing devices in keyboard-based systems. People could use pens to draw sketches, write notes, annotate text, select or point to objects on the screen. The third reason is that pens appear to be intuitively usable, in much the same way that speech appears to be intuitively natural. From this, it could be claimed that pen-based computing would make the technology more accessible for non-typists.

4.5.1 Technology for pen-based computing

Recall that a digitizing tablet basically consists of a flat surface which is treated in such a way as to detect pressure at different points on the surface (Chapter 3). The changes in pressure are transduced and passed on to the host processor. One way in which the user could interact with the tablet is by using a stylus or a pen. A slight extension of this concept brings us to the notion of "electronic paper" (Ellozy, 1990). In addition to responding to changes in pressure, this implies that traces can be made for movement of the pen's tip, i.e., simulating the use of ink. An approximation of the general form of the technology can be described thus: the digitizer is placed over a flat panel screen (the digitizer is transparent) and movement of a pen over the digitizer causes a corresponding movement of a line on the screen. Wolf (1992) reports a study which compares users' performance using a keyboard with a transparent digitizer tablet mounted on the computer screen and a digitizing tablet placed on the desk.

If the pen and paper metaphor is valid, then one would expect clear superiority of the transparent digitizer. Interestingly enough, while both tablets yielded superior performance to the keyboard, in terms of transaction time, there were no significant differences between tablets. However, while the mean times for the two tablets were marginally different (5.8 seconds for the screen-based tablet and 6.8 seconds for the desk-based tablet), the difference is possibly skewed by two sets of times in which the screen-based tablet appeared to permit slightly faster performance than the desk-mounted tablet: "insert row/col" (1.4 s vs. 2.1 s) and "enter" (4.7 s vs. 6.7 s). Given that, with the screen-based tablet the user marks the spreadsheet "directly" and with the desk-based tablet the user has to monitor marks made on the tablet in terms of changes on the screen, these time differences may simply reflect the difference between using direct and indirect interaction devices. Alternatively, the differences could reflect the "distance" from the pen and paper metaphor, and suggest that as one moves away from a direct application of the metaphor, i.e., writing on the screen, one begins to introduce additional task requirements, such as monitoring cursor movement, which can impact upon performance times.

4.5.2   Pen gestures

Pen gestures can either take the form of pointing to objects on the screen, in which case a pen will be used in much the same way as a stylus on a data tablet, or they can be used to make defined cursive marks to enter commands.

If we briefly dispense with the pen and paper metaphor, and simply consider pen-based computing as a variety of tablet device, then we recall that pointing to objects on a screen, using a pen or stylus, has been found to be faster and more accurate than pointing with fingers (Montaniz and Mack, 1991) or commensurate with mice (Mack and Montaniz, 1991). Thus, for the task of pointing to, or touching, objects presented on a display screen, pens could prove to be useful. However, one needs to bear in mind the potential problems arising from parallax in these tasks.

The phrase cursive gestures is used to distinguish between those types of gestures which a person can make bodily, e.g., signaling and signing, and those which a person can make using a pen. Examples of this latter type are shown in Figure 4.1. As with many of the devices considered in this chapter, the use of pens for making recognizable cursive gestures has a history of around 30 years. Sutherland (1963) used gestures made with a lightpen in his SKETCHPAD system. A potential problem lies in defining the legal set of cursive gestures which can be made by a user. One solution to this problem is to use established sets, e.g., there have been studies into the use of shorthand notation for cursive gesture systems which have shown

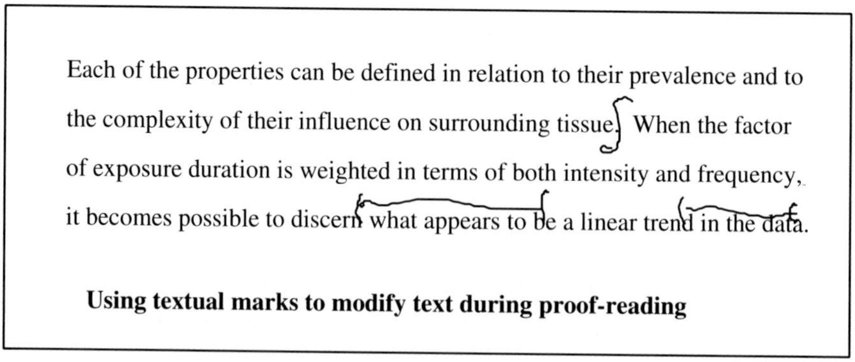

Each of the properties can be defined in relation to their prevalence and to

the complexity of their influence on surrounding tissue. When the factor

of exposure duration is weighted in terms of both intensity and frequency,

it becomes possible to discern what appears to be a linear trend in the data.

Using textual marks to modify text during proof-reading

Figure 4.1   Examples of cursive gestures in annotation

that an acceptable rate of data entry can be achieved using a pen-based system (Leedham et al., 1984; Leedham and Downton, 1986).

Gould and Alfaro (1984) found pen-based systems to be both faster and more efficient than either mouse- or keyboard-based systems for the annotation of text. Superior performance using pens has also been found for editing spreadsheets (Wolf, 1992) and editing drawings (Gould and Salaun, 1987). If we consider the types of gestures made in the examples in Figure 4.2, then a possible explanation of the superior performance of pens over keyboards suggests itself: a cursive gesture can represent a combination of typed characters, e.g., in the Wolf (1992) paper the command to sum the contents of columns is typed as "@sum (A2..G2)", whereas the cursive gesture involves drawing a line through the numbers and writing sigma, Σ. When the command to sum the content of columns is entered using the mouse, the action sequence can be defined as <move cursor to target cell>, <click button>, type "=sum", <press and hold button>, <drag cursor through range of numbers>. Comparing the mean time to enter the sum command between pen (7.4 s) and mouse (19.9 s) conditions, it is not too surprising that a difference occurs. Wolf (1992) suggests that "it is more difficult to map intentions to input for the mouse/keyboard conditions than the gestural operations" (p. 21). For the pen interface, a set of seven gestures had to be remembered. Of these gestures, one required users to write "ENTER" and another required the user to put a line through a letter and then write the correct letter. These gestures seem relatively unambiguous and similar to the meaning of the command. The remaining five gestures need to be remembered and applied. For the keyboard, on the other hand, commands appear to be less than intuitive. Thus, for the keyboard condition, users had to define a goal, specify the actions and subactions, then perform the actions. One might expect these differences to have an effect on error rate, but no data are supplied.

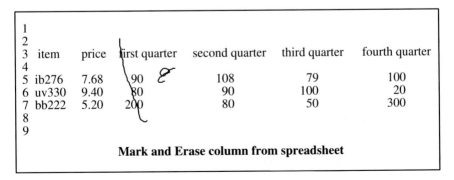

1						
2						
3	item	price	first quarter	second quarter	third quarter	fourth quarter
4						
5	ib276	7.68	90	108	79	100
6	uv330	9.40	80	90	100	20
7	bb222	5.20	200	80	50	300
8						
9						

Mark and Erase column from spreadsheet

Figure 4.2 Cursive gestures on a spreadsheet (adapted with permission from Wolf, 1992, *Business and Information Technology* **11**(1), 13–23, Taylor & Francis)

The point was raised in Chapter 3 that comparison of devices is often problematic, especially when performance data is measured at the level of seconds or below. Given that there are differences between device operation and the way in which a user can approach a task, it should not be surprising that performance differences arise between systems using the different devices. Furthermore, in the Wolf (1992) study, experience in using mice appears to be a significant role in users' performance, e.g., participants were "pen naive" and their mean time per task was around 13 s, but while the mouse-naive users had a mean time of 30.0 s, the experienced mouse users had a mean time of only 17.6 s (although the difference in performance time between pen and experienced mouse user was still significant).

4.5.3 Handwriting recognition

While it would appear that pen-based systems can be used for making simple "gestures", either through pointing or through specified textual marks, it is not readily apparent that this means that one can use the pens to write text. For this to be viable, the technology needs to be capable of recognizing either cursive script, or at least a constrained version of handwriting.

In some applications, there seems to be a tendency for the characteristics of digitizer tablets to hamper handwriting, specifically through misrepresenting pen position or movement. To a certain extent, these problems might be related to either display-digitizer resolution, or system response time and processing speeds, or parallax problems.

Frankish et al. (1995) found that average recognition accuracy, in their tests, was 87% (although this ranged from 76.1% to 90.9%). From this, and related studies, one can deduce that, given the current levels of technology, it is unlikely that handwriting recognition can be a viable technique for entering unconstrained text, even for passages of relatively short length (Oviatt et al., 1994; Frankish et al., 1995).

4.5.4 Conclusions

While handwriting recognition may not perform as well as people might expect, there has been a growing range of pen-based computers launched onto the market. Many of these products take the form of Personal Digital Assistants (PDAs), which combine note-taking facilities with diary and other information storage options. PDAs tend to combine pointing for command entry, with bit-mapped image capture of pictures and words. Thus, while the systems might not be able to accurately recognize text, they have the capability to capture and store it. This provides a device with some of the characteristics of paper, i.e., permanent storage without interpretation of information, but with some of the operational characteristics of a computer.

4.6 Speech-based computing

The idea of speaking to computers has been viewed as an attractive proposition in science fiction literature for decades; how else would one communicate with HAL or C3PO? However, the reader might be surprised to learn that attempts to produce voice-activated products can be traced back to 1911 (Baber, 1991). Large-scale industrial research into speech recognition really began in the 1950s, with a number of telecommunications companies looking for ways to expand the services they could offer. From this work came devices which could recognize digits or could use small vocabularies. In recent years the technology has advanced to a stage where it can be used in offices (Noyes and Frankish, 1989), in industrial applications (Noyes et al., 1992), and is being considered for military applications (Moore, 1989).

Linggard (1990) defines the "original *raison d'être* of speech recognition" as the facilitation of more natural human–machine interaction. Chapanis (1975) found that speech was the most effective communication medium for problem solving between two people. However, the analogy between human communication and the use of speech recognition is very limited, because the devices recognize rather than understand speech; in other words, while it might be natural to speak to other people, it is not natural to speak to a computer (Newell, 1984).

Speech recognition employs a wide range of techniques for matching speech with some stored representation of speech. The techniques vary in terms of the complexity of the stored representations used and the sophistication of matching algorithm employed (Ainsworth, 1988). It is often convenient to make a distinction between whether specific users need to train the device to recognize their speech (speaker-dependent devices) or whether people can use the devices without such training (speaker-independent devices). Baber (1991) suggests that recent years have seen a dramatic increase in the number of speaker-independent devices on the market, although there are still several applications for speaker-dependent devices, not least for applications in high-security domains. Furthermore, one can distinguish between devices which require users to pause between words (isolated word recognition) or which allow users to speak sequences of words (connected word recognition).

If we retain the view that speech recognizers match patterns (in much the same way as handwriting recognizers), then we can assume that perfect performance will be unlikely (this statement can be put into context when we consider the performance of a finely tuned speech recognizer, i.e., a human, when using a limited channel such as a telephone). The inherent variability of human speech poses problems for speech recognition (see Chapter 8). One could propose a number of solutions to this problem: provide additional information, e.g., use more than one communication modality (see Chapter 14), provide explicit information regarding what has been recognized, provide an efficient means of handling recognition errors, develop intelligence for the speech recognition system.

The requirement for error correction need not necessarily imply that speech technology is inferior to other interaction devices (see Figure 4.3). After all, most forms of computer interaction device have the potential to produce incorrect input, either through user error or technical malfunction. However, as Peckham (1986) has noted other forms of interaction device, such as a keyboard, appear to have a "standardizing effect" on user input, i.e., it does not matter how a user strikes a key (within tolerable limits), providing the user strikes the desired key. With speech recognition, the manner in which the user produces a spoken utterance can affect performance. In other words, the limits of tolerance are much tighter for a speech recognizer than other interaction devices. If efficient error-correction techniques are properly incorporated into the speech-based interaction, i.e., if they are both effective and unobtrusive, then they can be used to

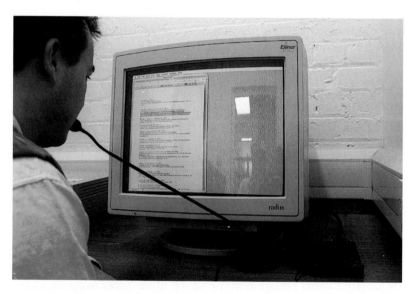

Figure 4.3   Using a speech recognizer for annotation

broaden these limits of tolerance and produce comparable performance. Thus, a prime requirement for the design of speech systems is the definition and comparison of error-correction strategies.

It has become customary to divide errors into three types: rejection, insertion and substitution. Rejection errors occur when a legal vocabulary item is spoken by the user and the speech recognition device does not respond. This suggests a problem in the communication between user and device. Brown and Vosburgh (1989) found that rejection errors accounted for 2–3% of recognition errors in their studies. Thus, while rejection errors can occur, they are rare and can often be dealt with by improving communications.

The next type of error, insertion, occurs when spurious noise, originating from either the user or the environment, is recognized as a legal vocabulary item. Brown and Vosburgh (1989) found that insertion errors accounted for 5–6% of recognition errors. This problem could be reduced using a number of techniques, such as altering microphone position, providing some means of masking for ambient noise, performing enrolment in similar ambient noise levels to task performance, etc.

The final type of error, substitution, occurs when a legal vocabulary item is spoken by the user and the device "recognizes" a different item. This type of error accounts for over 90% of recognition errors (Brown and Vosburgh, 1989) and is the main focus of efforts to develop error-correction techniques.

Baber and Hone (1993) discuss a number of approaches to error correction, ranging from using some level of device intelligence to simple repetition of misrecognized words by users to error-correction dialogues. They conclude

1. Error correction should rest with the user (although device assistance can be beneficial).
2. Error correction should be incorporated into the primary task (rather than require additional dialogue).
3. The choice of error correction will be influenced by the recognition accuracy of the device.

Unlike most other interaction devices, speech recognition does not have feedback inherent in its use (e.g., cursor positioning devices present movement of the cursor and provide visual feedback, keys on a keyboard move and provide tactile feedback). This means that some form of indication is required to inform the user that recognition has occurred, either in the form of an auditory tone, or a spoken response, or a visual response. Feedback can be provided at various points in the interaction, the most obvious of which are after each individual subunit of dialogue (word, digit, letter) or after each complete dialogue unit (command, phrase, digit string, etc.). It has been suggested that feedback be provided at the end of a complete dialogue unit (Hapeshi and Jones, 1989); depending on the definition of dialogue unit, this could be digit, word, sentence, command, etc.

Frankish and Noyes (1990) have shown that auditory feedback can reduce the possibility of users' either missing or misreading feedback. For visual feedback, it has been proposed that a text window is used for the complete dialogue unit (Schurick, Williges and Maynard, 1985). Baber et al. (1992) demonstrate that a determining factor in the use of feedback is its function in the task, hence different tasks are best supported by different feedback media. The most appropriate medium will be defined by user requirements and the function of the feedback (Baber et al., 1991; Baber et al., 1992).

4.6.1   Selecting objects and entering data

While speech recognition does not appear to offer much benefit for controlling the movement of a cursor, it can provide a means of selecting objects and entering limited amounts of information. Often people speak of the advantages of speech recognition as permitting "eyes- and hands-free" operation, e.g., by allowing people to perform object selection and data entry tasks while performing a primary task such as piloting an aircraft.

Welch (1977) compared the use of speech for "simple" and "complex" tasks. His study compared an isolated word speech recognizer with a QWERTY keyboard and a menu-based system for two types of data entry task. The tasks were defined as "simple", i.e., entering strings of three to ten characters, and "complex", i.e., composing flight data control messages in an air traffic control scenario. The data show that while the keyboard was fastest for simple data entry, speech recognition was fastest for the complex tasks (although it is fair to say that the relative error rates tend to paint a slightly different picture). Relating this to applications, speech may be more suitable to "complex" tasks, i.e., ones which involve more than simply entering digit strings. However, Damper (1988; 1993) questions the validity of such comparisons, pointing out that entering a word on a letter-by-letter basis is inevitably slower than entering it as a complete word. From this, one ought to consider comparisons of speech with function keyboards in order to produce equivalent conditions. It does suggest that entering some forms of data can be effectively performed using speech.

As one might expect from the discussion of device comparisons in Chapter 3, there is some disagreement in the findings from studies which compare speech with other devices. Some studies have found speech to be faster and more accurate than touchscreens (Crane, 1984; Reising and Curry, 1987), or function keyboards for large vocabularies (Mutschler,

1982), or menus (Dillon et al., 1990; Karl et al., 1993; Martin, 1989). Other studies have found speech to be slower and less accurate than touchscreens (Aretz, 1983), or function keyboards (Brandeau, 1982; Baber, 1991) or keyboard (Mitchell and Forren, 1987). Of note is the work by Reising and Curry (1987) who demonstrated that the superiority of speech recognition over touchscreens could be reduced by redesigning the dialogue used with the touchscreens. Thus, the issue would appear to be one of dialogue design as much as technology.

4.6.2 The talkwriter

Meisel (1986) notes that there is an enduring fascination with the concept of the speech-driven typewriter, which he terms the "talkwriter". Probably the earliest demonstration of a system which could be called a "talkwriter" occurred in the mid 1950s. Olson and Belar (1956) report a device which could recognize phrases such as "I can type this now". Several companies market speech recognition devices which allow for users to enter large amounts of unrestricted text for word processing (e.g., Dragon, IBM, Olivetti). However, there appear to be a number of human factors problems associated with these devices, although their performance is often very impressive. When I have used a "talkwriter", I find that it is necessary to monitor the recognition process; if a word is misrecognized, it needs to be corrected, otherwise the recognition algorithm will modify itself to match the speech pattern with that label. This tends to interrupt my train of thought, making direct dictation to the machine not only slower than typing, but also cognitively demanding. Carter et al. (1988) found that composition rates using a "talkwriter" tended to average around 12 words per minute (as compared to around 60 words per minute for a competent typist). Having noted these problems, I also know people who claim to be able to dictate to a "talkwriter" and produce text as quickly and accurately as when they type.

4.7 Conclusions

The range of application domains in which people wish to interact with computers is growing apace. This calls for new forms of interaction device. A number of these devices have been discussed in this chapter, together with some of the human factors which are associated with them. There is unlikely to be a single device capable of fulfilling all the requirements a user might have. Each of the devices considered in this chapter has potential application for a range of tasks, often in a range of environments.

Much of the work discussed in this chapter relates to work in progress; even products on the market can be considered "prototypes" or "concept demonstrators" rather than fully fledged devices. To a certain extent this reflects the competition within the computer marketplace. However, it also reflects two other factors: the pace of change and the lack of clear understanding of what people require from these devices.

With many of the best-designed products, we often do not realize that we are even using a product, so smoothly does the performance of a task appear. As task performance "breaks down", so our attention focuses on the tool rather than the task. The fact that so much effort is being put into various forms of "error correction" for these novel HCI devices might make one feel that, as a community, we are concentrating too much on the tools rather than on the tasks. Perhaps the reason for this is that we are unable to fully specify what the tasks are, and, instead, aim to produce tools which can be used by anyone for anything. The question is, to what extent will this approach lead to development, and to what extent will it lead to the reinvention of existing products and concepts?

4.8   Key points for practitioners

- System design should commence from user requirements and consideration of other tasks which the user might perform in conjunction with device use.
- Aim to match device requirements to user capabilities.
- Aim to match device operation with user knowledge and experience.
- Do not use pen-based computing for tasks which require large amounts of text entry.
- Design speech systems to incorporate error handling.

4.9   Key points for researchers

- Consider the relationship between human capabilities and device operation.
- Consider the requirements for device accuracy and performance.
- Consider ways in which performance can be quantified and compared across devices.
- Consider the ways in which user performance breaks down and develop ways to handle breakdown gracefully.

CHAPTER 5

Classifying devices

Abstract

In this chapter attention is shifted from device comparisons to device classification. Devices often appear to be most appropriate for specific tasks. If one could classify devices in an unambiguous fashion, then it would be possible to determine the suitability of specific devices for specific applications.

5.1 Introduction

With the vogue for new interaction devices, systems designers are faced with a bewildering range from which to choose the "best" interaction device for a specific application. Attempts to provide guidance on the basis of empirical device comparisons can be problematic, due to the interaction between a particular device and a particular task. However, it might be possible to define a set of tasks against which all devices can be considered. Thus, it is proposed that devices can be classified in terms of their suitability for certain tasks and in terms of the type of activity that they support.

5.2 Defining generic actions

The interaction between human and computer can comprise a wide range of different activities. One could begin the task of classifying interaction devices by suggesting that most tasks at the human–computer interface involve either entering data or moving objects around the screen, e.g., a cursor, an icon, or (in a drawing package) lines and shapes. At this simple level, one can argue that some of the devices will be useful for text entry and others will be useful for manipulating objects.

Further, for devices which can be used to manipulate objects, one can distinguish between those devices which allow users to operate directly on the object and those which are indirect. However, the "text entry/move object" and "direct/indirect" distinctions do not strike me as particularly fruitful as they add little to a common-sense understanding of interaction devices. Some authors have moved beyond these dichotomies and suggested that HCI activities can be decomposed into a set of generic actions (Carey, 1985; Foley and van Dam, 1982; Foley and Wallace, 1974; Foley et al., 1990; Wallace, 1976). In recent years, an ISO standard has been drafted which uses the concept of generic actions to describe graphic interfaces (ISO/DP 7942). On the basis of this work it is possible to propose a set of generic actions which characterize HCI (see Table 5.1).

For each generic action, the way in which the action is performed will be influenced by the information presented to the user and the type of device used. For instance, one could select an item from a menu by typing its number, or by typing its name, or by pointing to a menu heading, pulling down the menu and releasing on the item, or by pointing at the menu heading to call up the menu and then pointing to the menu item. The reader can probably supply further examples; suffice it to say that even for as simple a task as selecting an item from a menu, there is more than one

Table 5.1   Generic actions in HCI

Generic action	Example
1. Select objects	
Selecting objects on a display screen	"Clicking" on an icon
	Picking an item from a menu
2. Dragging objects	
Dragging objects around the screen	Dropping a file in the waste basket
	Dragging a file into a folder
	Moving a cursor
Drawing a line between two points	Drawing a straight line
	Drawing a freehand line
	Drawing a curve of defined diameter
3. Changing the orientation of objects	
Altering the orientation of objects	Rotating a picture through 90°
4. Entering data	
Entering numbers	Specifying a value
	Populating a spreadsheet
Entering text	Typing a report
	Naming an object

possible approach. A problem with the use of the term "menu selection" to describe action is that there is a further level of description which can be invoked to explain the differences in using a range of menu types. Thus, a set of generic actions needs to be described at a less ambiguous level than "menu selection". The problem is to define a level of description which will avoid ambiguity while retaining as much descriptive power as possible.

5.2.1 Selecting objects

The selection of an object could be approached in two principal ways: the object could be "named" and thus selected, or the object could be indicated and then selected. In the first approach users speak, write or type the object's identification (its name or code) which both indicates the object and indicates that it is to be selected. In the second approach, users indicate the object, perhaps by positioning a cursor on it, and then indicate that it is to be selected, perhaps by pressing a button.

While the first approach might appear appealing, in that it seems more direct, it could be prone to errors which cannot be dealt with until after the selection has been made; thus requiring additional confirmation action to signal that the selection was intended (Usher and Baber, 1989). The inclusion of this type of confirmation invalidates the distinction between the two types of selection. Therefore, it is preferable to subdivide selecting objects into the two stages of indicate object and indicate selection. The two stages are not of themselves generic actions because in some cases they are combined into a single action, thus making the distinction redundant, and in others they are performed using other generic actions, e.g., move cursor or enter text or numbers.

Table 5.2 contains a number of interaction devices classified according to the actions required to indicate object and selection. In a number of cases, a single action incorporates both object indication and selection. In these cases, the action is placed between the two columns. The sets of indirect and direct pointing devices indicate that devices in the set could be used in this manner.

There are clearly many options open to designers and users for performing this type of action. One could limit the choice by considering the action in slightly more detail. For instance, is it desirable for users to select objects with a single action, perhaps due to time constraints, or is it acceptable for users to perform two actions? If the answer is the latter, then one might decide to use an indirect pointing device. If the answer is the former, then one needs to decide whether objects will have a verbal identification (which can be spoken, typed, etc.), or whether the objects be represented graphically, say by an icon. In this case, one might use a direct pointing device,

Table 5.2 Interaction devices for selecting objects

Indicate object	Indicate selection	Interaction device
Enter object's number	Press key: e.g., return key	Keyboard Speech
Enter object's name	Press key: e.g., return key	Keyboard Speech
Position cursor on object	Press button	{Indirect pointing device}
	Touch object on screen	{Direct pointing device}
	Enter object's number	Numeric keypad Alphanumeric keyboard Pen Speech
	Enter object's name	Alphanumeric keyboard Pen Speech
	Press labeled button	Function keyboard Concept keyboard
	Mark object: e.g., draw a line across it	Light pen Tablet Pen
	Position cursor on object	Eye tracking Suck–blow devices
	Vocalize	Speech

e.g., touchscreens provide fast selection, providing the objects on the screen are of sufficient size and spacing.

Table 5.2 contains some approaches for selecting objects presented visually. There will be some situations in which objects are presented using a different medium, e.g., using sound. An example of this would be the presentation of a set of options over a telephone on a flight enquiry service. In this case, the interaction device used would be determined by the technology, i.e., some means of sending a signal over the telephone. One might anticipate that this would be speech recognition. However, speech recognition can be made to function in a number of ways and can require greater or lesser effort on the part of the user (Ainsworth, 1988; Baber, 1993). For instance, the user might have to wait until the end of the list before speaking the name of the desired item, or could simply say "stop" at the appropriate juncture. If the latter option is acceptable, then one could replace speech recognition with a telephone handset capable of sending an auditory tone in response to a button press, i.e., dual tone multi-frequency (DTMF).

5.2.2 Dragging objects

With the rise of the windows, icons, menus, pointing device (WIMP) interface, the increasing range of drawing and drafting packages on the market and the explosion in video games, has come a significant need for users to be able to move objects around the screen. The objects are not simply cursors or icons, but could be characters in a video game or lines and shapes in a drawing package. The generic action of moving an object involves three components, indicating the object, moving the object and dropping the object in a new location. However, while the action of selecting an object can be either discrete or simultaneous, indicating, moving and dropping objects are normally consecutive, i.e., one first indicates the object, moves it and then drops it. In some video games, the object is selected for the user, i.e., the object is the little character that the player moves through the game, and the direction of movement is limited to one direction (the player may have the option to turn the character in order to move in the opposite direction, and can make the character "jump"). In this instance, the "object" is already selected and is shown in Table 5.3 in square brackets [ ]. This means that the user is not explicitly required to either indicate or drop the object (although indication and dropping are inherent in the use of controls to move the character; move the control and the character is "identified", stop moving the control and the character is "dropped").

In many applications, the object only needs to move in two dimensions, e.g., up, down, left, right. There are some packages which limit movement to "one dimension", having selected the straight line tool the user can move a cross-hair cursor across the screen, leaving the trace of a straight line. The path of the cursor is anchored to the horizontal plane, so that even if the user does not hold the mouse steady, a straight line is always produced. Some movement can be effected in three-dimensional space, e.g., "exploring" a building in virtual reality. The task of drawing lines, etc., is usually confined to drawing and CAD packages, although it need not be their exclusive province, e.g., amending figures in graph packages. Generally, there are two approaches to moving objects: users specify the end-point coordinates of the object, or users indicate then move the object. CAD packages also permit the user to constrain and modify the resulting shape, and many drawing packages allow the user to select pre-drawn geometrical shapes which can be stretched, etc., at the user's discretion (Davies et al., 1986).

5.2.3 Changing the orientation of objects

Some drawing packages allow users to change the orientation of objects in a drawing by using menu commands such as "rotate left", "rotate right",

Table 5.3 Interaction devices for dragging objects

Indicate object	Move object	Drop object	Interaction device
[Specified]	Enter direction	Release button	{Indirect pointing device}
Touch object on screen	Drag object	Release touch	{Direct pointing device} Pen
Position cursor on object and press button	(i) Hold button (ii) Drag object	Release button	{Indirect pointing device}
Position cursor on object	(i) Indicate direction (ii) Move one unit or move several 'units'	(Press enter)	Cursor keys
Position cursor on object	Enter destination	Press enter	Numeric keypad
Enter object's ID	Enter destination	Press enter	Alphanumeric keyboard
Enter object's ID	Enter destination	Speak command	Speech
Enter object's ID	Point to destination		Speech and gesture or {Pointing device}

"flip vertical", "flip horizontal". In a video game, the objects of interest might be an aircraft which the user can control using a joystick to alter the roll, pitch and yaw of the display. Further, the majority of readers will be familiar with resizing windows on WIMP interfaces, in which the window is "grabbed" and its size and shape altered on the screen. Windows can be resized in several ways: they can be dragged (a combination of selecting the appropriate part of the window and moving the part), or they can be exploded (by selecting another part of the window to bring it from small size to full screen size), or they can be shrunk (some packages allow windows to be turned into icons by selecting another part of the window frame, with the opportunity to select the icon to recall the window). The square brackets [ ] in Table 5.4 signify that the action already has been performed, either by the computer or by the user. For the [select object] actions, refer to Table 5.2.

Table 5.4 Interaction devices for changing orientation

Indicate object	Change orientation	Interaction device
[Specified]	Alter roll, pitch, yaw	Joystick
[Select object]	Select menu command	{Indirect pointing device}
[Select object]	Enter new orientation	{Pointing device} Combined with: alphanumeric keyboard speech
Enter object's ID	Enter new orientation	Alphanumeric keyboard Speech

5.2.4 Entering numerical values

Numbers can be entered using a numeric keypad, pen or speech. However, the discussion of "virtual interaction devices" in Chapter 3 shows that packages can include a representation of a potentiometer which the user can manipulate to increase or decrease the relative value of a specified quality, e.g., brightness or contrast of the display. Alternatively, a popular means of altering numeric values is through the use of a scrolling number window (see Figure 5.1).

The user selects the up or down arrow to increase or decrease the value. In some applications of this idea, the amount of force the user exerts in selection or the amount of time the arrow is selected is related to a ramp function which increases the rate of change in the window. Having said this, a problem with the approach comes from the user "overshooting" the desired value.

Thus, there are two classes of device for entering numerical values: devices which allow the user to alter or modify the value, e.g., rotary or

Figure 5.1 Scrolling number window

linear potentiometers, or scrolling number windows; and those which require the specification of numeric values, e.g., using numeric keypads, or speech, or pen.

5.2.5 Entering text

Text entry is the most common form of computer activity. However, with the development of CD ROM encyclopedia and interactive computer technology, it is credible that the importance of text entry might diminish over the coming decade, to be superseded by selection of items.

The alphanumeric keyboard is still the most common form of interaction device (readers are challenged as to whether they would be prepared to have a computer which did not have a keyboard on which to perform all their work) although there are several potential alternatives to the keyboard, e.g., handwriting and speech recognition systems. Finally, for highly restricted entry of text, one can treat text entry as a form of object selection (e.g., selection of commands from a menu or a function keyboard).

5.2.6 Conclusions

While the generic actions described above can cover many aspects of HCI, they do not of themselves describe some of the common actions involved in working with WIMP systems, e.g., multiple selection of objects. The user might want to select more than one object on the screen, e.g., when putting files into a new folder or into the waste basket. Rather than repetitively selecting one object and acting upon it, many packages allow multiple selection, either through "rubber banding", i.e., dragging an imaginary rubber band around a collection of objects to select them, or repeated selection, e.g., by allowing the user to hold down the <shift key> while selecting one object followed by another, etc. However, these actions represent variations on the themes of dragging and selecting objects which have been discussed above. It is important to note the distinction between generic actions (which involve similar activity) and generic goals (which lead to similar outcomes).

The classification of devices in terms of generic actions has been received with some favor by the HCI community (Jacob et al., 1993). However, I have deliberately avoided prioritizing the devices in the tables. The approach is clearly arbitrary, with different definitions of actions leading to different conceptions of appropriateness. One could argue that the very arbitrariness of the approach tends to mitigate against its usefulness. However, this approach does allow designers to consider devices against different types of action, which could allow for some early human factors input into system design decisions.

5.3　Generic actions and widget-level design

In his discussion of HCI, Eberts (1994) illustrates the utility of the concept of "widgets" in interface design. In specifying the requirements of a particular system, one can begin at the level of partially described tools which will be used to perform specific functions, i.e., widgets. Thus, the "push button to select" widget will be a tool on the interface which requires the user to operate it in a certain way under certain conditions. From this, we can see that widgets have definable properties and can be used in definable circumstances. Eberts (1994) points out that many interfaces seem to share a common widget set, especially when one considers the WIMP-paradigm. It strikes me as a simple matter to extend the concept of generic actions, discussed above, from a classification scheme to design principles via the use of interaction device widgets.

To illustrate this point, let us focus on the generic action of selecting an object. This is assumed to comprise two components (which may or may not be performed concurrently): indicate object and indicate selection. The designer might decide that the widget has to allow the actions to be performed simultaneously, i.e., that the act of indicating an object will also indicate selection of the object. In this case, the widget would need to permit object selection with a single action, e.g., using a touchscreen, lightpen, pen, tablet, speech recognizer. It might further be required that the widget will be employed under specific operating conditions, e.g., on a hand-held compu-ter, which could rule out one or two options. By further restricting the definition of the widget, the designer can reduce the set of possible devices to a set which can be evaluated through prototyping and testing.

There is an obvious problem with this widget-level approach to design of interaction devices, and that is that one's choice will be heavily influenced by the size of the initial set, i.e., by the range of devices which are known to the designer. While a reading of this book, for instance, could expand the initial set, there is no guarantee that the appropriate device for an applica-tion has actually been designed. It might be feasible to consider the widget-level approach as a device design tool, e.g., through careful task description and elucidation of possible circumstances in which the task is to be performed, one might be able to arrive at a novel design proposal. For instance, the "light handle" (discussed in Chapter 3) is a device which combines several concepts into an ingenious tool for manipulating numer-ical displays along several dimensions.

5.4   Operational characteristics of interaction devices

While some authors have attempted to classify devices on the basis of generic task descriptions, there has been some interest in using objective descriptions of device characteristics as the basis of a classification scheme (Buxton, 1983; Card et al., 1991; Card et al., 1992).

The approach begins with the assumption that interaction devices can be considered as transducers (Buxton, 1986) and will convert user behavior into system activity. In order to describe this process, a set of basic properties is defined as:

- expressiveness
- effectiveness
- operation
- state of device.

From these basic properties, it is credible that devices possessing certain properties will be more usable than other devices. For instance, the property of device expressiveness can be defined in terms of the ratio between the number of possible actions in the input domain to the number of possible responses in the output domain. If the number of possible display responses exceeds the number of user actions, the user could mistakenly select an undesired input action, and alternatively, if the number of display responses is less than the number of user actions, the user might feel unable to perform the desired action. If there was a discrepancy between the ratio between the action in the input domain and the response in the output domain, one could propose that either error or frustration would ensue.

The property of effectiveness comprises a number of factors based on relationships between the primitive movements. Card et al. (1991; 1992) suggest that effectiveness can relate to performance speed and accuracy, users' preferences, the time it takes to reach for and grasp a device, the required desk space and the cost of the device.

While Card et al. propose that indices of expressiveness and effectiveness can be empirically derived, they propose that one means of classifying devices is through the operation of the device in three-dimensional space. In this case, movement can be in the X, Y or Z planes, and rotational movement can also occur about these planes. Furthermore, one can incorporate some indication of the type and degree of movement permitted by devices. In Figure 5.2, devices can respond to indication of a position in space (P) or to continuous changes in position (dP); devices can respond to the application of some force (F) or to changes in force (dF); devices can respond to some rotary movement (R) or to continuous changes in rotation (dR); devices can respond to the application of torque (T) or to changes in torque (dT). Several interaction devices have been placed onto

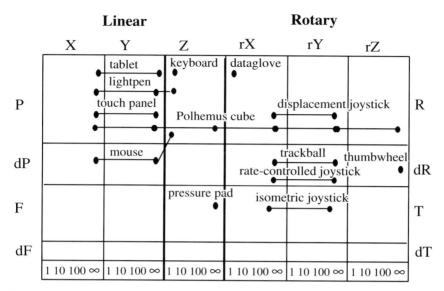

Figure 5.2 A selection of devices plotted on Card et al.'s (1992) taxonomy (from Card, S.K. et al., 1992, in M. Blattner and R.E. Danneberg (eds) *Multimedia Interface Design*, ACM Press)

the taxonomy to illustrate its basic plan. For instance, a mouse can respond to continuous changes in position (dP) and its movement in the X and Y planes is largely unconstrained, i.e., ∞, although moving it in the Z plane has no effect. The mouse also contains a button which can be moved only in the Z direction. On the other hand, changing the position of a trackball has no effect on its performance, but it does respond to continuous change in rotation (dR). If one wanted to indicate a button on the trackball, then it would be necessary to include a line from the dot in dR-rX to P-Z, i.e., to where the mouse button is indicated. From this classification of mouse and trackball, one can see that, whatever actions they are used for, there are inherent differences in the performance of the devices. The question, for this book, is whether these devices will have an impact on user performance.

5.4.1 Conclusions

Card et al. suggest that the approach offers a means of classifying interaction devices independent of task requirements, and so could allow objective comparisons to be made between different options for device selection. However, one might wonder whether it is precisely the use of a device for a particular task which defines its functionality, and that such classification tends to miss this important point. Although the approach might appear attractive, it is somewhat limited in that one cannot include speech into the taxonomy (speech does not lend itself to descriptions of spatial movement), and it is difficult to see how combinations of devices could be represented.

5.5 Performance-shaping factors

In Chapter 1, it was proposed that one needs to consider the use of interaction devices as part of the human–computer system, and to consider the influence of additional contextual factors of device use. When studying the reliability with which people can perform tasks and activities in complex systems, researchers often make reference to a concept of performance shaping factors. Basically, performance-shaping factors (PSFs) are those aspects of the task, human and situation which can be assumed to have a bearing on performance, e.g., in terms of human error. I do not believe that the notion of performance-shaping factors has been applied to the study of interaction devices, but suggest that it provides a useful framework within which to study the broader issues associated with their use. Of course, it is possible to identify large numbers of performance-shaping factors (the only obstacle being the creativity of the analyst). However, from a review of several studies, Stanton (1995) proposes that relatively few factors are needed to account for much of the variance in human performance. In this section, attention is given to four factors which are intended to describe the various components of the context of interaction device use.

5.5.1 Device

In this section the relationship between design and operation of a device is considered. At a coarse level, one could describe this factor as the ease of operation of a device, or its usability. After a discussion of the concept of usability, it has been decomposed into three subfactors: device handling, $C:D$ ratio, reliability.

The most commonly cited definition of usability was proposed by Shackel (1981). This definition concentrates on the operational aspects of using a computer, and comprises four factors:

1. learnability: a system should allow users to reach acceptable performance levels within a specified time from installation.
2. effectiveness: acceptable performance should be achieved by a defined proportion of the user population, over a specified range of tasks and in a specified range of usage environments.

3. attitude: acceptable performance should be achieved within acceptable human costs, in terms of fatigue, stress, frustration, discomfort and satisfaction.
4. flexibility: the computer should be able to deal with a range of tasks beyond those first specified.

These four factors provide a collection of basic requirements of a "usable" system and one can classify interaction devices simply on the basis of these criteria, using the general findings of studies reported in Chapters 3 and 4. This classification is applied to a selection of interaction devices in Table 5.5. The reader will recall that the results of the studies presented in Chapters 3 and 4 were treated with a degree of caution, and might feel that simply presenting the information in the form of a table does little to hide the problems associated with the derivation of the data. I would agree. However, the approach of relating devices to these usability factors has its attractions. The approach can allow one to draw up a matrix for device evaluation, at least at a global level, to consider device comparison.

The definition of usability presented above has proved popular; indeed it features in ISO 9241. However, it has been criticized for failing to consider several important points (Booth, 1989; Eason, 1984; Stanton and Baber, 1992). For instance, there is no consideration of the *perceived* usefulness of the system, i.e., do users believe that the system will help to make their work easier? In order to answer this question it is necessary to focus on the notion of task-fit. This raises the performance shaping factors pertaining to user, task and environment to be discussed below.

The design of mice encourages some physical activities rather than others; specifically, mice appear to be designed to support actions resulting in small movements of the cursor with the base of the user's hands resting

Table 5.5 Interaction devices classified in terms of usability

Usability issues	Interaction devices					
	Touchscreen	Lightpen	Tablet	Mouse	Joystick	Trackball
Learnability	+	0	0	0	0	0
Effectiveness (speed)	+	+	0	0	−	−
Effectiveness (accuracy)	−	0	+	+	−	0
Attitude	+	+	0	0	−	−
Flexibility	−	−	0	0	+	+

KEY: + better than average; 0 average; − worse than average

on the desk, curving over the mouse and fingers resting over the buttons. Adjusting the hold to make larger movements requires raising the forearm from the desk surface, leading to possible increase in strain. The shift from control movements centered about the elbow would be less precise than those centered about the wrist. Thus, the physical design of a device encourages specific types of grip and physical activity. Kroemer (1986), in a paper on the design of hand tools, proposes a classification scheme for what he terms the hand–handle interface. This scheme is applied to a selection of interaction devices in Table 5.6.

Some of the devices listed can be used with more than one type of handling. In the table, I have tried to indicate a possible reason for using one form of handling over another, e.g., whether moves are precise or fine, or whether they are coarser. Having differentiated devices in terms of the type of hand–device coupling they support, one can begin to ask questions about the user's posture when operating the device, about possible situations in which the couplings may break down, e.g., under severe environmental stresses, such as vibration, about the relative precision with which different activities might be performed using the different devices, and about how the design of the device can influence its use.

Table 5.6 Interaction devices classified in terms of grip

Grip	Example	Interaction device
Finger	Finger on device, no hold	Button touchscreen tablet trackball (fine)
Palm	Inner surface on device, no hold	Trackball (coarse)
Finger–palm	"Hook grip" (e.g., beer pump)	?
Thumb–fingertip	"Tip grip"	Joystick (fine) toggle switch
Thumb–finger–palm	"Pinch grip"	Joystick (coarse)
Thumb–Forefinger	"Lateral grip"	Mouse (fine)
Thumb–Two fingers	"Pen grip"	Pen stylus
Thumb–fingertip	Disk "grip"	Puck mouse (coarse)
Finger–palm	"Collett enclosure" e.g., ball	Air-mouse
Hand	"Power grasp" e.g., hammer	?

Consider displacement and isometric joysticks: the former provides a direct mapping of displacement to cursor movement, while the latter allows for some acceleration of cursor movement. This illustrates a distinction between orders of control. A zero-order control translates device displacement directly into cursor displacement. A first-order control translates device displacement into a velocity-linked cursor displacement. A second-order control requires a movement to accelerate the cursor towards a target and then a movement in the opposite direction to decelerate the cursor onto the target. Lower-order controls are preferable for target acquisition tasks (Poulton, 1974; Hammerton, 1962). The control:display ratio of an interaction device is simply an expression of the relationship between device and cursor movement. A low ratio allows a high degree of "play" in an interaction device. The defining factors of $C{:}D$ ratio are the amplitude of movement for the device (A_d) and for the cursor (A_c), together with the amount of permissible movement of the device (W_d) and the width of the target to which the cursor is aimed (W_c). There seems to be some evidence to suggest that speed of performance is related to A_d and W_d (Buck, 1980), whereas accuracy of performance is related to A_c and W_c (Tränkle and Deutschmann, 1991). This would lead to the proposal that tampering with the C:D ratio need not lead to more efficient performance. Indeed, studies of "powermice" and their variants have shown that altering the $C{:}D$ ratio has no effect on performance (Jellinek and Card, 1990; Tränkle and Deutschmann, 1991).

Direct pointing devices, such as lightpen and touchscreen, have a C:D ratio of 1:1. It is simple to calculate gain for zero-order devices such as optical mice or tablets; one simply ensures that maximum permissible movement of the device (W_d) is related to maximum display size (W_s), i.e., so that movement of an optical mouse from one corner of its pad to the other will cause the cursor to move from one corner of the screen to the other. Thus, one can propose values of 0.3 to 1.0 for mice and tablets. For the displacement joystick, the full extent of joystick displacement (W_d) relates to (W_s), and is defined using equation (5.1).

$$C{:}D \text{ ratio} = \frac{\text{fraction of circle movement} \times \text{circumference of circle}}{\text{cursor movement}}$$

$$(5.1)$$

Consideration of the mechanical mouse is slightly more difficult, although one could assume that W_d can be defined as the size of the mouse mat. For first-order devices such as the isometric joystick, calculating appropriate values of gain are complicated by the fact that W_d is effectively set at infinity. At present this means that defining gain requires trial and error rather than calculation.

From equation (5.1), if one assumes zero slippage between trackball and holder; C:D ratios for small trackballs on portable computers can be calculated. If one assumes that the trackball has a diameter of 20 mm, then its circumference is given by $2\pi r = 62.83$ mm. If one then assumes either a 9 in (c. 230 mm) or 12 in (c. 300 mm) monitor, it is possible to relate cursor movement across the leading diagonal to trackball rotation, depending on how many revolutions correspond to 1 mm cursor movement. If the trackball has to be rotated 1.5 full revolutions to traverse the screen, a value of 0.4 for the 9 in screen and 0.3 for the 12 in screen is obtained. If the trackball has to be rotated 2.5 full revolutions to traverse the screen, the values of 0.6 and 0.5 respectively are obtained. Even with acceptable $C:D$ ratios for trackballs on portable computers, there is often a problem with screen refresh such that the cursor appears to disappear on fast movements or to leave a trace in its wake.

Much attention has been given to the setting of $C:D$ ratios to match the speed of cursor movement to that of device movement, principally to reduce the perception of lag between movement although it is possible to incorporate some acceleration in the cursor. However, $C:D$ ratio may not be as important as previously believed. Tränkle and Deutschmann (1991) argue that movement is far more likely to be influenced by factors such as target size, distance moved and, to a lesser extent, screen size.

5.5.2 User

From a simple model of human–computer interaction, such as Shneiderman's (1980) "syntax semantics object action" (SSOA) model, it is possible to consider the relationship between how a device is designed to be used and how a person actually uses the device. The SSOA model describes a users' syntactic and semantic knowledge of objects and actions in the interface. At the syntactic level of knowledge, the user must be able to recall the appropriate action for each command, e.g., on a three-button mouse, which button can be used to select an object, or on a single button mouse, when should one "double-click". At the semantic level of knowledge, the user needs to understand the basic operations of the computer and the task requirements. The user must also be able to recognize and understand the objects displayed on the computer screen, and to use the required action appropriately. Buxton (1988) proposes that the use of appropriate gestures to perform a task with a device can simplify syntax. If a user wishes to move an object on the screen, they should be given the opportunity to physically move the object. If the action they can perform matches that of the object, so much the better. Suffice it to say that, for this task, one might hypothesize that performance using a device which moves in a similar fashion to the object, e.g., a displacement joystick or a mouse, would be preferable to one which is stationary, e.g., an isometric joystick or a trackball. Ergonomists refer to such properties as compatibility (Sanders and McCormick, 1992). For some writers, compatibility is seen as a property of the device. I feel that this is not true; rather compatibility describes the relationship between the expectations that a person brings to the use of a device and the design of the device. In other words, compatibility can be said to be as much a consequence of the context of the interaction between person and device as an influence on user performance. In this section five types of compatibility will be considered (movement; spatial; operational; conceptual; modality), and their relationship with the design of computer input devices.

Movement compatibility is said to be present when the action required to move an object corresponds to the user's intention. This means that if the movement is opposite to intention or if it requires translation, then error is possible, and if the movement needs to be fully completed before the user can detect its outcome, then it is not possible to correct errors. The issue of movement compatibility for interaction devices would appear to be relatively straightforward. Many of the available devices can be used to move a cursor on the VDU. In this case, movement of the device will result in a corresponding movement of the cursor. Providing the orientation of the device is correct, one should be able to move the cursor with relatively little difficulty in the appropriate direction. However, in Chapter 9 it is suggested that, for interaction devices, movement compatibility must be translated, i.e., rather than being a simple matter of using an input device to move the cursor around the screen, the interaction device is used to move the cursor to specific targets. For some interaction devices, there is a clear relationship between movement of the device itself and movement of the cursor (mice and displacement joysticks), for others there is a relationship between action of the device and cursor movement (isometric joysticks and trackballs). Thus, although these indirect pointing devices pair device action with cursor movement, they do not all offer the same level of movement compatibility.

The second form of compatibility to be considered is spatial compatibility, and it is said to occur when a control and the object it controls (or a display of the object's state) are positioned proximally. Proximity can result from placing the control adjacent to the object, or it can result from placing the controls in a similar arrangement to the objects. It can be difficult to define how an interaction device can have spatial compatibility with the object(s) it is being used to control. One can draw a distinction between direct pointing devices, such as touchscreens and lightpens, in which the users will physically touch a specific object, and indirect pointing devices, such as mice, trackballs, joysticks, in which the user moves a cursor to an object and then performs some selection action, such as a button press. In the former, spatial compatibility is simply a matter of permitting an object to act as its own button, i.e., an icon of a valve on a touchscreen could be touched to change its state. However, this relates to the design of the display rather than the use of the device. In the latter case, one might propose that object selection requires a degree of translation (or at least, imposes some additional task on the operator). A point worth considering is, given the drive to design and implement multi-purpose controls, is there a possibility that errors could arise due to a lack of spatial compatibility.

The potential for violation of spatial compatibility offered by reconfigurable displays is clearly illustrated by a case reported by Moray (1992). A training unit for ship control consisted of a computer with three screens. Each screen was capable of displaying all of the information relevant to the control task, although the central screen was reserved for overview information. However, sets of controls were positioned under each screen and were dedicated to the screen, i.e., the right-hand control only controlled the right-hand engines. When a problem occurred, one of the trainees called up information pertaining to the left engine on the right-hand screen. Using the controls positioned under the screen had no effect on the state of the left engine (although, of course, it did reduce power to the right engine and made the situation worse). One could propose design solutions which allowed controls to be reconfigurable as well as displays, but that could only exacerbate matters. Alternatively, one could attempt to label displays to indicate what the operator was looking at. However, as this example illustrates, people are likely to read information they are looking for (which may not always be what they are looking at). Alternatively, one could attempt to design the interaction so that specific control actions are performed on specific objects, i.e., in this example, having the engine throttle incorporated into the display could permit the operator to select that object on that display and act upon it. In this latter case, spatial compatibility would be achieved by having the control placed within the representation of the object.

Operational compatibility occurs when the design of an object permits an unambiguous set of actions, e.g., the shape of a mouse permits a certain set of couplings. I have heard of people who were able to learn to use inverted mice, i.e., they placed the mouse with its lead facing away from the computer (assuming the lead was the mouse's tail) and learned that movement of the mouse to the left would lead to a movement of the cursor to the right. Other anecdotes tell of people who, when told to use the mouse to move the cursor, placed the mouse on the computer screen. These anecdotes raise interesting questions of how the design of an interaction device suggest its use. One could answer this question with reference to an everyday object, such as a door handle (Norman, 1988). A flat plate on a door is clearly intended to be pushed, a door knob, on the other hand, would appear to be designed to be grasped and pulled. However, while the flat plate is unambiguous, in that there is only one operation available, the door knob has a degree of ambiguity, in that one could also grasp and push.

For some computer interaction devices, as noted above, users might have an initial difficulty in interpreting the correct set of actions. While this problem can be addressed by training, one needs to bear in mind that during periods of high workload or stress, people could revert to pre-training assumptions and perhaps respond to the operational compatibility of a device. As an example, consider a trackball which is designed such that the ball is mounted in a holder which also houses a button at the top of the housing. Movement of the cursor will result from fingertip control of the trackball, how will the button be pressed? One could suggest that the button is positioned such that its operational compatibility invites pressing using a finger, but the fingers are already engaged in operating the ball and if moved they could shift the cursor. Alternatively, users could attempt to press the button using their thumb but this would require even greater contortion of the hand.

The feedback that people receive from a computer will shape their actions (see Chapter 9). This illustrates conceptual compatibility and is most likely to occur when the design of information permits unambiguous interpretation by users. It is important for the user to be informed of the success or otherwise of an action. This type of feedback incorporates a number of levels, and one needs to consider the compatibility of each of these levels with the task in hand in order to provide sufficient information without distraction.

There has been recent interest in cognitive ergonomics in the notion of codes of processing. For instance, Wickens (1992) has suggested that pairing the presentation of information with an appropriate response code leads to improvements in performance when information is presented in a format suitable for its interpretation, and when actions are performed using appropriate responses. The issue of modality compatibility is developed further in Chapter 14. The principal issue here is how one should define the information displayed to the user.

The principles of compatibility relate to earlier design principles, but one needs to reconsider them in terms of computer interaction devices. Computer interaction devices permit users to manipulate objects on computer screens. This means that the manipulation will be dependent upon the design of the objects and the operational characteristics of the devices. Problems in compatibility could lead to increases in the perceived difficulty in using a device and in the level of workload experienced by the user (Table 5.7).

Some users will be unable to exercise complete physical control of a device, because they are disabled, either temporarily, e.g., recovering from an accident, wearing clothing which restricts their movement, working in domains with high environmental stress, or permanently. Such disability can require novel device designs to permit users to gain full functionality from their computers. Finally, one can also classify interaction devices comparing the relative loads they place on users (see Table 5.7). The loads selected are cognitive, perceptual, motor and fatigue. The ratings are

Table 5.7   Interaction devices classified in terms of workload

Interaction device	Cognitive load	Perceptual load	Motor load	Fatigue
Lightpen	Low	Low	Medium	Medium
Touch panel	Low	Low	Low	Low
Tablet (stylus)	High	Medium	Medium	High
Alphanumeric keyboard	High	High	High	High
Function keyboard	Low	Medium	Low	Low
Mouse	Low	Medium	Medium	Medium
Trackball	Low	Medium	Medium	Medium

largely subjective, although some of the information is drawn from Foley et al. (1990).

5.5.3   Work domain

There are several PSFs which can be included under this heading, depending on one's definition of the task. Some of these factors will be considered in Chapter 13, when the sociotechnical aspects of using interaction devices will be discussed. However, an important task PSF would seem to be how well the device operation matches task requirements. The definition of the work required can have a bearing on the use of a specific device. This point is illustrated in Chapter 13.

5.5.4   Work environment

There are several ways which might characterize these factors. In Chapter 11, the influence of the environment on device use will be considered, including discussion of the effects of such factors as noise, vibration, acceleration, etc. on human performance. In this section, attention will be limited to the issue of the amount of space a device requires in order to be used effectively.

As the design of portable computers becomes more advanced, there is a pressing need to develop means of allowing cursor control without using separate devices. Two approaches which are proving popular are the trackball and the tablet. However, the inclusion of such devices necessarily has an effect on the size and arrangement of the keyboard and other controls. For computers used on the desk top, the interaction device which has minimal requirement for desk space is the touchscreen, which is mounted over the VDU. Devices can be classified in terms of their relative space requirements, by making some simple assumptions about their operation (Table 5.8).

Informal discussion with designers suggests that the use of the trackball is based primarily on its limited space requirements and its lack of trailing lead during operation. The mouse requires an area of desk space, preferably with a pad (this is, of course, very important for use with an optical mouse). Devices can be classified in terms of their relative space requirements, by making some simple assumptions about their operation. If a mouse is used to move a cursor around a 230 mm screen, assuming a mapping of 1:1, then one might anticipate that the requisite mouse mat would be 200 × 110 mm.

5.6 Conclusions

Devices were compared in terms of performance measures in Chapters 3 and 4. A number of problems were considered in relation to such research, primarily concerned with the bias introduced into studies using tasks which favor a particular type of device. In this chapter a number of approaches to the classification of devices have been considered. One of the aims of using such approaches is to develop a more objective means of performing device comparisons. For instance, by moving away from the problems of experimental context.

The notion of generic actions is useful for HCI, and can be particularly beneficial in the study and classification of interaction devices, by providing

Table 5.8 Interaction devices classified in terms of desk space requirements (measurements in millimeters)

Device	230 mm screen (200 × 110)	300 mm screen (270 × 150)
Keyboard	415 × 200	415 × 200
Mouse (1:1)	200 × 110	270 × 150
Mouse (1:2)	100 × 55	135 × 75
Tablet (1:1)	200 × 110	270 × 150
Touchscreen	0	0
Lightpen	0	0
Trackball	50 × 75	50 × 75

a core set of actions against which devices can be compared. An alternative to device classification maps devices onto basic movement properties, such as direction, force, etc. This approach is being developed by Stuart Card and his colleagues and can also allow for devices to be compared objectively. The generic action and device operation approaches share a similar goal of classifying interaction devices and both share a similar failing in that they do not explicitly address the context of the user–device interaction. However, both approaches, ultimately, might allow comparison of devices against a set of standard benchmarks.

In terms of the general argument underlying this book, it is suggested that a description of the relationship between specific devices and generic action omits a central issue: the knowledge, skills and abilities of the user. In order to consider these factors, the concept of performance-shaping factors has been briefly illustrated. While this approach has not been used before, it does allow a range of issues to be introduced into the analysis and classification of devices. It is necessary to determine these factors with greater precision through field study and laboratory work. The point of this discussion is to broaden the approach taken to the study of interaction devices and to illustrate how a wide range of factors will have a bearing on how a device is used.

5.7 Key points for practitioners

- Consider the range of generic actions in specific applications.
- Consider whether generic actions are performed in an optimal manner.
- Consider performance-shaping factors in the operation of the applications.
- Consider the issues of task-fit, usability and compatibility in device use.

5.8 Key points for researchers

- Consider the use of generic actions for widget-level design.
- Develop bench-mark tests for device comparisons, based on generic actions.
- Consider the issue of compatibility in device design.
- Consider the influence of population stereotypes on compatibility.
- Consider the range of generic actions in future computing, e.g., in 3D.
- Compare devices in terms of their operating characteristics.

Part II
Using Interaction Devices

Chapter 6 Modeling device use
Chapter 7 Typing
Chapter 8 Writing and drawing
Chapter 9 Pointing
Chapter 10 Speaking

Modeling device use

Abstract

In the preceding chapters some of the many forms of interaction device which are available have been reviewed and classified. While device classification can provide some insight into device use, there is a need for predictive models of device use. Some possible approaches to the modeling of user behavior with interaction devices are considered in this chapter.

6.1 Introduction

In Chapter 5, approaches to the classification of interaction devices were discussed. While the approaches have some utility, they would be more useful if they contained a description of how people used the devices. This is a major aim in writing this book. There are several techniques which could be used for modeling user behavior with interaction devices. In this chapter, modeling is defined as the formal description of activity which can be used for predicting some future activity. Primarily, the modeling techniques focus on what has been termed "transaction time" (Peckham, 1986), in other words, the total time taken to perform a task or sequence of tasks. The obvious criticism of such approaches is that they do not need to contain information on how or why actions are performed in one way or another; indeed, from this point of view one could argue that they represent versions of the "one best way" philosophy of Scientific Management (Greif and Gediga, 1987). However, there are benefits to be gained from using modeling techniques.

6.2   Modeling in HCI research

There are occasions when it is useful to test a concept prior to building a working system. While the best way to test a product (in terms of human factors at least), may be to get people to use it, there may be problems in terms of time and logistics with running usability trials. A fundamental problem with usability trials is that some version of the product needs to exist in order to be tested; in other words, such testing will occur at a point when a number of key design decisions will have already been made and implemented.

If one could define models of human performance, then initial designs could be "tested" against the models. This would allow for consideration of the effects of different system configurations on user performance. Using the models could also permit testing of different parts of the design for consistency, and for prediction of overall system performance.

Of course, defining the properties and parameters of models is not a trivial matter. While many of the current models employ time as their main source of data, it is not clear what should be timed or what level of timing should be used, e.g., should one time to the most basic physical action or to the basic mental process? how can one time mental processes? should one use milliseconds (in the belief that this will be precise) or should one use seconds (in the belief that this will be robust)?

An early model of human physical performance was developed by Fitts in the 1950s (see Chapter 9). He noted that there was a relationship between speed and distance for discrete, repetitive movements, and encapsulated this relationship into a mathematical equation. Given that contemporary interfaces require a great deal of cursor movement and positioning, there has been interest in the possible use of Fitts' law for the description of pointing behavior. However, simply describing the time to move a cursor across the screen will not be sufficient basis for a model of user performance in the majority of HCI tasks. More recent approaches have sought to break a task sequence into constituent units and then to examine the performance of these units both in isolation and in combination.

Furthermore, transaction time is not the only measure of performance. One might wish to incorporate some measures of the types and frequency of errors which people could make when performing a sequence of tasks, or the length of time that it would take a new user to become proficient in the operation of the system. Finally, while time and error data may give an indication of overt performance, it would often be useful to know how users were deciding what action to perform, i.e., what knowledge people possess in HCI and how they apply this knowledge. There is an assumption in many models that one can describe "expert" performance, and that such performance is "error free". This latter assumption is manifestly false. For instance, Roberts and Moran (1983) estimate that between 4% and 22% of transaction time, for experts, is spent in recovering from errors. Further, the "expert user" hypothesis assumes that experts have learned the single, most appropriate sequence of tasks to achieve a goal. However, it is in the nature of expertise to exhibit flexibility in task performance (Ericsson and Smith, 1991). Experts might be characterized, not as users who have rote-learned a task sequence for fast execution, but as users who possess a repertoire of alternative approaches to the performance of a task and who select an approach from this repertoire on the basis of a number of contextual factors. Thus, modeling techniques require a number of simplifying assumptions. In broad terms, the aim is less to model the process than to capture its outcome, i.e., to predict transaction time rather than to describe the details of performance. In the remainder of the chapter, seven techniques will be considered. These techniques have been selected to illustrate the range of approaches used rather than as a review of the area.

6.3   Three-state device description

In Chapter 5, the notion of generic actions was introduced. Taking this notion further, it was proposed that it is possible to use generic actions as the basis for widget-level design of interaction devices. From the resulting generic devices, one could begin to construct a model of user behavior. For instance, knowing the components of the "select object" action allows one to consider the user activity required to perform the task using a specific device. Assume that a device can be in one of a number of states at any one time, and that user behavior will change the state of the device. For instance, the generic action of "select object" can be performed by either moving a cursor and pressing a button, or by touching an object on the screen with one's finger (see Table 5.2). This is the gist of an approach proposed by Buxton (1990b).

6.3.1   Defining the three states

The three-state description employs a relatively simple version of state-transition networks. These networks have proved popular in HCI for many years (Harel, 1988; Wasserman, 1985). The popularity of state-transition networks is, presumably, due to the fact that they allow one to model an ordered sequence of operations (usually to describe the progression of a "dialogue"). A common problem associated with the use of such networks is that, beyond a few nodes, the diagrams can become unwieldy and difficult to follow (Dix et al., 1993). However, one can attempt to reduce the problem by considering the human–computer system and focusing on specific, goal-driven activities (Harel, 1988; Baber and Stanton, 1994). In other words, one could use the goals of the user to define a sequence of activities and exclude some activities from the network. Buxton (1990b) proposes that for interaction devices transitions from one device state to another will be made on the basis of user activity. Transitions in device state result from a discrete signal, e.g., a button press. Figure 6.1 shows the state-transition diagram for a direct pointing device (e.g., touchscreen, tablet or pen).

In state 0, user activity has no effect on the device. This state can be considered recursive in that the actions of aiming at, and moving one's finger towards, a target are performed until the user is ready to make the selection. Bear in mind that the action could consist of something entirely unrelated to the task at hand; state 0 indicates no interaction between user and device. Once the target is located, the user touches it. Touching the screen leads to a change in state of the device, which corresponds to selecting an object. On the type of touchscreen modeled here, lifting one's finger off the screen signals selection, and returns the device to state 0. On other types of touch device, touching the object corresponds to selection (see Chapter 3). Here, state 1 is not recursive but leads straight back to state 0 (i.e., the "release" transition is automatic rather than the result of user activity).

Thus, the model can be used to describe the interaction between user behavior and device state. However, the description tends to focus more on

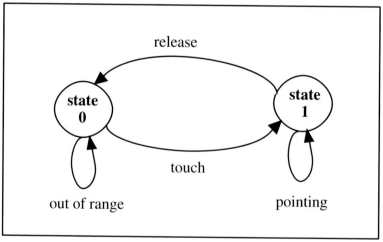

Figure 6.1   Three-state description of selecting using a direct pointing device (from Buxton, 1990b, in D. Diaper et al. (eds) *Human–Computer Interaction: Interact '90*, pp. 449–456, Elsevier Science Publishers B.V.)

the device than on the user, especially when one considers the amount of activity which could be performed in state 0.

Many devices permit the user to manipulate the object, e.g., by dragging it. Consequently, Buxton (1990b) adds another device state, state 2, to describe this activity. Figure 6.2 describes an indirect pointing device (such as a mouse or trackball or joystick), which can be used to select and drag objects. In this case, there is no valid use for state 0 (not directly interacting with the device serves no useful purpose), and the initial state is state 1, i.e., the user has grasped the device and is moving the cursor. Once an object has been indicated, it can be selected by pressing a button, i.e., state 2. It is now possible to remain in state 2, while performing an additional action, i.e., holding the button down while moving the cursor. Releasing the button will take the device back to state 1. Thus, the model describes both cursor positioning and object dragging (indeed, it was argued in Chapter 5 that dragging is simply a class of cursor positioning, in which the cursor is transformed into an object).

Some direct pointing devices also permit object manipulation. For instance, some touchscreens allow users to drag objects and many stylus tablets allow users to drag objects and draw. Figure 6.3 describes such devices. State 0 involves the user in preparing an action. This could simply be positioning of the finger, or, in the case of drawing, could involve preparatory "sketching movements" prior to drawing (see Chapter 8).

In state 1, the user is directly acting upon an object on the display. Lifting off the finger or stylus in this state will take the device back to state 0 and

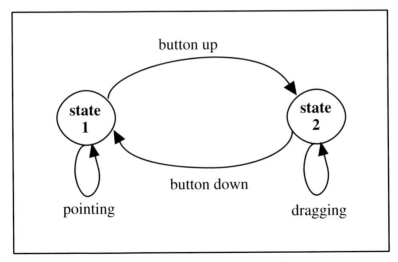

Figure 6.2   Three-state description of selecting and dragging using an indirect pointing device (from Buxton, 1990b, in D. Diaper et al. (eds) *Human–Computer Interaction: Interact '90*, pp. 449–456, Elsevier Science Publishers B.V.)

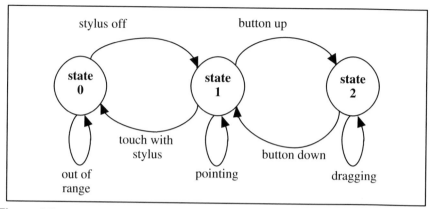

Figure 6.3 Three-state description for selecting and dragging using a direct pointing device (from Buxton, 1990b, in D. Diaper et al. (eds) *Human–Computer Interaction: Interact '90,* pp. 449.456. Elsevier Science Publishers B.V.)

the object will be selected. If the user maintains contact and then moves the finger or stylus, the object will be dragged around the screen until the device is returned to state 1. It might be necessary to allow users to signal that they wish the device to remain in state 2, perhaps by pressing a button.

Thus, the three-state description provides a device level description which allows designers and researchers to map specific user actions onto specific device states, and to start interrogating the transitions between states in terms of usability. Table 6.1 illustrates the relationship between interaction devices and provision of states 0, 1 or 2. The reader will notice that the main conclusion to be drawn from this table is that indirect devices do not provide state 0. This could be seen as simply supporting the "common-sense" distinction between direct/indirect devices which was criticized in Chapter 5. However, I would argue that the strength of the three-state description of device use lies in the manner in which device use is represented. It allows researchers to consider the type of activity which users engage in when using devices and, ultimately, could replace the * in Table 6.1 with descriptions of user actions with each of the devices. Thus, one could view the three-state description as the framework for the approach taken in this book; the study of how people use interaction devices.

The three-state description allows one to describe the relationship between task, user and device (albeit from the perspective of the device). Having defined the states in which a device will operate for a specific task, one can begin to ask questions about the similarities and differences between devices in the same class. This information is not explicitly contained in the description. However, MacKenzie et al. (1991) compare a mouse and a trackball for state 1 and state 2 in selecting an object. Their analysis draws on Fitts law to define transaction times for the devices in

Table 6.1 Interaction devices classified in terms of states

Interaction device	State 0	State 1	State 2
Direct			
touchscreen	*		*
touch tablet	*	*	*
tablet and stylus	*	*	*
light pen	*	*	*
Indirect			
joystick		*	*
trackball		*	*
mouse		*	*
tablet and puck		*	*

each state (see Chapter 9), and they conclude that performing the task with the trackball will take longer than performance with the mouse.

6.3.2 A critique of the three-state description

There are several problems with the three-state description, if one wishes to use it for modeling user behavior. The first problem is that it does not, of itself, permit prediction of relative performance of devices. Hence, according to the remit of this chapter, it is not strictly a model. However, it is included in the chapter for two reasons: it aims to extend the notion of generic tasks introduced in Chapter 5, and it can be supplemented to include performance time data. Having noted that the three-state description aims to extend the notion of generic actions, it is difficult to see how it functions beyond a description of selecting and moving objects; for instance, how would one describe the orientation of objects or data entry with the description? The description is not only limited in terms of the tasks that it can describe but also in the devices which can be described, e.g., it cannot handle pressure devices or speech systems. Furthermore, while it can distinguish between broad classes of devices (direct/indirect) it does not seem to be able to differentiate devices within a class. However, it is suggested that the description should serve as a cue for asking how the devices within a class perform the various transitions. This means that much of the analysis is performed after the description has been drawn, rather than as a result of the description. For instance, returning to the mouse/trackball comparison of Mackenzie et al. (1991): one could assume that a factor in the difference in performance time was the type of user activity performed in state 2. For the mouse, it is quite easy to move the mouse while keeping the mouse button pressed, but for the trackball it is more difficult.

The description can provide a useful framework for over-viewing devices. However, the main problem is one of focus; by focusing on the device, rather than the human–device system, the approach fails to respond to the goals of the user and the context of the task, e.g., it cannot distinguish between drawing and dragging. Further, by focusing on the device state transitions, rather than user behavior, the description cannot explicitly say what the user is doing, e.g., what is happening during state 0 when selecting objects on a touchscreen? Finally, the description appears to consider action in isolation, i.e., not as part of an ongoing dialogue. While Figure 6.3 implies that the description can be extended to accommodate more information, the approach describes the interaction device as object rather than the interaction device in use (see Chapter 1).

6.4   The keystroke level model

Card et al. (1980; 1983) developed an engineering approximation of human performance, which they termed the keystroke level model (KLM). KLM relies on the assumption that a sequence of actions performed at an interface can be decomposed into unit tasks, and that each unit task can be assigned a standard time. The performance of the task sequence can then be described by summing the unit times. In order for the unit task times to be combined into the total time, it is necessary to assume that there will not be any extraneous times inserted into the performance, e.g., due to error or to unscheduled pauses. Furthermore, in order for the computation to be tractable, it is necessary to make assumptions about the manner in which the task will be performed, e.g., that users will tend to order the sequence of actions in a similar manner, that users' performance will be consistent, that unit time will be constant across different instances of the same unit task. Consequently, the approach seeks to describe transaction time for consistent, error-free use of the device.

6.4.1   Defining unit times

KLM requires the assumption that task performance involves acquisition and execution of a task. Acquisition involves preparation and planning of the task, and could be affected by memory demands, such as the requirement to recall an appropriate command from memory in order to type it, or could be affected by the complexity of the task, e.g., the number of actions which need to be combined. There are, of course, problems with this stage, the most obvious being the difficulty with which one can assign times to mental activity. Card et al. (1983), on the basis of a series of studies, propose that mental activity can be represented by the single time of 1.35 s per mental operation.

Execution involves the physical performance of the task, and comprises the act of reaching for the interaction device, pressing a key or button, moving a cursor, etc. In order to reach for a device, one would anticipate that the location of the device and the type of grasp required would influence movement time. However, this action is described using a standard time of 0.4 s (Card et al., 1978). We know that typing speed can be influenced by expertise, and so Card et al. (1983) permit some flexibility in the unit times assigned to keypressing, ranging from a "hunt and peck" typist with no knowledge of the keyboard, to a highly fluent typist. The average typing speed is assumed to be 55 words per minute, and the standard time for keypressing is 0.2 s per keypress. As far as movement of the cursor is concerned, KLM simplifies Fitts' law into a standard time of 1.1 s. Finally, drawing is defined as an action performed using a cursor to create straight lines. An initial set of standard times is presented in Table 6.2.

The transaction time for a specified operation will be given as the sum of standard action times involved, i.e., $T_{exec.} = T_m + T_k + T_h + T_p + T_r$ (see Table 6.2 for definition of times). There are additional rules for the use of the T_m values. Generally, if the sequence of tasks can be considered to be planned as a coherent unit, then only one T_m value is required, e.g., in typing an alphanumeric string, it will only be necessary to include one T_m before the string of keypresses rather than a T_m prior to each keypress.

1. Insert M before all K's which are not part of argument strings, and before all P's which select commands;
2. If an operator following an M is part of an ongoing sequence, then delete the M, e.g., if one types a three letter word, it is not necessary to include M before each letter;
3. If a string of MKs belongs to the same cognitive unit, then delete all but the first M;
4. If K is a redundant terminator, e.g., a return key press, then delete the M, and if K terminates a constant string, then delete M.

6.4.2 Using KLM to predict performance

Baber et al. (1992) used KLM as part of a study comparing the use of a graphical-user interface (GUI) with an interface which employed commands entered via the keyboard. The GUI required the user to select menu options and icons using a mouse in order to perform a simple text-editing task. In order to compare the interfaces, it was decided to use an activity which required a sequence of tasks.

Table 6.2   Unit times for KLM

Action	Definition	Label	Standard time (s)	Comments
Keystroke, or button press	Pressing a key or button	K	0.08	(135 wpm)
			0.12	(90 wpm)
			0.2	(55 wpm)
			0.28	(40 wpm)
			0.5	(random letters)
			0.75	(complex codes)
			1.2	(worst typist)
Pointing	Using a mouse or other pointing device to move a cursor	P	1.1	$[0.8 + 0.1 \times \log_2 (d/s + 0.5)]$
Homing	Positioning finger over a keyboard or mouse	H	0.4	
Drawing	Draw n straight line segments of length l cm	D	–	$0.9n + 0.16l$
Mental operation	Performing cognitive processes prior to keystroke	M	1.35	
System response	Performance characteristics of computer system	R	–	a defined constant

The first stage of conducting a KLM-based study is to describe the actions which the user will perform. This is known as task analysis, and there are several methods which the analyst can use for this purpose. Readers are advised to consult Diaper (1989) to see the application of task analysis to HCI.

In this particular example the task analysis method used in this study was hierarchical task analysis (Annett et al., 1971). The tasks were analyzed to a sufficient level of detail to allow us to apply standard times to each operation. Note that some of the operations require combinations of more than standard time, e.g., the first operation. The transaction time was calculated by summing the times, taking care to consider whether the times formed separate or integrated actions (see above). Table 6.3 presents the tasks for the GUI, together with standard times used in the prediction of transaction time.

Table 6.3 KLM times for a simple text editing task using a mouse

Task	Action	Label	Time (s)
1	*Select line*		
	move cursor to start of line to move	H	0.4
		M	1.35
		P	1.1
	press mouse button	K	0.2
	move cursor to end of line to move	P	1.1
	release mouse button	K	0.2
2	*Cut line*		
	move cursor to edit menu	P	1.1
	open edit menu	K	0.2
	move cursor to "cut"	P	1.1
	release mouse button	K	0.2
3	*Select insert point*		
	move cursor to insert point	P	1.1
	press mouse button	K	0.2
	release mouse button	K	0.2
4	*Paste line*		
	move cursor to edit menu	P	1.1
	pull down edit menu	K	0.2
	move cursor to "paste"	P	1.1
	release mouse button	K	0.2
	$T_{\text{exec.}}$		11.05

In order to validate the prediction made from the data in Table 6.3, a number of users were asked to perform the task. Figure 6.4 shows the empirical results against the predicted times for both the task described in Table 6.3 and for a task using commands entered using the keyboard. The reader will notice that the performance times for the command-based user interface (CUI) are more sporadic than those for the GUI. Baber et al. (1992) suggest that this is largely due to the nature of the CUI used in the study, which required the users to recall often obscure command abbreviations in order to perform the task. Thus, the main difference in results could be explained by the differences in memory load imposed on users. Despite the limitations of the approach, KLM does appear to provide a useful, if approximate, method for predicting transaction time.

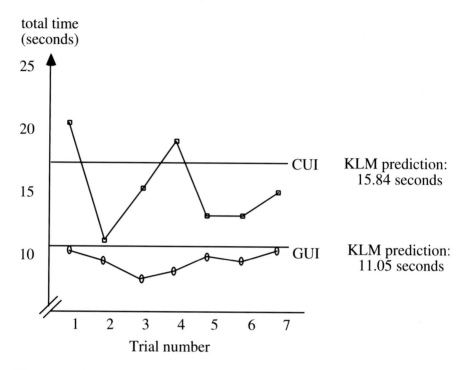

Figure 6.4   Comparison of predicted times with actual times (from Baber et al., 1992)

6.4.3   Using KLM to compare devices

The above example gives one a rough idea of how well KLM can be used to predict user performance, and also an indication of how KLM can be used to compare devices, in this case, a mouse with a keyboard. The reader may well object that what is being compared in this instance is not so much a pair of devices as a pair of quite distinct forms of interaction, i.e., GUI and CUI. If one accepts this, then one is faced with the recurring problem of how devices can be compared; in Chapter 3, it was argued that device comparisons are difficult precisely because different devices require different forms of interaction. Thus, the criticism which had been leveled at other approaches to device comparison can be applied to KLM.

If one does wish to consider KLM for device comparisons, one might feel that the approach is highly limited. For instance, on the basis of the data provided in Table 6.2 there seems little chance of comparing two pointing devices, say a trackball and a mouse using KLM. However, notice that the movement time is defined using Fitts' law. In Chapter 9, values for these terms are presented for a range of different types of device. Card et al. (1983) suggest substituting the appropriate value into the equation and then proceeding as normal. However, it is only fair to warn the reader at this point, that there is by no means a consensus of opinion as to these values, as will become apparent from the discussion in Chapter 9.

Assume, for the moment, that it is possible to define data for pointing devices. Thus, it is possible to compare predicted performance times for different types of keyboards and different types of pointing device; indeed, Card et al. (1983) report a number of such comparisons. However, there is no data pertaining to, for instance, gesture or speech-based devices. It is proposed that, should such data exist (see for instance, 6.5), the values could be inserted into the KLM equation if the logic of the approach is accepted.

6.4.4 A critique of KLM

Card et al. (1983) accept that KLM simplifies the interaction between user and computer. The question is whether this simplification can be defended on the grounds of parsimony or criticized as misrepresentation. It seems to me that the problems that one sees in KLM will be a function of one's background. An engineer might find the approach attractive and be willing to accept the simplifying assumptions in order to have a method which produces useful data. On the basis of this attitude, the use of KLM would be similar to the use of work study methods in industry (ILO, 1982). From the point of view of a human factors specialist, some of the assumptions might be too extreme. For instance, the problem of assuming that expert performance was consistent and error-free has been discussed above. One might argue that the approach should not attempt to provide a description of human performance so much as a prediction of the likely performance time when using a particular device in a particular fashion. Indeed, by explicitly stating the sequence of actions to be performed, one might feel that the "model" of the user is contained in the task analysis.

The definition of "unit task" sequences is problematic; experts tend to employ short-cuts, they use the fewest number of actions possible to perform a task, they select task sequences from a repertoire of possible actions. This means that the choice of a particular action will be influenced by expertise and past experience; hence, the times assigned can only function as approximations. Furthermore, the use of standard times cannot accommodate flexibility in performance strategy nor can KLM deal with time spent correcting errors.

6.5   Network models

In Buxton's (1990b) three-state description, there was an assumption that devices could be represented in terms of their states and that user action could result in changes in device state. An alternative perspective on this assumption is that, rather than devices being in different states, a dialogue between user and computer progresses through states. From this notion, it should be possible to suggest the device properties required to perform actions in a state, and to develop a model of the developing dialogue. If one follows this line of thought and includes the notion of standard times from KLM, it might be possible to develop network models which can predict the transaction time for a given sequence of task activity. Ultimately, this would allow one to move beyond the simple summing of standard times to allow for some degree of stochastic variation in performance, perhaps to include points where the user can choose from several alternative courses of action or perhaps to indicate the likelihood and consequence of user error. In this section, two network modeling approaches are presented: Markov models and task network models.

6.5.1   Markov models[6.1]

Rudnicky and Hauptmann (1991) propose the use of Markov models to describe human–computer interaction. Given that one can describe the sequence of actions between a user and device, and given that one can assign times to each stage in the sequence, then it ought to be possible to define HCI in terms of progress through a network of states.

Movement from one state to the next will be dependent upon the states to which a transition can be made. For instance, if there is only one state following the initial state, the probability of moving to that state will be 1, whereas if there are four states, each with an equal probability of following the initial state, the probability of moving to a particular state will be 0.25. Of course, the actual probability of moving from one state to another will depend on a number of features of the system. One approach to describing the movement through these states is to use Markov models.

Figure 6.5 shows a network, describing the entry of a word into a speech recognition system. In this example, the user speaks a word and, if the word is not correctly recognized, the user simply repeats the word until it is recognized correctly. The system begins in state I. A word is spoken by the user and recognized by the device, which takes the system to state C. This transition takes time u. The user then decides whether the device has

---

[6.1] I am indebted to David Cleaver for his assistance in preparing this section.

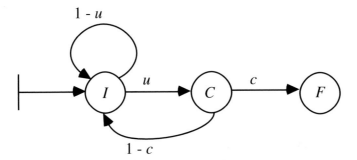

Figure 6.5 Example of a Markov chain

correctly recognized the word, and issues a confirmation command to take the system to the finish state F. This takes time c. If the recognition is incorrect, then the user issues another command to take the system back to state I (via path $1 - c$).

In order to predict performance time, we apply Markov chain theory to each state in the network. First construct an initial transition matrix for time spent in each state (all values are set at 0 prior to running), i.e.,

	F	I	C
F	0	0	0
I	0	0	0
C	0	0	0

The rows in this matrix correspond to the start states and the columns to the finish states of each move within the transaction. As F is the end state, it does not have routes leading from it, so it remains at F and does not travel to I or C, i.e., $F = 1$ and I and $C = 0$. Further, the spoken word enters at state I, and the system can proceed to state C or back to state I depending on the recognition accuracy of the device.

	F	I	C
F	1	0	0
I	0	$1-u$	u
C	c	$1-c$	0

Ignoring the possibility of transitions from F, matrix Q can now be derived by considering the flow of operation within the system.

$$Q = \begin{bmatrix} 1-u & u \\ 1-c & 0 \end{bmatrix}$$

In order to describe the system, it is necessary to apply the standard Markov chain transformation (Iosifescu, 1986), as shown in equation (6.1).

$$N = (I - Q)^{-1} \tag{6.1}$$

Applying the standard Markov chain transformation (equation (6.1)) to matrix Q, it is possible to define matrix N as

$$N = \begin{bmatrix} 1/cu & 1/c \\ 1-c/cu & 1/c \end{bmatrix}$$

Predict of transaction time requires some measure of the time spent in each state, i.e., residence time. The residence time is calculated as the relationship between the time (d) to input a string of length (l), in a system with processing overheads (e). These factors are combined into a cost vector such that

$$t = \begin{bmatrix} e + dl \\ e + d \end{bmatrix}$$

The values of d, e and l will be set according to different system parameters. For instance, e can be defined in terms of recognition accuracy of the device, u. If the device was 100% efficient then u would be 0, if the device was 90% efficient, u would be 0.1 and if the device was 75% efficient, u would be 0.25. Transaction time for the network shown in Figure 6.5 can be calculated by applying the cost matrix t to matrix N.

$$\text{Transaction time} = \begin{bmatrix} e + dl \\ e + d \end{bmatrix} \begin{bmatrix} 1/cu & 1/c \\ 1-c/cu & 1/c \end{bmatrix}$$

From these equations, it is possible to produce performance graphs (for example Figure 6.6). Thus, one can prove a relationship between recognition accuracy of a speech recognition system, length of string to be entered and transaction time.

6.5.2   Task-network models

Task-network models have been used for a wide range of applications by ergonomists (Meister, 1990). They stimulate the performance of events or tasks within a specified segment of activity. The tasks are described in terms of time requirements and a probability of either successful completion or progression to a further task. Thus, it is possible to define differences in overall performance in terms of time and success between different networks.

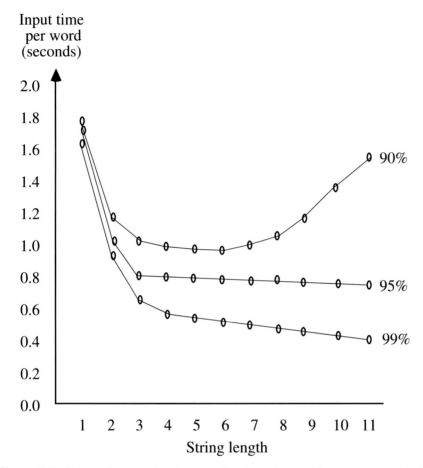

Figure 6.6   Predicted transaction time as a function of recognition accuracy and string length

MicroSAINT is a simulation package, run on a personal computer or Macintosh, which can be used to model performance of a specific network. The package has been used to model performance of both manufacturing processes and human performance. In Birmingham, Kate Hone has been exploring its potential for modeling another aspect of human performance. Given that it is possible to describe human–computer dialogues in terms of flow diagrams, it ought to be possible to use a task-network modeling package to vary the parameters of the dialogues in order to compare different system configurations. Figure 6.7 shows a network version of the dialogue described by Figure 6.5. Recall that in this dialogue, the user speaks a word and then, if the word is not recognized, repeats the word until it is recognized correctly.

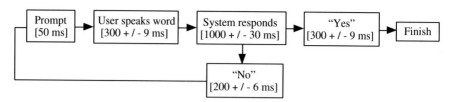

Figure 6.7 Task–network description of a dialogue

Each node in the network is assigned a mean time with a standard deviation around this mean. A Monte Carlo technique is used to randomly extract numbers from this range. The probability of transiting from one node to another can also be expressed numerically. In Figure 6.7, the probability of moving between nodes is dependent upon the recognition accuracy of the speech recognizer. At 99% accuracy the probability of correct recognition of a word or phrase is assumed to be 0.99, and the probability of an error is 0.1. As recognition accuracy is reduced, so the probability of error, and hence deviation from the optimal path, is increased.

While it is possible to gather data pertaining to performance of physical tasks from the KLM approach (see Section 6.4), there appears to be a dearth of similar data for speech-based interactions. In our work, we have made a number of simple assumptions concerning the production of speech (Baber and Hone, 1993). These figures are shown in the figure and represent 100 ms for each "unit" of speech, i.e., in this case each syllable, together with times for processing by the recognizer. The overall probability of successfully transiting a node is given using equation (6.2):

$$N_{ra} = [100 - (100 - P_{ra})] * [(C - 1)/(V - 1)] \qquad (6.2)$$

where N_{ra} represents the new recognition accuracy. P_{ra} represents the previous recognition accuracy, C represents the current vocabulary size, and V represents the previous vocabulary size. The number of errors in a string to be entered has a multiplicative effect (Schurick et al., 1985), such that the probability of a complete string being accurately entered is P^N. This is taken as a rule to capture the benefit of reducing the number of words entered during different phases of error correction.

Mean transaction times (for a digit entry task) were modeled for interactions with feedback in different positions, i.e., after each digit (concurrent), after two digits, after three digits and at the end of the string (terminal). A full description of the model and the data is reported in Hone and Baber (1995). The models produced a similar pattern of results

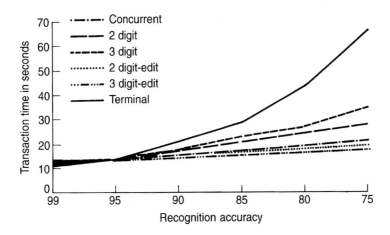

Figure 6.8 Results obtained from a task–network model (reproduced with permission from Hone and Baber, 1995, in S.A. Robertson (ed.), *Contemporary Ergonomics 1996*, published by Taylor & Francis.)

to the Frankish and Noyes (1990) data. The advantage of using the model was that we could run simulations using different levels of recognition accuracy in order to examine how the performance would be affected by decreased recognition accuracy.

6.5.3 Conclusions

The network modeling approaches discussed in this section can be considered extensions of the basic KLM approach. The nature of the extension offered by network modeling is twofold:

1. In terms of data, by allowing inclusion of probabilities, it is possible to accommodate variation in performance, e.g., to the level of considering error.
2. In terms of task description, by considering performance in terms of a network with a number of routes, it ought to be possible to represent variation in performance strategies, e.g., to consider alternative routes through the network and analyse the impact of these routes on transaction times. From this, one could attempt to define the most effective route, perhaps through the use of critical path analysis (Olson and Olson, 1990). Alternatively, one could use the approach to examine

the effects of specific parameters on performance, e.g., recognition accuracy (Baber and Hone, 1993).

6.6 Cognitive models

The previous sections have been concerned with modeling physical performance, primarily in terms of predicting transaction times. While these approaches can produce useful data, especially in the initial stages of research and development of products and systems, they can be criticized for over-simplification. In particular, the approaches pay little or no explicit attention to the cognitive aspects of human performance. Consequently, there is no room for discussing why a particular user has chosen to perform a particular task in a particular fashion. This section considers two (of the myriad) approaches to the issues surrounding the definition and use of knowledge in HCI. I have chosen approaches which are related and which are widely reported. GOMS is probably the best-known modeling approach in HCI, and CCT is, at least in part, a derivative of GOMS.

6.6.1 The GOMS approach

The GOMS approach of Card et al. (1983) can be considered to be a framework within which to build and test models of human performance, specifically with reference to HCI (although the approach has been extended to consider human interaction with other technology). Broadly speaking, the framework comprises three components: a model human processor, which aims to synthesize research in cognitive psychology; a description of the knowledge required by the user in order to perform basic tasks; a set of standard times to allow performance prediction. The standard times represent an extension of KLM (see above) with the important addition of information processing times.

Figure 6.9 illustrates the basic components of the model human processor (MHP). Initially, MHP comprises three stages (roughly corresponding to the stages of input–processing–output), termed perception, cognition and response. This description not only typifies much of the research in cognitive psychology on which the MHP draws, but also highlights a possible limitation in the approach; while the stages of processing hypothesis is popular in cognitive psychology, there has been a great deal of debate in recent years as to the extent to which human information processing also contains elements of parallel processing and whether such parallelism can be modeled (Quinlan, 1991).

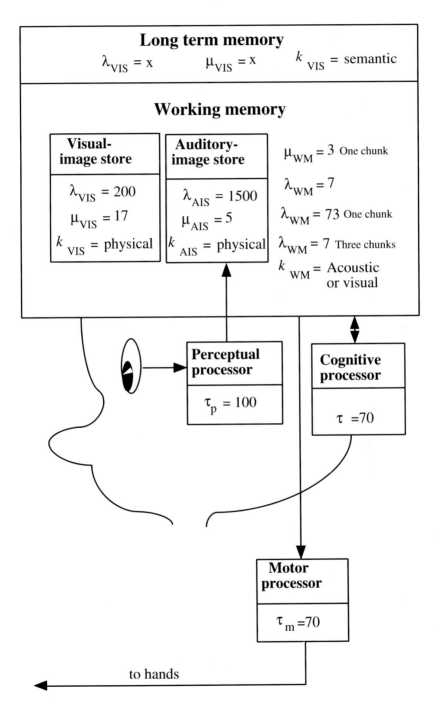

Figure 6.9 Model Human Processor (adapted from Card et al., 1983)

MHP is provided with several parameters relating to the storage capacity of a particular part of memory (μ), the decay time of an item (λ), and the main type of code processed by the part of memory (k). These parameters are then provided with mean times, shown in the figure, and standard deviations around the means. The model, therefore, combines a range of times, assuming no recursion and no error, in order to provide a prediction of the total time required to perform a specific task. The values in Figure 6.9 are derived from the work of Card et al. (1983), which combined both reviews of previous research and new research. In recent years, a number of researchers have added to these basic times (Bovair et al., 1990; John and Newell, 1987, 1989; Olson and Nilsen, 1988). While the MHP can be used to define the scope of performance, specifically in terms of processing and performance times, it is necessary to add an extra dimension to describe how performance is sequenced. Figure 6.10 maps the stages of the MHP onto the model of human action proposed by Norman (1988).

Users' knowledge could be decomposed into a number of levels, and a principal focus for developing models of users is to define the relationship between users' goals and the means by which they can achieve those goals. To a certain extent, goals are quite easy to define; they represent the state of affairs which the user wishes to achieve through acting on the computer.

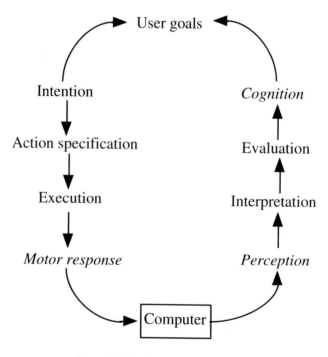

Figure 6.10   Stages of action in HCI

However, in the GOMS approach, goals can also be considered as representing addresses in human memory which can be flagged, and to which the user can return, should the selected method fail. Thus, goals are both users' intentions and particular manifestations of declarative knowledge. As a psychological model, this is the point at which GOMS begins to develop some problems. However, GOMS is primarily an engineering tool and is content to over-ride problems of psychological validity in its pursuit of performance prediction.

Following the specification of goals, the analyst must determine the possible operators. These represent similar units of analysis to those used in KLM, although it is possible to employ a coarser grain of analysis and to consider groups of physical actions, e.g., at the level of generic actions. Operators can be perceptual, cognitive or motor activities and are defined by their output and their processing time.

The methods are used to specify particular combinations of operators in order to achieve the user's goal. Methods can be seen as ready-to-hand solutions to task demands, i.e., they are programs rather than plans for performance. The selection rules determine which methods will be preferred in a given situation. As GOMS assumes no errors in performance, it seeks to produce a performance prediction based on selection of the most appropriate method. GOMS has been applied to a wide range of applications from using spreadsheets (Olson and Nilsen, 1988) to touchtyping (John and Newell, 1989) to playing video-games (John et al., 1994).

6.6.2   Problems with, and refinements of, GOMS

There are many problems associated with GOMS. These can be categorized as problems of expertise, parallelism and functionality. The assumptions which underlie GOMS stem from the belief that expert performance is error-free, consistent and represents minimum performance time. The problem with this assumption is that experts are not always fast and accurate. Thus, GOMS can best be considered as an approximation rather than as a description of human performance. However, it was noted above that a characteristic of expert performance is the possession of a repertoire of methods from which an expert can select a particular course of action. This aspect of expertise can be captured by GOMS in the guise of operations and methods. The focus on expertise does mean that the model cannot account for sub-expert performance nor can it describe how people learn new skills.

GOMS assumes that tasks are performed in series. In the chapters on using interaction devices in Part I, it is clear that expert performance contains a large element of parallelism. Olson and Olson (1990) demonstrate that GOMS can lead to over-estimation of transaction times as a result of this problem. There have been several attempts to circumvent these problems. For instance, John and Newell (1989) propose that perceptual, cognitive or motor operations can occur in parallel, if the context allows the user to predict events.

While GOMS can describe and model what the user needs to do in order to use a system, it does not indicate whether these actions represent the most appropriate approach to the performance of the task. For instance, there may be faster or more efficient approaches which can be used. Of course, one could perform GOMS analysis for each of the alternative approaches to ascertain their relative utility. However, the focus of GOMS is on one aspect of the usability of the system, rather than on the full complement of performance-shaping factors discussed in Chapter 5.

6.6.3 Cognitive complexity theory

Kieras and Polson (1986) have extended the basic notions of GOMS by introducing two additional elements: a description of the users' knowledge in terms of production rules, and a state transition description of the system being used. This section will focus on the use of production rules in cognitive complexity theory (CCT). Basically, the production rules follow the traditional format of:

$$If \text{ (condition) } Then \text{ (action)}$$

For example, consider the use of cursor keys to move a cursor to the right. This can be described in the following rule:

```
(MOVE-RIGHT
    IF (AND (TEST-GOAL move-right)
            (TEST-CURSOR BELOW %LINE))
    THEN    ((DO-KEYSTROKE '>') ))
```

In this example, having defined the goal to move the cursor to the right, the position of the cursor is determined and the action of pressing the appropriate cursor key is performed. It is worth noting that the rules can follow when the conditions are true (irrespective of sequence).

CCT contains a set of rules for sub-expert users which, broadly speaking, require the user to constantly monitor and check performance (Bovair et al., 1990). In other words, in terms of learning a skill, the naive user can be considered to function at the level of procedural knowledge (Anderson, 1990). Furthermore, it is proposed that CCT can allow analysts to determine the relative training time required to master a particular task using equation (6.3).

$$\text{Training time} = t \times n + c \qquad\qquad (6.3)$$

where $t =$ training time per production rule;

$n =$ total number of production rules
                    (excluding ''common rules'';

$c =$ time required to perform existing tasks

From this equation, learning a new task is seen as building on existing knowledge (both in terms of existing tasks and in terms of "common rules", i.e., rules which are assumed to be known to the user from experience with other tasks). The equation does, however, rely on the assumption that all production rules take the same amount of time to learn. This would only be true if all of the production rules were of equal complexity, which strikes me as a difficult proposal to justify.

6.6.4 Problems with CCT

Knowles (1988) has used CCT to evaluate learning of a CAD system and proposes that the approach has a number of limitations. Her criticisms are presented in the following quotation:

1. No underlying theory of knowledge sources and their interaction.
2. Restricted in application, by virtue of its reliance on GOMS, to tasks involving problem solving.
3. No empirical validation of the hypothesis Kieras and Polson put forward in their paper.
4. There is no clear separation of the components of CC, if they cannot be identified how can they be measured?
5. An over-reliance on quantitative aspects of representing knowledge at the expense of qualitative aspects.

[Knowles, 1988, p. 295]

Thus, CCT would appear to allow some comparison of tasks in terms of the number of production rules they require. The psychological validity of production rules as representations of user knowledge is difficult to justify. Further, the attempt to define training time seems to rely on the dubious assumption that all tasks are of equal complexity and will take equal times to learn and master.

6.7   Predicting human error

In Chapter 5, a number of possible measures of performance were listed. One of these approaches was to study the types of errors that users make. Many of the modeling approaches either explicitly exclude error by focusing on "expert" performance, or implicitly exclude error by focusing only on performance time. Traditionally, human error has been classified in terms of errors of intention, or mistakes, and errors of execution, or slips (Reason, 1990). To a certain extent, mistakes can be represented by CCT by describing production rules to capture erroneous planning of action. However, while this can describe error it is difficult to see how it could be used to predict error.

"Slips" represent a common form. For instance, when typing users may inadvertently hit a key next to the one they intended to hit, or when moving a cursor the user may overshoot a target. No doubt the reader can add to these examples. As one increases the types of error which are both possible and credible, it becomes increasingly necessary to develop some structured approach to the analysis.

In other spheres of human factors, researchers have been developing a number of approaches to the prediction of human error. Kirwan (1992 a,b) presents a critical review of the most well-known approaches. In general the prediction of human error tends to be performed in safety critical domains, as part of the human reliability assessment process. However, Baber and Stanton (1994) have proposed that human error prediction methods could be profitably applied to the evaluation of consumer products and computer systems. Furthermore, Baber and Stanton (1996) have shown that error prediction methods can capture some 80% of the errors observed in the actual use of products. In general, error prediction methods share the assumption that, if the analyst can describe what the user *ought* to do then it is possible to describe how such behavior can break down. Thus, the methods begin with a task analysis and proceed to interrogate the description of the task.

One possible approach is now known as SHERPA: systematic human error reduction and prediction approach (Embrey, 1986). In SHERPA, the analyst constructs a hierarchical task analysis and then interrogates the action level, using the error types in Table 6.4. For instance, if the user needs to press a particular key, one could define possible errors as pressing the wrong key.

This approach allows one to define a number of possible errors, and can be applied to task analysis of a wide range of activities. The drawback with the approach is that it can be very time consuming, and there is little indication of how critical the predicted errors are to system operation or how probable the errors are.

Table 6.4 Error types in SHERPA

Planning errors
P1 Plan preconditions ignored
P2 Incorrect plan executed
P3 Correct but inappropriate plan executed
P4 Correct plan executed but too soon/too late
P5 Correct plan executed in wrong order

Action errors
A1 Operation too long/too short
A2 Operation mistimed
A3 Operation in wrong direction
A4 Operation too little/too much
A5 Misalign
A6 Right operation on wrong object
A7 Wrong operation on right object
A8 Operation omitted
A9 Operation incomplete

Checking errors
C1 Check omitted
C2 Check incomplete
C3 Right check on wrong object
C4 Wrong check on right object
C5 Check mistimed

Retrieval errors
R1 Information not obtained
R2 Wrong information obtained
R3 Information retrieval incomplete

Information communication errors
I1 Information not communicated
I2 Wrong information communicated
I3 Information communication incomplete

Selection errors
S1 Selection omitted
S2 Wrong selection made

Thus, it is possible to predict errors which users could make in their interaction with a computer. However, a plain listing of errors can only tell the analyst that such errors are possible. Combined with predictions of transaction times, one might be able to predict possible outcomes of user performance. However, the prediction of outcome (either for time or error) has no need to consider the process involved in performing the tasks. Without an adequate explanation of how the action is planned and performed, it is not possible to say why the action was performed in a specific way and why errors occurred. Consequently, in order to develop solutions to user problems, it is necessary to develop a more detailed understanding of how people use interaction devices. This will be the substance of Part II.

6.8 Conclusions

In Chapter 5, the notion of generic actions was introduced. The first approach to modeling user behavior presented in this chapter can be seen, in part, as an extension of the generic action concept. The three-state description allows one to consider the components of the generic actions of selecting and dragging objects. It was noted that combining the state descriptions with performance times allows one to predict transaction time. While this approach could capture some aspects of the human–computer interaction, it was felt that the focus was a little too limited. In all of the approaches discussed in the chapter, it is necessary to define standard times and the principal approach to generating and defining standard times in HCI is the keystroke level model. Two alternative approaches to state transition modeling were introduced. Both Markov and task-network models allow the analyst to describe the progression of a dialogue through a series of states with probabilities of moving to the next state and residence times for each state. Running the models can provide transaction time data, which has been shown to bear some resemblance to human performance data. It is suggested that the notion of standard times also requires acceptance of "one best way" to perform tasks, which is highly contentious when considering expert performance and the fact that the majority of HCI tasks allow the user some flexibility in their performance. While transaction times can be predicted (albeit with varying degrees of accuracy), it is proposed that one needs to understand how a task is performed, and not simply how quickly it can be performed. To this end, the popular approach to GOMS was reviewed. It was felt that although the approach could represent an extension of the previous approaches, it lacked the ability to predict either variation in performance or learning time. CCT, on the other hand, attempts to predict learning time and can allow for comparison between different styles of interaction (if not between different interaction devices). Finally, the issue of human error was considered and the approach of SHERPA briefly presented.

In this chapter a number of approaches to modeling human performance have been considered. The approaches share the theme of describing activity in sufficient detail and with sufficient data to allow prediction of user performance. Thus, the focus has been primarily on quantifiable models of performance. This approach can be contrasted with the discussion of performance-shaping factors in Chapter 5, which can be considered as a qualitative approach to studying performance. Bearing in mind the problems associated with the "hard" approaches presented in this chapter, Part II contains a number of models of performance which, while based on performance data, tend to describe rather than predict human performance.

6.9 Key points for practitioners

- Consider the possibility of introducing modeling into the design process as a means of evaluating early prototypes.
- Consider the use of modeling in product evaluation.
- Define the operation of a system in terms of different states and consider how user tasks and activities map onto these states.

6.10 Key points for researchers

- Continue collection and validation of standard times.
- Investigate ways of representing parallelism in user models.
- Consider how to represent both learning and skill in models.
- Consider how to predict and model human error in task performance.
- Extend models which combine user knowledge with action.

CHAPTER 7

Typing

Abstract

The keyboard stubbornly refuses to be shifted as the prime means of interaction between people and computers. Thus, typing is a major skill in the interaction between people and computers. Of course, not all people who use keyboards approach the proficiency of touch typists. However, in this chapter typing is considered as a motor skill which can be performed with greater or lesser fluency by all keyboard users, and the implications of this for the design of keyboards are discussed.

7.1 Introduction

While the QWERTY keyboard is the most common form of interaction device in use with contemporary computer systems, there are some problems inherent in its design (as discussed in Chapter 2). In Chapter 12, the potential physical problems associated with keyboard use are discussed, while in this chapter the focus will be on the psychomotor factors involved in using keyboards. In order to consider such problems, it is necessary to examine the extensive literature on the skills involved in using keyboards.

A description of typing can be obtained by breaking the activity into its main parts (a common initial step in ergonomics research) and then studying these parts, separately and in combination. Thus, the first section will focus on the apparently trivial task of pressing a button. Even this task can be described in terms of controlled movement, and can be affected by specific, external factors, such as the size of the button, its distance from the person, the position of other buttons in its vicinity. Next the activity involved in pressing a sequence of buttons is examined, along with the problems of timing and coordinating such an activity, before moving to consideration of pressing a sequence of buttons in a specified order, i.e., an order defined by the spelling of words which are read from a page of text.

Attention is directed to the use of chord keyboards, and the use of keyboards with a limited number of keys, such as numerical keypads. The chapter concludes with a discussion of the possible relationships between keyboard design and typing performance.

7.2 Basic elements of typing skills

If one assumes that typing is a skilled activity, it is important to determine what distinguishes a skilled typist from an unskilled typist. One can state the obvious and say that highly skilled typists are faster than unskilled typists. West and Sabban (1982) report a very wide range of typing speeds from the people who took part in their study: from 10 words per minute (wpm) to 114 wpm. The average speed at which a skilled typist, using the QWERTY arrangement can produce text lies between 60 and 90 wpm. Assume an average typing speed of 60 wpm, with average length of words of 5 characters plus a space, i.e., 6 keypresses. This gives around 360 keypresses per minute, for our mythical average typist. From this, a figure of around 166 ms per keypress can be defined (i.e., 60 seconds/360 keypresses). The time needed for the human visual system to process information has been estimated to be around 200 ms, i.e., from 165 ms (Young and Zaleznick, 1992) to 290 ms (Beggs and Howarth, 1970). This means that it is not possible for skilled typists to perform each keypress in isolation, i.e., there is not sufficient time for a skilled typist to press a key, evaluate visual feedback and then press the next key. Thus, in order for typists to reach even an average speed, they need to be able to combine sequences of keypresses. This implies some form of plan for typing.

There is also some evidence to suggest that "incorrect" keypresses, i.e., those in which the typist has pressed the wrong key, are often less forceful than "corrrect" keypresses (Rabbit, 1978). We can demonstrate this by asking typists to type passages onto several sheets of paper (using a manual typewriter); the harder a key is pressed, the more sheets of paper will bear the impression of that letter. It would seem that "errorful" keypresses result in fewer sheets bearing an impression of the wrong letter. This implies that, not only are sequences of keypresses planned, but also that performance is monitored before it has occurred. This, in turn, implies a hierarchy of levels in plans, with checks being carried out at each level. The checking does not require conscious attention so much as a well-defined feedback loop.

7.3   The timing of typing

Let us assume that typing is simply a matter of pressing a sequence of keys (ignoring the fact that the sequence is determined by various rules governing the combinations in a language). Our first question should be how quickly can a person press a key?

7.3.1   Pressing a single key

From the earliest work in the field of motor skills, researchers noted that the timing of keypressing seemed to increase as the number of possible keys increased (Donders, 1868). This represents a version of choice reaction time, i.e., the time to react to a stimulus when the respondent has a choice of responses. This is presumed to be due to two factors: the uncertainty as to which key should be pressed, and the selection of the appropriate key. (It is customary in such research to prompt people as to which key is required, for instance, by illuminating a light on, or near, the key, or by placing the keys in a pattern similar to those in which the lights are arranged). In the 1950s, researchers defined a law to govern this relationship between the time a person takes to react to a stimulus and the number of choices they could possibly make (Hick, 1952; Hyman, 1953). This is known as the Hick–Hyman law and is defined thus,

$$\text{Choice reaction time} = K \log (n + 1) \qquad (7.1)$$

Note the use of $(n + 1)$ in equation (7.1). This is to cover the possibility that uncertainty will arise not simply due to which stimulus has appeared, but also as to whether a stimulus has appeared, thus the equation is designed to cope with conditions in which $n = 0$. However, it is customary to indicate a value of N, which is a measure of the total number of equiprobable stimuli. Taking data derived from equation (7.1), it is possible to construct a graph which will present a linear relationship between number of choices and reaction time and the slope of the graph tends to give a value of around 150 ms for each additional choice (Rosenbaum, 1991). From the Hick–Hyman law, one might assume that making a response to a stimulus involves a definable time, and that the time is influenced by the number of choices which need to be made. This gives a simple model of reaction time in which a person rejects possible responses in order to arrive at the correct response. While it is possible to gather data to support the Hick–Hyman law, it is also possible to produce data which refute it.

   If we vary the way in which choice stimuli are presented, we can produce results contrary to those predicted by the law. Let us take two studies as examples. Crossman (1956) arranged the stimulus lights in one of two patterns. In the first, he used a straight line which corresponded to the arrangement of keys on the response board. In the second, he used the same arrangement of keys but placed the lights in a random configuration. Not surprisingly, he found that the second configuration produced longer reaction times than the first. This finding supports a notion of spatial compatibility between stimuli and responses (see Chapter 5). This implies that reaction is influenced not simply by the number of choices but also by the amount of processing the person needs to make; in this case, the second configuration required the respondent to translate from light number to key number, whereas the first simply required a translation between positions. We also know that reaction time will be influenced by factors such as stimulus intensity or uncertainty (Teichner and Krebs, 1972), practice or experience (Woodworth and Schlosberg, 1954), and which limb segment is used for the response, e.g., finger, hand or arm (Anson, 1982).

Leonard (1959) ingeniously combined stimulus and response material into the same item (a switch was vibrated under the participant's finger). If the Hick–Hyman law held, one would expect the number of switches to yield a linear increase in reaction time. However, the actual results showed little change in reaction time as the number of switches increased. This is proposed to result from the high degree of compatibility between stimulus and response; the participants in Leonard's (1959) study were able to respond very efficiently to the stimuli because there was little need for additional processing. Thus, it is possible to improve reaction time performance by defining compatibility between stimulus and response. More importantly, even the relatively simple task of pressing the correct key in response to a stimulus can be shown to be mediated and influenced by a number of factors.

7.3.2   Pressing a sequence of keys

In the previous section, the activity of pressing a single key was considered. Consider what happens when a person is requested to press a sequence of keys. Several studies have shown that performance on this task is faster if people can use alternate hands, rather than the same hand; we can suggest that using alternate hands for key pressing can produce key pressing rates roughly twice those of using the same hand, e.g., Salthouse (1986) suggests that typing using alternate hands is some 30–60 ms faster than when using the same hand. We also know (from Rabbitt, 1978) that performance on sequential key pressing tasks decreases in the following order:

1. second keypress using same finger as first keypress but other hand, e.g., left-index followed by right-index;

2. second keypress using different finger but same hand, e.g., left-index followed by left-middle;
3. second keypress using different finger on different hand, e.g., left-index followed by right-middle.

This suggests that some sequences of keypresses are easier to prepare than others, as reflected in their relative performance times. If people can use alternate hands, then they might be able to prepare the second action when the first is still being performed, whereas, if they use the same hand, they will have to wait until the first action has finished before they can commence the second. This certainly seems plausible, especially when one considers that the hands of skilled typists appear to be in constant motion. However, while this explanation explains the difference between (1) and (2), it appears to be contradicted by the difference between (2) and (3). Let us suppose that (1) is superior to (2) because the same finger is used on different hands, and (2) is superior to (3) because the same hand is used for (2). From this, we could propose that the first action somehow "primes" the second, i.e., having a common feature might facilitate planning. This implies that the plan for typing a sequence of letters should have within it a code for the fingers to be used and one for the hand. Thus, if the action requires a person to specify a different hand and different finger (3), preparation might take longer than if they had to specify just a different hand (1) or a different finger (2). From this account, one would anticipate that planning of typing action would first define a finger and then define which hand to use. This might appear to be somewhat counter-intuitive; after all, one might expect the hand to be selected first, and then the appropriate finger.

Rosenbaum et al. (1983) asked people to perform simple sequences of key presses using middle and index fingers. The sequences were first learned by participants, and then performed from memory. Each sequence was performed six times in succession, and participants were told to respond as quickly as possible. The results suggested that the times between keypresses were related to the fingers used to press the keys. This was explained by a tree-traversal model, shown in Figure 7.1. Start at the top node. Assume the first keypress requires the use of the left middle finger, move down the tree to one of the left middle nodes. This will take you through three nodes. Assume the second keypress will also use the left middle finger, move to the other left middle node. This will take you through four nodes. Assume the third keypress will use the right middle finger, which will take you through two nodes. Following this logic, it is possible to construct a route through the tree, with different keypress pairs taking different numbers of nodes.

Rosenbaum et al. (1983) demonstrate that the number of nodes passed through in Figure 7.1 gives a good approximation of the relative times between each keypress, and also relates to the order of sequential key-

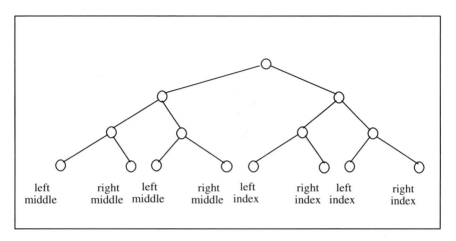

left   right   left   right   left   right   left   right
middle   middle middle   middle index   index   index   index

Figure 7.1   Rosenbaum et al.'s (1983) tree–traversal model for sequential keypressing tasks

pressing tasks given above. Note that the route specifies finger (e.g., middle or index) and then hand (e.g., left or right). There is some further evidence to consider in support of the notion of a plan which specifies finger and then hand. In one study, Larochelle (1983) analyzed videotape of touch typists and was able to show that the initiation of a movement to strike a key occurs 32 ms before the termination of the previous keypress when using alternate hands, but occurs 39 ms *after* the termination of the previous keypress when using the same hand. In another study, Salthouse (1984) found that the initial keystroke of a word is some 20% longer than successive keystrokes within that word.

7.4   Typing considered as skilled behavior

When researchers investigate skilled behavior, one of the best places to begin is the consideration of what happens when the skill breaks down, i.e., when people make errors. We will begin this section with a discussion of the types of error made by typists. However, it will be useful to refresh our memory with the layout of the QWERTY keyboard and the advised positions of the fingers for touch typing (as shown in Figure 7.2).

7.4.1   Errors in typing performance

In an early study of typing behavior, Lessenberry (1928) compiled a corpus of 60 000 typing errors. He analyzed this corpus in terms of which key

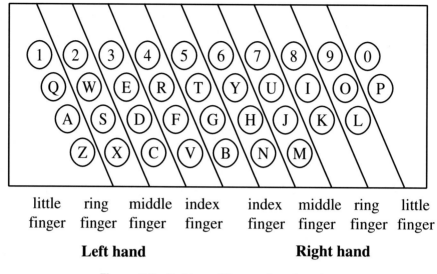

Figure 7.2   Positions of fingers of touch typing

was pressed when a specific key was intended, e.g., by taking typographical errors and asking which letter should have been typed in place of the erroneous letter. He noted that a large proportion of the errors could be explained by the typists hitting a key which was in close proximity to the intended key. The most common form of this error involved hitting a key adjacent to the intended key, e.g., typing "habe" instead of "have" (assume that the typing is performed on a keyboard using the QWERTY arrangement).

The next most common group of errors could be explained by the typist hitting above or below the intended key, e.g., typing "hafe" for "have". One might suggest that such errors are simply a matter of the slips of the hand, i.e., the finger simply missing the desired key. However, the next class of error identified by Lessenberry (1928) implies that this is not the whole story.

The third group of errors often involved widely spaced keys, e.g., typing "hane" for "have". This cannot be explained by a simple account of slips, but can be explained if we notice that the finger used to type the "n" in the incorrect word is the same as that used to type the correct "v", albeit on the right hand rather than the left. This reintroduces the notion of planning being "primed" by previous actions. Pursuing this argument further leads to the proposal that the wrong keys are typed not by the "correct" finger, i.e., in terms of the finger slipping, but are typed by the "wrong" finger, i.e., rather than the "n" of "hane" being typed by the first finger missing the "v", it could be typed by the middle finger which "normally" types "n". This is precisely what Grudin (1983) has found.

From these studies, one might propose that typing errors imply that each key has a "correct" finger associated with it (at least for touch typists). Recall, in Chapter 2, that the typing competition of 1888 was won by a typist who used all ten fingers and who had memorized the arrangement of the QWERTY keyboard. The implication of this is that typing involves learning the spatial arrangement of the keys on a keyboard and also learning the pairing of specific fingers with specific keys. One might feel that, at this point, the skilled typist and novice typist will part company. While I am not aware of any work on the spatial knowledge of a QWERTY keyboard for novice typists, the discussion of numeric keypads below suggests that spatial knowledge could play an important role in the use of keyboards by novices. Consider where you expect to find the "b" key; if you use the keyboard on a daily basis (even if you are not a touch typist), I suspect that you have an expectation as to which quadrant of the keyboard to look first in order to find the key. Furthermore, I would suggest that novice typists attempt to alternate typing between left and right hand (assuming that they have reached the level of proficiency which allows them to use *two* fingers).

Finally, there is another common class of errors in typing, in which the correct letters are typed in the wrong order, i.e., "haev" instead of "have". This implies a breakdown not at the level of finger selection, but of sequencing the movements. Finally, the fact that incorrect keypresses are made less forcefully (Rabbitt, 1978) and with longer latencies (Shaffer, 1975) than correct keypresses, implies that typists must, somehow, know in advance of pressing a key whether they have made a mistake or not.

7.4.2 Typing performance

Combining typing speed and errors, we have a skill which appears to require people to combine sequences of activity into chunks (in order to overcome the limits of processing), where units within the chunks can interfere with accurate performance (in order to produce substitution errors), where units can be mistimed (in order to produce transposition errors) and the execution of which can be monitored. This raises the question, how large are these "chunks" and what form do they take? The common-sense answer to this question would be that "chunks" in typing are the same as words.

If we assume that the "chunk" used in typing was equivalent to words, then we would expect non-words to take longer to type than words. This is, indeed, the case (Fendrick, 1937). Furthermore, Shaffer (1978) has shown that if the rate at which letters are revealed is controlled, so that, for instance a person sees eight letters at a time, typing is faster when those letters form words than when they do not form words. We might also follow this line of logic and suggest that words arranged according to conventional rules of syntax would be typed more quickly than words presented randomly. However, this is not the case. West and Sabban (1982) show that typing "meaningful text" is only 2.8% more efficient than typing random text. This suggests that typists do not read for meaning. Indeed, when Marton and Sandqvist (1972) compared typing performance between a group of typists who were asked to think about what they were typing, with a group who were told simply to type the material, the results showed a significant difference in comprehension between the two groups but no difference in typing performance.

If the chunk was equivalent to a word, then we might predict that the movement of a typist's eyes reading text to be copied will mirror that of the fingers across the keyboard, i.e., that the eye will read a word, and the fingers will type that word. However, it appears that the hand–eye span (or the number of letters the eye reads in advance of the hand) is between 6 and 8 characters. Cooper (1983) suggests that the locations of eye fixations are not necessarily related to word boundaries. As an early researcher argued, the typist will read sufficient text "to supply the copy to the hand as it is needed." (Butsch, 1932, p. 113). Thus, typists do not need to comprehend what they are typing. This suggests that the chunk is not a word so much as a sequence of letters, restricted by limits in the span of attention.

If the "chunk" into which people combine units is equivalent to a word, then the information that typists hold in short-term memory should consist of words. One might also expect that the short-term memory could serve as a buffer, feeding the next word to the fingers for typing. Considering the speed with which skilled typists execute keystrokes, one might then assume that asking a typist to stop typing would lead to them emptying the buffer, i.e., typing a complete word. However, this does not happen; typists can stop within one or two characters of the command to stop (Long, 1976). This means that either the buffer is quite small, i.e., limited to only a few characters, or that the typist can exert some control over the extraction of items from the buffer. The latter proposal seems implausible. Therefore, we must assume that buffer size is limited. Furthermore, we know that variation in interkey intervals can be influenced by a number of factors, such as the preceding and succeeding characters to be typed, whether the typist can alternate hands, whether the succeeding character forms part of a common digram, e.g., "t" followed by "h" might have a shorter interkey interval than "t" followed by "s" (as in "tsar").

These context effects are limited to only a space of 2–3 characters (Shaffer, 1978). We also know, from analysis of hand movements, that typists seem to commit themselves to keystrokes within 2–3 strokes of the current stroke. This would suggest that the "chunk" is also limited by attentional constraints. It also seems that the notion of a detailed plan would appear excessive for typing. If planning only considers the next 2–

3 characters, then an overall plan seems extravagant. Having said this, the fact that initial keystrokes take longer than successive keystrokes implies that some form of planning is taking place. The following sections contain some of the models which have been proposed to account for the evidence presented above.

7.4.3 Salthouse's model of typing

Taking these findings presented in the preceding sections, Salthouse (1986) proposed a parsimonious model of skilled typing. He assumes that text is read (which defines the input to the model), and then decomposed into character strings. The length of these strings could well depend on the proficiency of the typist; for novice "hunt and peck" typists, the strings could be limited to single characters, whereas more skilled typists would use a limit of 2, 3 or more characters. At this point, there might well be some additional syntactical knowledge which facilitates parsing (thus, explaining the superiority of words to non-words in terms of typing performance). The character strings are then translated into their relative movement sequences, so that such a sequence of finger movements is defined for a sequence of keypresses. For instance, the model uses a code for identifying hand (H) as either left (L) or right (R), finger (F) as being 1 to 4 and reach as up (u), down (d) or on same row (-). The model allows that sequences of keypresses could be performed in two distinct ways: either as serial processing, i.e., "hunt and peck", or as parallel processing, i.e., touch typing. Finally, the keypresses are executed (see Figures 7.3a and b).

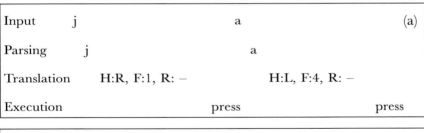

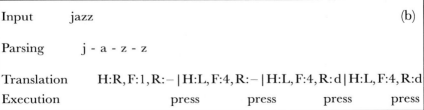

Figure 7.3 Salthouse's model of typing for (a) serial and (b) parallel processing

In addition to describing the basic processes through which typing is executed, the model can be used to define likely causes of error in typing (as shown in Table 7.1). The model can be used to propose, for instance, that substitution errors arise at the translation stage and transposition errors arise at the execution stage. However, the model does not seem to be able to deal with the fact that errors can be detected prior to execution.

From Table 7.1, one can see that it is possible to relate specific types of error to specific points in the performance of the typing activity. One might propose that some of the causes of errors require further decomposition in order to provide a useful description, e.g., the term "perceptual confusion" applies across error types at the input stage. "Perceptual confusion" could be influenced by compatibility between keyboard layout and user's expectations such that people aim for a key in a position where they expect it to be.

Table 7.1   Classification of typing errors (after Salthouse, 1986)

	Error types			
Stage	Substitution	Intrusion	Omission	Transposition
Input	Perceptual confusion	Perceptual confusion	Perceptual confusion	Perceptual confusion
Parsing	Capture by high frequency digram	—	—	—
	Failure to preserve sequence	Failure to preserve sequence	Failure to preserve sequence	Failure to preserve sequence
Translation	Faulty movement specification	Failure to deactivate previous action	Inhibition by previous action	—
	Failure to preserve sequence	Failure to preserve sequence	Failure to preserve sequence	Failure to preserve sequence
Execution	Misplaced finger	Keypress between two keys	Inadequate force; inadequate reach	Out of sequence
	Inaccurate trajectory	—	—	—

7.4.4 Rumelhart and Norman's model

Rumelhart and Norman (1982) proposed a connectionist model of typing in
which nodes allow fingers to be associated with keys. When a particular
string of characters is read, the nodes associating each character to a finger
to a key are activated. The approach is illustrated by the schematic diagram
in Figure 7.4.

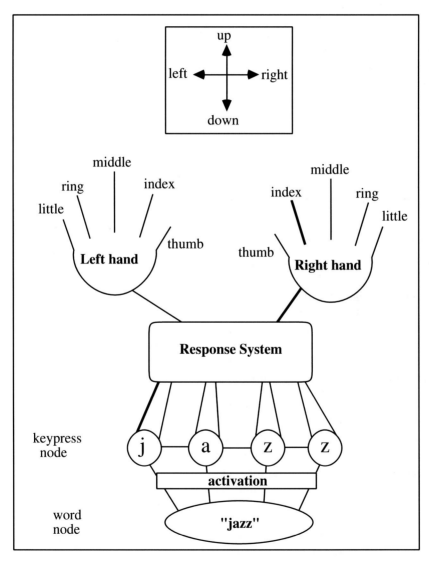

Figure 7.4   Schematic of Rumelhart and Norman's Model

A set of connections determining the sequence of firing will also be activated. Each node, on activation, will inhibit the activation of other nodes in the sequence. As soon as the keystroke is effected, the active node will inhibit itself. This means that self-inhibition can occur during a keystroke, and so explain overlapping of movement in touch typing. The strength of activation can be primed by previous activity. If the next keystroke uses the same finger, then the node will need to be reactivated (as it was inhibited on previous firing), but if the keystroke uses the homologous finger, it could be primed and activated before the previous keystroke had finished. These assumptions are similar to those illustrated by the tree-traversal model (Figure 7.1).

Norman and Fisher (1982), using the Rumelhart and Norman (1982) model with keystroke timings derived from their own work and that of Kinkade, 1975), suggested that while the Dvorak keyboard could yield a 5.4% increase in typing speed, five other alternative arrangements they considered led to decreases in typing speed of between 1.8% and 8.9%.

While the Rumelhart and Norman (1982) model can explain many of the effects found in typing research, it does not easily allow co-articulation of keypresses, nor can it explain how typing performance can improve with practice. Furthermore, it does not appear to have any lexical knowledge, and so cannot explain the superior performance of words over non-words in typing.

7.4.5   Computational models

While one can consider the relationship between levels of processing and typing activity, it is useful to operationalize this relationship in terms of activity timing so that we can begin to make predictions about typing performance. Kinkade (1975) measured keystroke intervals and timing from a number of skilled typists using the QWERTY arrangement. From these data, he extrapolated possible performance times for an alternative arrangement, i.e., the Dvorak keyboard (see Chapter 2). Kinkade's (1975) data suggest that the Dvorak layout would yield an increase in performance of only 2.6% for a skilled typist. He also proposed that it ought to be possible to produce a maximum increase of around 7.6%, on the basis of further changes in design and operation. Card et al. (1983), using a keystroke level model of typing behavior (see Chapter 6), proposed that an alphabetic arrangement would reduce typing performance by 8%.

What do these results tell us? They provide some indication of relative performance limits which might be expected in human performance, suggesting that the redesign of keyboards would lead to relatively small gains in performance. This certainly helps us appreciate the fact that some of the more extreme claims for performance improvements voiced for alternative keyboard designs may be based more on fancy than fact (and suggests that efforts should be directed not at getting people to type faster, perhaps, but more comfortably, see Chapter 12). While a number of factors have been shown to contribute to the activity of typing, one can illustrate the main factors with the following quotation:

> The layout of the keyboard and the physical constraints of the hands appear to be the most important determinants of keystroke timing in skilled typing.
>
> [Gentner, 1983, p. 117]

7.5 Psychomotor skills and chord keyboards

There have been few studies which examine skills in the use of chord keyboards. Rabbit et al. (1975) used a choice reaction time paradigm in which participants were required to respond to stimuli using combinations of key presses. They found that the reaction times were shorter when people were able to use homologous fingers than when they used different fingers (perhaps due to priming effects). There also appeared to be a carry over of effect, in which a high reaction time for one chord increased the reaction time of the next chord, although this might well have been due to the effort required to monitor previous keying.

Gopher et al. (1985) studied the effect of different arrangements of chord keys on performance. They used horizontal and vertical layouts with two chording protocols, i.e., homologous fingers to form the chords or symmetrical chord shapes. They found that performance was fastest when the keyboard was vertical and participants could use symmetrical chord shapes, and worst if participants were required to use homologous fingers. The horizontal, symmetrical chord shape condition came between these two. This, at first glance, seems to disprove the priming hypothesis, in which homologous fingers produce fastest performance. The results could be explained by the proposal that priming may occur not at the finger but the hand (chord shape) level.

7.6 Typing with limited keypads

Conrad (1967) reports a study on the arrangement of numeric keypads. He used two layouts: the first corresponds to conventional telephone arrangement, i.e., 1–2–3, and the second had the keys arranged randomly. The results for the conventional arrangement showed superior performance (both in terms of speed and accuracy) to the random arrangement. This suggests that, when using a numeric keypad, people do not simply search the keypad for each digit, but rather can aim for where they might expect the digit to be. Conrad (1967) suggests that the 1–2–3 arrangement has a higher operational compatibility than the random arrangement. Furthermore, the random arrangement led to a measurable disruption to recall performance, suggesting that there was an interaction between search for keys and maintenance rehearsal in short-term memory.

It is interesting to consider whether the differences between calculator and telephone arrangements of numeric keypads might also relate to the compatibility hypothesis. For example, assume that we expect to read from left to right and from top to bottom, and that we tend to treat numbers as increasing values. This would suggest that the telephone arrangement would have higher compatibility than the calculator arrangement. Next assume that, through practice, we have become highly proficient at treating number sequences as left to right, bottom to top, i.e., on the calculator arrangement. Problems will arise specifically when we move to the other arrangement, or if we change the arrangement yet further, e.g., by placing the "0" key at the side of the other keys rather than at the bottom. While this suggests a relationship between user's expectations and keyboard arrangement, it does not tell us how people perform simple data entry, i.e., involving short strings of information without syntactic constraints, such as numbers.

Verwey (1993) asked people to enter 3-digit strings using a 7–8–9 arrangement numeric keypad (as on a computer). After practice, the time between a prompt and the first keypress decreased. The time between first and second keypresses remained about the same, but the time between the second and third keypress also decreased with practice. In a subsequent study, Verwey (1994) varied the length of the digit string, 2 or 4 digits. The data again suggest a decrease in the time between prompt and first keypress, as a result of practice. As one might expect, the time between prompt and first keypress was shorter for 2 than 4 (by about 20 ms. on average), and the interkey times were longer for 4-digit strings than for 2-digit strings. Finally, the results also showed a decrease in time for the final keypress, either the second or the fourth depending on string size. This suggests that even with as simple an activity as entering digits, people have a tendency to construct short plans to regulate their action, with the first and final keypresses improving with practice as the plans become better described and more efficiently performed.

Robertson and Black (1986) designed a study in which participants used a simple text editor with 8 function keys to make changes to sentences. There were two ways in which this task could be performed: either by positioning the cursor and overtyping the desired word, or through removing one word and inserting another. Each task was attempted twice, and the residual times reported (i.e., the difference between the keypress without planning and the keypress during task performance). The authors made several interesting findings. First, the relative distribution of the two correction techniques changed with practice, with the majority of participants moving to the overtyping technique. Second, as one might expect, performance improved with practice. Third, the inter-keystroke times were higher at points which were defined as plan boundaries. Fourth, the inter-keystroke time for the initial plan boundary for the overtyping technique actually increased with practice. The authors propose that this latter finding indicates that participants were evolving more complex plans, covering a larger sequence of keypresses. However, overall the plans used by participants seemed to be restricted to two to three keypresses (as with the literature concerned with typing).

7.7 Conclusions

Following the Rumelhart and Norman (1982) and Salthouse (1986) models we can say that in addition to the physical constraints of the hand and keyboard layout, one must consider the ability of the typist to prepare and use unambiguous plans linking key position to finger. The plans for sequences of keypresses appear to be limited to two or three items.

From Conrad's (1967) study of numeric keypads, one can consider that the relationship between keyboard arrangement and user expectation might influence keying performance, particularly in users who have not developed sufficient familiarity with the layout to establish the key–finger relationship described by Salthouse (1986) and Rumelhart and Norman (1982).

From this, it is feasible that the main problem with the alphabetic keyboard lies, not so much in its arrangement, as in the potential ambiguity arising from people's knowledge of the sequence of letters in the alphabet which could slow search time (Norman and Fisher, 1982).

Thus, as we shall see in Chapter 12, improvements in typing performance are most likely to be obtained from keyboard designs which allow keystrokes with alternating hands and which minimize muscle loading during typing.

7.8 Key points for practitioners

- Consider the relationship between the design and layout of the keyboard and the constraints of the users' hands, in terms of possible physical problems.

- Provide training for keyboard operators, rather than simply allowing them to develop their own techniques.

7.9 Key points for researchers

- Develop models of novice typists and consider the implications of these models for keyboard design.
- Develop models of the use of minimal keyboards.
- Develop models of one-handed keyboard operation.

CHAPTER 8

Writing and drawing

Abstract

The use of keyboards has been discussed in terms of psychomotor skills in Chapter 6. In this chapter the skills involved in drawing and handwriting are considered. The issues raised will be considered in terms of current approaches to pen-based computing systems, and to computer-aided design.

8.1 Introduction

The rise of pen-based computer systems in recent years has been breath-taking in its speed; one can be forgiven for thinking that such systems had no sooner been "discovered" than they were marketed. However, the notion of pen-like interaction devices has a relatively long history, with several early graphics systems using some form of pen or stylus (see Chapter 3). Furthermore, from the discussion of pen-based computing in Chapter 4, it is clear that not all forms of the technology permit the user to either write or draw. For instance, on personal digital assistants (PDAs) user activity can be limited to using the pen as a stylus to "tap" menu-items and icons, and a common use of a "pen-like" device is for "wanding" bar-codes in warehouses and shops. Thus, there is a wide range of pens and related products in HCI. This means that to speak of pen-based computing, without defining the types of user activity which the technology supports, may lead to confusion.

For many people the idea of pen-based computing conjures up an image of a computer which allows one to jot down notes, sketch pictures and write commands simply with the aid of a pen. As the technology advances to a stage at which it can comfortably perform these functions, it would be beneficial to consider the type of activity which will be supported by pen-based computers in the near future. In order to do this, the psychomotor skills involved in handwriting and drawing are discussed in this chapter.

Finally, one of the areas where pen-based computing could make a significant impact is computer-aided design (CAD). A comparison is made between drafting by hand and by CAD at the end of the chapter, with particular reference to the role of sketching in design.

8.2   Using writing instruments

Kao (1979) considered the relationship between type of writing instrument, i.e., pencil, ballpoint pen, felt-tip pen or fountain pen, and performance on a series of writing tests, e.g., write the letter "a" ten times in succession. His findings are illustrated by Figure 8.1. Notice that there are differences in both performance time and mean writing pressure between the different pens. One can propose a number of reasons for these differences. However, the two which will be advanced here are that the writer needs to maintain sufficient pressure on the writing surface in order to leave a legible trace and that the characteristics of the trace will have an impact on writing speed.

Increasing the pressure needed to leave a trace on the paper could have a bearing on the way the pen is held and on the style of writing used. With reference to pen-based computing, simply using a stylus with no friction is likely to produce a different experience of writing to using a pen, e.g., the

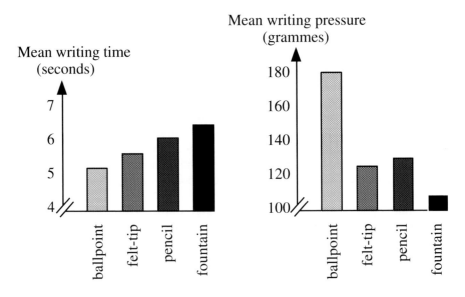

Figure 8.1   Mean writing time and pressure for a selection of writing instruments

degree of tactile and kinesthetic feedback will be greatly diminished. Furthermore, the presence of a trailing lead could have implications for postures which are "permitted" by the device which, in turn, could influence the usability of a particular device. In order to consider these points further it is necessary to consider how people manipulate writing instruments.

8.2.1 The activity of drawing

There are a number of factors which influence the ways in which people can comfortably use writing instruments, not least of which relate to the mechanics of the human hand. The first factor can be observed quite easily by the reader. Holding a pencil in your hand, place your little finger on a desk, so that the tip of the pencil rests on a piece of paper. Trace a loop without raising your wrist off the desk surface, so that the pencil is controlled by your fingers. Try to maintain as little control of the movement of the pencil as possible, i.e., do not try to draw a "perfect" loop. Once you have performed this exercise a couple of times, ask yourself the following questions: Did you trace clockwise or anticlockwise? Did you start the loop in the same position on each occasion? Is the loop larger in some places than others? Does the loop resemble an ellipse or a circle? The answers to these questions will depend upon a number of factors, such as whether you are left or right handed. However, there are sufficient consistencies between the ways in which people draw simple pictures to allow some predictions to be made. In an extensive study of drawing, van Sommers (1984) suggests that drawing and writing will be influenced by a small set of constraints. A number of these constraints have been illustrated in the exercise presented above.

The trajectory of the pencil is the result of an interaction between the movement of the hand about the wrist and the control movements of the fingers. The lateral movement of the hand is limited to around 30° either side of the wrist (with the forearm held steady). If one wishes to extend this range of movement, then it is necessary to move the rest of the arm around the elbow and around the shoulder. The movement of the hand will also be constrained by the orientation of the arm. These constraints define the "excursion envelope" of the hand. Movements up and down the page will be easier to perform than movements to the left or right. While these findings hold for writing on flat surfaces, such as a table, I am not sure what would happen when people write on near-vertical surfaces, such as black- or white-boards. Presumably, the excursion envelope would be further constrained, requiring additional activity around the elbow and shoulder. Furthermore, surfaces for pen-based computing could be held in a "clip-board" fashion, i.e., in the crook of the non-writing arm. Presumably, this posture has implications for the definition of the excursion envelope of the hand and, ultimately, for the degree of control the writer can influence over the formation of letters.

Van Sommers (1984) proposes that people approach drawing tasks in a similar fashion. For instance, stroke direction (for right handed people) tends to be about the axis 2 o'clock to 8 o'clock (for left handed people, the axis is 11 o'clock to 5 o'clock). Thus, the first prediction (pertaining to the exercise above) is that the loop you drew would be on a diagonal about one of these axes (depending on whether you are right or left handed). The excursion envelope about this axis will not be symmetrical, but will take the form of an ellipse (as a result of biomechanical constraints). Furthermore, there appears to be a preference for movements to travel from left to right and from the top to the bottom of the page (for right handed people). This suggests that, providing you were right handed, you would have drawn the ellipse about the 2 o'clock to 8 o'clock axis, starting at 11 o'clock and moved clockwise around the ellipse.

In addition to variation in drawing activity as a result of whether one is right or left handed, there also appears to be a difference in the ways in which people hold pens. The two most common forms can be described as palm up and palm down. The palm up posture allows freedom of most drawing and writing movements, but makes downward strokes more difficult, while the palm down posture supports downward strokes. Bearing in mind that people have a tendency to write down (rather than up) the page, one would anticipate that people who adopt the palm up posture would be more likely to manipulate and alter the position of the writing surface when they are writing or drawing. From this point of view, the "sketching" motions that people make prior to drawing might represent a means of checking the position, orientation and direction of movement of the subsequent strokes in terms of their writing or drawing posture.

8.2.2   The activity of handwriting

Handwriting is, for many people, a well-practiced skill. Interestingly, it is a skill which shows a high degree of motor equivalence (Bernstein, 1967). This means that, regardless of the muscle effectors used (i.e., dominant or non-dominant hand, foot, etc.), the writing patterns an individual produces will be qualitatively similar. This suggests that people aim to produce similar patterns in the writing that they produce, perhaps stemming from a notion of writing as an expression of an individual's personality. However, Wright (1993) has shown that despite the qualitative similarities, there are observable differences in the basic properties of the writing activity per-formed with different muscle effectors, e.g., differences in kinematics, stroke decomposition and stroke fluency. It is these differences which make the process of recognizing handwriting by computer so difficult. Furthermore, cursive handwriting seems to vary in response to a range of contextual factors, which result in variation in stroke size and duration (Thomassen and Schomaker, 1986). Teulings et al. (1983) suggest that even repetitions of the same pattern performed in constant conditions can vary slightly due to "motor noise" during writing. This notion could be seen as analogous to problems of speech production (see Chapter 10), in which muscle movement is continuous and passes through acceptable approximations of the desired state in order to produce the pattern. From this, one might anticipate that, as with typing, the production of writing will be controlled by a hierarchy of processes, from general goals to the control of specific actions.

Maintaining the analogy with typing, the reader will recall that touch typists probably work too quickly to be able to effectively use visual feedback. Visual feedback appears to play a role in monitoring handwriting, in that people often look at what they are writing. The removal of visual feedback can lead to disruption in writing performance, primarily in terms of increasing movement time and character size (van Galen et al., 1990; Smyth and Silvers, 1987). However, this effect appears to depend on the type of letter written, with frequently used letters being less susceptible to the problem than less frequently used letters (van Doorn and Keuss, 1993). This implies that some aspects of writing can be performed with minimal reliance on visual feedback, possibly due to the fact that the "motor program" associated with the production of letters is well learned and practiced. Furthermore, given the speed of handwriting, it is unlikely that visual feedback can be used in "real time", i.e., to correct errors as soon as they occur. Additionally, while tactile and kinesthetic feedback ought to play an important role in monitoring and executing writing performance (Teasdale et al., 1993), these take a period of time to process and will lead to corrections after several strokes have been made. This latter point has been demonstrated by studies which change the friction of the pen–paper contact (Denier van der Goon and Thuring, 1965).

As with drawing, there are clear differences between the manner in which people hold pens and the activities involved in writing. Levy and Reid (1976) suggested that the posture adopted during writing could reflect differences in hemispheric localization, with people who use the hand in an inverted position, i.e., palm down, using different parts of their brain to control the actions of writing. Moscovitch and Smith (1979) have countered this claim with the assertion that "palm down" writing requires a different form of visual processing of information, possibly due to the fact that their hand moves across the previously written text while for the palm up posture, the hand moves in front of the writing.

8.2.3 Conclusions

From this brief discussion, one can deduce a number of important points. The manner in which one holds and uses a pen will influence the way in which writing is performed, primarily by imposing certain constraints on movement. These constraints will also be influenced by the relationship between the pen and the writing surface, e.g., in terms of friction and pressure required to make a mark. While there is a degree of motor equivalence in writing, there are sufficient differences to lead one to suppose there are several levels of control in producing writing. The limited importance of visual, tactile and kinesthetic feedback during the actual production of writing suggests that, as with typing, people develop plans prior to the action. However, there are differences in the ways in which people process information as they are writing. The differences in writing posture and processing of visual information lead to differences in the ways in which people "prepare" surfaces prior to writing or drawing, e.g., by turning the paper at an angle before they begin to write, or by moving the paper around as they are drawing.

8.3 Planning and handwriting

Several researchers have found that simply varying the information that a person is required to write can have an impact on the rate at which words are written. For instance, Hulstijn and van Galen (1983) have shown that the mean velocity of strokes is higher in the first three letters of real words than for the same letters of non-words. Furthermore, the frequency of word use has an impact on writing performance and phonological factors also influence writing, e.g., the "ght" trigram has different timings associated with it when written in "daughter" and "laughter" (van Galen, 1990). These findings call to mind the differences found between words and non-words in typing, and suggest that writing involves several levels of control. One way in which to investigate this proposal is to look at the errors that people make when writing.

8.3.1 Errors in handwriting

As with many studies into skilled activity, research into the skill of handwriting has received a considerable input from study of breakdowns in performance, in this case slips of the pen. An interesting account of these slips is provided by Ellis (1979), and based on the analysis of his own handwriting errors over the period of a year. Examples of these errors are presented in Table 8.1. These errors are intended as illustrations and it is possible to extend the list to include such additional errors as "stroke omitted" and combinations of the other errors such as extra stroke and case change.

On the basis of the classification scheme applied to the different errors, Ellis proposed a four-stage model to account for the production of handwriting (Table 8.2). There are four stages through which writing is initiated (Ellis, 1979; 1982). In his model, Ellis (1979, 1982) distinguishes between the selection of an abstract representation of a letter (an allograph) and its physical execution (graph). Graphs can be defined in terms of temporal and dimensional parameters, and are assumed to be associated with appropriate activity of muscle groups for execution. This suggests that handwriting requires control at the level of generating the appropriate words and letters to write, and control at the level of manipulating particular muscle effectors in order to move the pen across the page.

8.3.2   Levels of control in handwriting

Van Galen (1990) investigated allographic programs. He proposed a distinction between retrieving a motor pattern, stored as ordered sequences of movements, and estimating parameters for the execution of movement. The motor patterns are hierarchically organized in terms of recency and frequency of use, e.g., Hulstijn and van Galen (1983) show that reaction times are faster for familiar letters than for novel shapes. On retrieval, the motor pattern will be defined by temporal and spatial parameters, calculated at execution, using general rules. This is defined in terms of a three-stage model of motor pattern retrieval–parameter setting–motor initiation (activating specific groups of muscles).

Teulings et al. (1983) presented subjects with a single handwritten letter on a screen, with a second letter presented either to the left or to the right,

Table 8.1   Classification of handwriting errors (from Ellis, 1979)

Intended	Written	Error type
too	two	lexical error
lapse from	lapse trom	letter substitution
looks	loooks	letter repetition
Cognitive	yognitive	letter substitution and case change
Wednesday	Wednesdauy	extra stroke

Table 8.2 Stages in handwriting production

Words	These are the entities selected at the first stage of a handwriting program.
Graphemes	These are the individual letters of the alphabet.
Allographs	These define such factors as the case of the written letter (upper or lower), and the appearance of the letters (straight or curved).
Graphs	These are the actual writing strokes used to produce a letter.

after a short time period. The subject was asked to copy the pair of letters as quickly as possible. It was found that, if the letters matched, the time to start writing was shorter than if they did not. This suggests some support for the notion of a grapheme selection process; if the letters are the same, the process can be accessed more quickly than if they are different.

While both these models seem to assume the graph as a base unit, it has been shown that, on writing a string of letters, there is an increase in time between the first letter and those subsequent to it (Hulstijn and van Galen, 1983). This suggests that it is only the first letter which is preprogrammed, and that subsequent letters are programmed during actual execution, i.e., in parallel with the writing. Finally, van Galen (1990) found a relationship between both word length and letter length (e.g. "l" vs. "b") and the latency between word presentation and commencement of writing. This suggests that preparation precedes execution, at least at more abstract levels, e.g., word or grapheme. Furthermore, in writing longer letters, the movement times of the preceding letters were also increased (up to two letters back). Finally, there is evidence to suggest that the shape of a letter is related to the shape of both preceding letters (Wing et al., 1983) and succeeding letters (Teulings et al., 1983). When people are asked to produce the same letter a number of times, writing speed is faster than when they are asked to alternate letters (Greer and Green, 1983), which suggests that repeating a letter requires the activation and maintenance of a single timing and force program. Taken together, the work of Ellis and van Galen and colleagues suggests that handwriting has a hierarchical level of control, which works from an abstract level to a motor control level in a temporal relation to the activity of writing; the execution of actions at different levels can affect performance at lower levels. Furthermore, recent work suggests that there are levels of control at the motor stage, with vertical stroke size being planned before stroke duration and peak force (Teulings et al., 1983; Wright, 1993).

8.4 Planning and drawing

While one might feel that drawing is less well-practiced as a skill than handwriting, it is interesting to reflect upon how often people use drawing in their day-to-day communications. Some professions, such as teaching, employ all manner of drawings as didactic aids; indeed, it is often useful to explain a concept (say, how the human ear works) by using the gradual construction of a diagram to structure the "narrative" of the lecture. Drawings can also be useful in organizing our thoughts, e.g., through the use of "mind maps", and for describing our environment, e.g., through the use of maps of our town or neighborhood and plans of our houses.

Children produce progressively more refined pictures as they grow older, moving from apparently random scribbles to more controlled movements to representations of objects and people (Kellogg, 1969). Given that drawing appears to follow the progression of skilled activity, and that most people can exercise this skill with sufficient ability to support communication, it would be useful to consider how drawing is performed and whether it would be possible to support the activity with pen-based computing.

8.4.1 Levels of control in drawing

Goodnow and Levine (1973) examined the drawing paths produced by children who had been asked to copy simple two-dimensional shapes, e.g., squares and triangles. They proposed a number of rules which governed the sequencing of strokes.

        Keep the pencil on the paper at all times.

    Start at the top, start at the leftmost point of the figure.

  IF the figure has an apex THEN start at top and descend down the
                    left oblique.

      IF lines horizontal THEN draw from left to right.

      IF lines vertical THEN draw from top to bottom.

These studies suggest that people tend to use a definable subset of possible actions when drawing. As mentioned in Section 8.2.1, biomechanical constraints, relating pencil and hand positions, require satisfying. Lacquaniti et al. (1983) have demonstrated that people draw equal angles in equal times, i.e., if a person is asked to draw a figure "8", the angle of pen movement plotted against time follows a sinusoid of equal frequency and amplitude for both circles of the figure. Furthermore, when drawing tight curves the angular velocity of the pencil decreases. These factors suggest some degree of control during the execution of drawing activity. Wann et al. (1988) propose that a goal of people engaged in drawing is to draw smoothly, i.e., to minimize jerky movements.

8.4.2 Higher-order control

Taken together, these studies suggest some similarity between drawing and writing, at least in terms of plausible models of cognitive control. Drawing can be described in terms of rules governing both figure production and pencil movement. However, we have not yet shown whether there is a higher-order level of control which could correspond to the "word" unit of writing. Van Sommers (1984) asked people to copy a simple figure (Figure 8.2) to which he assigned one of two verbal labels: either a cocktail glass or a man holding a telescope. He found that there were noticeable differences in stroke patterns for the two labels.

For the "cocktail glass" label, the subjects tended to draw the glass first and then the cherry, but for the "man holding a telescope" label, subjects tended to draw the head first, i.e., the object in the centre of the drawing was drawn either first or last depending on the label assigned to the overall figure. This suggests that, for copy drawing at least, semantic factors determine representational goals, which then determine the order in which parts of the figure are drawn, which then influence choice of rule for moving the pencil. In other words, both drawing and writing appear to follow a similar pattern of cognitive-motor control.

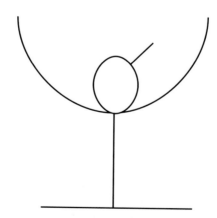

Figure 8.2   Picture used by van Sommers (1984)

8.5 Writing with pen-based computer systems

One of the major classes of application which could benefit from the application of pen-based computing can be termed note-taking. For instance, a secretary in a large organization takes a telephone message by jotting down a few key points on a notepad and then types these details onto an email system to the addressee of the message (Rhyne and Wolf, 1992). Using a pen-based interface could allow the secretary to jot down the information using a pen and to have the information transcribed and ready to place in a field for transmission over email. Alternatively, in Chapter 11, a number of "hostile" environments are discussed, e.g., forestry work and civil engineering surveys. Like speech, pen-based computing offers the opportunity to both liberate users from the desktop and capitalize on well-learned skills. Also, like speech, the process by which the computer recognizes handwriting is sufficiently different from that of humans to lead to problems in using the system.

People tend to perceive handwriting on the basis of the finished product, i.e., on the characteristics of the shapes of the letters and the shapes of their combinations into words (Garnham, 1985). Of course, it is possible to use this information as the basis for template or pattern-matching algorithms in handwriting recognition. However, due to the lack of a knowledge of the linguistic context in which the letters occur, handwriting recognizers also include some stochastic models of the production of the letters, i.e., on the characteristics of stroke direction and velocity. While this can, in principle, improve recognition accuracy, it raises a difficult problem for users. If a mistake has been made, simply over-writing the letter will serve to confuse rather than help the recognizer (Wolf, 1990). Users' assumptions that the recognition of letters will be based on the finished product leads them to believe that correction and over-writing will not influence performance, but the algorithm for stroke tracking can "see" the new strokes as extra characteristics of the letters rather than the replacements they are intended to be.

In an effort to keep the recognition problems within tractable limits, some handwriting recognition systems require users to enter letters discretely (the fashion for providing "grids" in which to write is, fortunately, going out of favor, although it is by no means obsolete). Thus, rather than allowing cursive script, these devices require users to print letters individually. The degree of spacing required depends on the recognition algorithms (in much the same way as the distinction between isolated, connected and continuous word recognition in speech recognition systems, see Chapter 4).

From this, it would seem that, far from being natural extensions of an everyday skill, handwriting recognition systems impose certain constraints on users. One could suggest that these constraints will be sufficient to slow down the process of handwriting and will require the user to focus on the formation of letters and words, rather than on the construction of the message. From this, one would not expect current pen-based computing systems to support detailed note making, say in the preparation of notes for a lecture, book or technical report. Further, given the range of applications on the market, pen-based computing seems most appropriate for use with short, highly constrained forms of information (Oviatt et al., 1994; Frankish et al., 1995).

8.6 Drawing with pen-based computer systems

While there is a growing body of literature on how people can use pen-based computing systems for tasks using handwriting, there is less interest in the use of drawing in such applications (with the exception of sketch recognition in CAD, see below). Van Sommers (1984) has proposed that one can consider everyday drawing to fall into a number of classes, which he terms "graphics acts" (after the notion of speech acts, discussed in Chapter 10). From surveys of a range of different people, van Sommers (1984) concludes that the main functions of drawing are for drawing maps and plans, e.g., in order to describe routes for people or in order to plan domestic tasks such as laying carpets. Certainly the idea of using sketches in planning has been considered in a number of the "whiteboarding" applications, i.e., shared workspace on which people can write or draw.

Not all everyday drawing is for public use; a number of us use drawings to organize material for lectures or reports. In this case, drawings become tools for organizing and arranging ideas and thoughts into more structured formats. For instance, I often lay out each paper or lecture that I am working on in the form of a "spider diagram", in which a central point has links growing out of it to exterior parts, and with links between these exterior parts. Applying this activity onto a pen-based computing system would allow me to draw and edit the initial plan before I began writing. Furthermore, the approach could be particularly useful for project management techniques, such as critical path analysis. Of course, software exists which allows users to build and modify flowcharts, e.g., for developing software or for performing task analysis or for project planning. However, often this software takes text input and converts it into diagrams. The proposal here, in effect, takes a diagram and turns it into text.

8.7 Computer-aided design

Given the discussion of drawing skills above, one can consider the human factors of computer-aided design (CAD) systems. The first issue that becomes apparent is that CAD, in its current guise, appears to be less about drawing than about manipulating objects. Indeed, much of the work on the design of CAD systems is focused on how best to support designers working with three-dimensional representations on the two-dimensional surface of the computer screen (Sandford et al., 1987; Barfield et al., 1988; Osborn and Agogino, 1992). While this research will allow designers to exploit the potential of CAD systems to allow detailed visualization of designs, it relies on the designs being created in the first place (often from the construction of standard orthographic projections). It is at the point of creating the designs and entering these designs that one can consider the role of interaction devices.

Manual design involves roughly equal time spent on creative design work, physically drawing and updating the designs, and other activities. The benefits of CAD are that, in the first place, it allows storage and manipulation of drawings (Davie et al., 1991), and, in the second place, it can reduce the requirements for creative design work (see Chapter 13). Drawing with CAD can take significantly longer than on conventional drawing boards (Beitz et al., 1990), often because more discrete actions are required on CAD (Müller, 1992). Consider the task of drawing a circle, using a pencil and a compass. Compare this activity with the activity illustrated in Figure 8.3.

The CIRCLE menu has been selected, and the user has selected the option for a circle to pass through a center point and has a specified radius. The other options allow the user to specify whether the circle should pass through two of the points, or whether it should be tangential (TTR). The "Command" line below the drawing indicates the command selected (in angled brackets) and requires the user to specify the co-ordinates of the center of the circle. The "Diameter" line indicates that the user must specify a radius.

There are a number of points to note from this simple illustration. First, while manual design involves the use of a number of tools, each with limited functions, e.g., compass, set-squares, rulers, etc., CAD involves the use of a single tool with a range of functions, i.e., the software package (Frieling et al., 1987). One might object, given the discussion concerning interaction devices as tools in Chapter 1, that the interaction device the CAD operator uses can also have several functions. However, in many applications, the role of the interaction device is simply to select objects. Second, there are clear differences between the type of "device knowledge" required by designers for manual design and CAD operation (Dillon and Sweeney, 1988). The traditional tools of manual design have evolved to suit

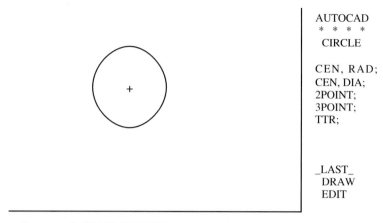

```
                                                          AUTOCAD
                                                          *  *  *  *
                                                          CIRCLE

                                                          CEN, RAD;
                                                          CEN, DIA;
                                                          2POINT;
                                                          3POINT;
                                                          TTR;


                                                          _LAST_
                                                          DRAW
                                                          EDIT
```

Command: CIRCLE 3P / 2P / TTR / <Center point> : [side-menu] 150, 100
Diameter: <Radius> 50

Figure 8.3 Drawing a circle in AUTOCAD (from Davies et al., 1991)

specific functions; and designers have developed a range of skills to allow them to represent all manner of objects. On the other hand, the CAD operator needs to learn and remember the appropriate commands for the package being used. This requires a knowledge, not of the outcome and results of using tools, but of the process required to effect specific outcomes, as the following quotation illustrates:

> On a drawing board, you're thinking construction all the time. The pen just flows, you move your hand around. You've got one train of thought, how you construct, how you design. With CAD you've got to think of construction, of how to do it using the software and the best way to do it, because there is always six ways of doing it, you haven't got that option on a board. You just draw it. There's more thought processes going on with CAD.
>
> [from McLoughlin and Clark, 1988]

Third, as Dillon and Sweeney (1988) suggest, the traditional approach allows the designer more opportunity for direct manipulation of objects than on CAD. For instance, consider the task of drawing a circle. The manual version of the task embodies the well-learned pairing of physical movement with visual representation. The CAD version, on the other hand, separates representation from execution.

Cognitive psychologists draw a distinction between declarative and procedural knowledge, i.e., between knowing facts about something and knowing how to do something. In Chapter 1, it was proposed that tools mediate human performance; mediation can be considered as an extension of procedural knowledge. Thus, when considering design, one can begin to see differences in procedural knowledge required for manual and CAD approaches. While manual drawing relies on an intimate relationship between visual representation, physical movement and knowledge of the tools to be used, CAD relies on visual representation and knowledge of the procedures required to present this representation. At an extreme, it is possible to argue that the representations should be standard and CAD work be performed like any other office job (see Chapter 13).

As noted above, designers often spend an appreciable period of time in creating and testing new ideas. Often this process of creation and testing is seen as a transitory stage in the production of the final design; initial drawings and sketches are drawn on scrap paper and scribbled over and modified. What is apparent is that sketching represents work in progress, the immediate capture of initial ideas in a format which the designer can develop and change. Given the increasing pressures in the design world to minimize the time spent designing (in order to reduce lead times and maintain market share), there has been pressure to short circuit this process. In Chapter 13, the use of standard designs and solutions is discussed as a means of deskilling the work of draftspeople. In this section, technology for supporting and enhancing existing skills is considered.

At present, existing CAD software is difficult to use for sketching (Foley et al., 1990). One of the reasons for this difficulty is the fact that the CAD software acts as a barrier between the immediacy of the designers' ideas and the requirements of the software language. Furthermore, the interaction devices used on contemporary CAD systems often bear little resemblance to the pencil and paper used for sketching. Consequently efforts have been directed towards the production of pen-based systems which can handle sketches (Endo et al., 1993; Stolpmann and Roller, 1993; Zhao, 1992; Zhong et al., 1990). While the applications differ in the manner in which they handle and interpret sketches, they share common goals. Using pens, rather than other interaction devices, can allow designers to sketch as they would on paper. However, the pen-based systems allow sketches to be "beautified" on-line, so that they can be produced with sufficient clarity and esthetic quality to be used in design meetings. Further, the sketches can be converted into CAD files and stored on a database for distribution and consultation by other members of the design team.

Thus, it is now possible to use sketching as a means of creating graphics on a computer. While this has a number of benefits (not least of which being the linking of sketching as a design process with CAD as design production), it does seem to require further modification in order to combine what has traditionally been an activity involving non-design-related work and competing ideas, e.g., in the form of doodles, scribbles and other "graphical junk", with an activity aimed at producing finished drawings. I wonder whether the sketching recognizers would handle this graphical junk, and whether such activity may play a more important role in the initial stages of creating designs than we realize; for instance, design involves not simply the definition of shape, but also selection of materials and consideration of the relationshp between production, manufacture, use and appearance of the finished product. The graphical junk around the sketch will probably contain observations pertaining to these factors, as well as modifications to the view and structure of the design. As should be clear from these last comments, not all of the information used by designers will be best presented using graphics. This raises the thorny problems of how to combine sketching with the entry of other information. I have termed applications which support such activity "multimodal" interfaces (see Chapter 14).

If one can envisage sketching tools (and indeed, some have already appeared on the market), then one can also envisage larger-scale drafting aids, such as an active drafting table (again such a device is on the market). This comprises a drawing board with conventional drawing tools. However, rather than drawing paper, the user draws onto a large tablet. The marks made on the tablet can be translated by the host computer, and modifications can be made via CAD software or via the board. This would allow conventional drafting skills to be supplemented by the capabilities of the computer. Drawings could be stored and called onto the "table", modified using a pen and other tools and saved. This would provide an opportunity for direct manipulation of the design which is difficult to achieve using conventional CAD.

Finally, one might feel that a major problem with CAD is that it uses two-dimensional technology to create three-dimensional deigns. While there have been exciting developments in technology which allow designers to represent their designs in 3D (either on a computer screen or as physical objects using stereolithography) there seems little to allow the designers then to work directly on these 3D models. However, recall the discussion of haptic interfaces in Chapter 4; it might be possible to allow direct manipulation of 3D objects to either create or modify designs. This could allow the process of prototyping and model-building to link directly with design and CAD; in other words, the interaction would be primarily with the object being designed rather than a computer.

8.8 Conclusions

The scientific study of how people produce drawings and handwriting has advanced rapidly in recent years. It is clear that both activities represent a skill (in much the same way that typing and speaking are skills), and a great deal of research has been undertaken to determine how these skills are learned and practiced. With reference to pen-based computing, a number of issues have been raised, not least of which concerns the problems of transferring a skill from one audience (i.e., people) to another audience (i.e., computers). The manner in which computers deal with information is sufficiently different to human information processing to lead to users having difficulty in performing the computer-based tasks. These difficulties could ultimately limit the usefulness of handwriting recognition systems.

Considering the manner in which people use drawings leads to a number of proposals for research and development of new technology. Sketching has been shown to be a valuable part of the design process and a number of research groups have been considering ways in which sketching could be supported using pen-based computing systems. Many of the systems have achieved an impressive level of performance, albeit in limited domains, and products are being launched on the market which build on some of these successes. On the other hand, people use drawings in their everyday life. Applications of pen-based computing to support drawing maps and plans and organizing ideas for reports etc. were discussed.

8.9 Key points for practitioners

- Consider how to inform users about how pen-based systems function in order to reduce misconceptions and misunderstanding.
- Consider extending the possible range of applications and looking to introduce pen-based computing into new domains such as maintenance work.

8.10 Key points for researchers

- Consider the appropriate friction between pen and writing surface: should we aim for no friction or is a limited amount of friction necessary?
- Extend technology to support sketching and drafting.
- Consider the uses of drawing in everyday life and work, and consider techniques to support this activity.

CHAPTER 9

Pointing

Abstract

The limitations of current approaches to modeling use of interaction devices have been considered in Chapter 6, where it was suggested that a more fruitful line of exploration arises from considering the psychomotor skills involved in the performance of a range of tasks at the interface. This suggestion led to discussion of the skills of typing, writing and drawing in Chapters 7 and 8. In this chapter, the psychomotor skills of using pointing devices are considered.

9.1 Introduction

In this chapter consideration is given to one of the dominant types of interaction technique in contemporary HCI: the selection of objects on a screen, which is often known as "pointing". This might at first glance appear to be a trivial matter, but it is a topic which has increasing relevance for systems growing ever more reliant on the use of icons, menus and other objects to which users point on computer screens. In Chapters 7 and 8, the study of typing and writing was shown to be beneficial for an understanding of how people interact with computers and the sort of problems produced by these forms of HCI.

When considering pointing, it is worth noting that there does appear to be a minority of users who, despite the claims that such devices are easy to learn (Milner, 1988), find difficulty in both learning and using mice (Taylor and Hinson, 1988). It would be useful to have some idea of why such problems occur, and also to ask why some devices appear to produce better performance than others.

9.2 Direct manipulation

Before tackling the question of usability of pointing devices, it is necessary to consider the reasons why pointing has become so central to modern computer systems, in the guise of direct manipulation. With the development of the windows, icons, menus, pointing device (WIMP) interface, has come a shift from command-based to object-based software, i.e., rather than typing commands to open a file, the user is now in a position to select an icon which represents that file. Thus, rather than having to decompose the command into its constituent parts (recall name of file, recall appropriate command, recall appropriate command formulation and syntax, type command using correct syntax), the user can move a cursor onto an object and then has to "click" a button. Pointing has now become a staple part of many interfaces and of an increasing amount of software; so much so that we speak of interfaces allowing users to directly manipulate objects on the screen (following Shneiderman's coining of the term "direct manipulation" in 1982). Direct manipulation has been a significant development for both HCI theory and HCI design practice (Frohlich, 1993).

"Direct manipulation" is one of the many terms in HCI literature which manage to be both self-explanatory and ambiguous. The term "direct manipulation" is self-explanatory because it indicates that users no longer have to type command expressions, but can issue commands by manipulating objects on the screen. This requires a number of additional factors to hold: the representation of the file should be displayed continuously, i.e., rather than remembering the name of a file, I should be able to look at the screen and recognize the icon for that file (usually with a file name attached to it); the syntax of a command language is replaced by physical actions of pointing and clicking; the consequences of user actions are made immediately apparent and consequently, it will be easy to "undo" the action.

Consider the screen shown in Figure 9.1. The user can move the cursor, shown as an arrow in the center-right of the window, onto an icon, e.g., the "System" folder, changing its state from non-highlighted to highlighted; pressing and holding a button will allow the user to move that object from one place to another, perhaps even to move it into a new folder or onto a disk; pressing the button twice in quick succession will cause the file to open. We do not currently possess a means of combining several state-changes into a single action, e.g., it is not possible to use a single action to move a spreadsheet file from the drive to hard disk, causing it to open (from the hard disk) in a specific part of the screen.

Users seldom see pointing as anything other than a means to the end of effecting changes in the states of objects. An exception to this comes under

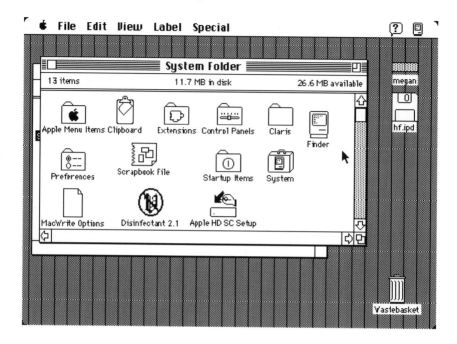

Figure 9.1 Objects on a computer screen

the more advanced forms of graphical manipulation such as drawing (see Chapter 8). For many experienced users of WIMP interfaces, the task of "pointing" is sufficiently burdensome for them to seek fast-key commands on the keyboard; ironically, in this case the use of commands would appear to be more direct than pointing. As Whiteside et al. (1985) note, the effective use of an interface is as much to do with the relationship between interface design and user goals, as it is with the style of interaction employed.

The term "direct manipulation" is ambiguous because it is not always direct, in that the user normally needs to use an additional device to move the cursor to select the object, and it does not involve manipulation in any real sense of the word (with the exception of some of the current virtual reality applications): direct manipulation typically allows the user to toggle between the current state of an object and another state. Furthermore, while it is clear that direct manipulation has superseded command languages, it is not clear that it has completely done away with the problems of syntax or recall. Indeed, one could suggest that the syntax of direct manipulation is as obtuse as that of command languages, the only difference being that direct manipulation employs far fewer elements in its language. By way of illustration, novice users of a Macintosh often encounter problems when opening files because the "double-click" command (used primarily to extend the functionality of a single button mouse), can be difficult to pace; until they have spent a period of time mastering the pace of press, they continue to select, rather than open, the file. As far as problems of recall are concerned, users do not have the problem of remembering obscure combinations of the letters which make up commands when using icons and menus, unless the icons are given obscure labels. However, there is still a potential memory problem associated with the use of icons; if the icons are difficult to associate with specific commands or functions, then users will find them difficult to use.

9.3 Pointing

Before we consider pointing in human–computer interaction, we will first discuss the act of pointing in general, to see what characteristics it exhibits and how these characteristics could be applied to computer operation.

Let us begin with a "common-sense" model of pointing. Pointing to an object requires a person to have identified the object and then perform some physical act in order to draw the attention of another person to that object. At a gross level, the ensuing physical action could be a matter of directing the index finger towards the object. However, the precision with which the finger is directed will differ according to the aims of the speaker. For example, if I point towards the computer on which I am currently typing, and say "have you seen this?" I could be referring to the computer (an old Macintosh Classic), or perhaps, to the package (MacWrite), or to a specific feature of the screen, or to a specific part of the text, or to some other object related to the computer. Already, pointing seems to combine a number of functions: indication, identification and selection.

Anchoring my speech to a specific object is an example partly of using a word to point to a thing, i.e., "this", and partly an example of physical gesture. The use of words to point to something is known as deixis (Bühler, 1934), and in the above example, the combination of physically pointing and the word "this" represents a type of place deixis (Levelt, 1989). A speaker indicates a specific object by making reference to its place. The physical act of pointing can be considered to have several levels of accuracy, depending on whether it is the object itself or a specific part of the object to which reference is being made.

Precisely how the listener can accurately respond to this action will relate to the ongoing conversation and the salience of the reference. Nunberg (1979) argues that identifying requires both speaker and interlocutor to recognize the relationship between what object is being pointed at and what aspect of the object is being indicated. Returning to the example above, the object is a Macintosh Classic computer on which, for the sake of argument, I am indicating the somewhat archaic word processing package MacWrite 5. In order for this to make sense, therefore, I must already be engaged in a conversation in which "word processing packages" constitutes a meaningful topic. At this stage pointing can only be effective if it is performed in a definable context with a second party to whom the reference is meaningful (it is difficult to imagine pointing as a solitary activity).

The question still remains as to why a speaker would choose to say "look at that" and then perform a physical action, rather than say "look at that icon". Surely the latter would be far less demanding both cognitively and physically? In terms of planning and coordinating the physical act of pointing, there would appear to be several points at issue. The speaker would need to decide whether a physical reference is required, or whether the desired effect can be achieved linguistically. One could argue that pointing would be appropriate for either introducing a new topic into a conversation, e.g., "look at that" – pointing to an icon, or for reducing any ambiguity in a reference, e.g., "look at that icon". In terms of computing, pointing is the term given to specifying objects on a computer screen. The context in which "pointing" occurs can be defined as selection of a specific object presented with a range of other objects, i.e., pointing would require the selection of an icon from a screen containing several items (the fact that I have introduced the word "selection" indicates that the term "pointing" in HCI has a narrower meaning than in everyday parlance). By "pointing" in HCI, we do not tend to mean making linguistic reference to an object, but "selecting" or "choosing" from a group of alternative objects. The concept becomes muddled when we consider the function of these pointing actions. In Figure 9.1, if I use the cursor to point to the "System" folder, then I am indicating an object (which requires an additional physical action of pressing a button). If I use the cursor to point to the "File" menu heading, I am indicating an intention, i.e., the intention to issue a command contained under this heading. If I point to the "System" folder and press the button twice, I am issuing a command.

Hayes (1988) suggests three issues of deixis in natural language interfaces. It is necessary to determine *when* pointing relates to language input to the computer, and when it is intended to serve another function, e.g., when talking to another person. Most computer systems achieve this by using a very simple protocol for pointing, i.e., moving a cursor. It is necessary to minimize the ambiguity of pointing. In terms of HCI, "pointing" could present a number of problems, principally how can a computer understand the linguistic context in which pointing occurs? Most computer systems require pointing to be explicitly directed at a single object, and for some form of confirmation action to be performed. For a natural language interface, it is necessary to have a representation of the object in a language string, e.g., referring to the object as "that" or "it". In Chapter 14, recent developments in multimodal HCI are considered, particularly systems which allow the combination of physical gestures with spoken commands. Thus, we can say that, by and large, "pointing" in HCI tends to lack much of the subtlety of deixis.[9.1]

The gist of this section is that, although we consider the use of pointing in HCI to be visual and to allow ease of interaction between user and computer, pointing is a linguistic concept. As is often the case, as we extend the metaphor, we introduce ambiguity. As we move from pointing as identifying an object, to indicating an intention to entering a command, we are moving to situations in which user behavior is, again, constrained partly by syntax and by the vagaries of "commands" which the software deems acceptable, and partly, by the users' knowledge.

9.4   Users' knowledge

Direct manipulation is often considered as a useful means for reducing the amount of knowledge required of users in order to use a computer; the notion of pointing and clicking at "self-explanatory" icons and labels is fundamental to much of the recent development in interface design. However, direct manipulation places some demands on users in terms of what they need to know.

There is still a load on the user in terms of hunting for and finding the appropriate object. For instance, I regularly "save" the material that I type. When I am typing (on an Apple Macintosh), I tend to perceive "saving" as an editing function, i.e., overwrite current temporary storage with new material. Many times, when using menu commands to perform this "save" function, I look under the "Edit" menu, and am unable to find the command. Of course, "save" refers to the manipulation of files, and is kept under the "file" menu. In order to minimize this problem, I tend to use

---

[9.1] Bolt (1984) posits that pointing can also be considered in terms of distance between hand and object. He suggests that there will be a "cone of indication" (p.41), through which pointing becomes increasingly precise, e.g., taking our example of pointing at a Macintosh screen and saying, "have you seen this?", one could reduce the ambiguity of this phrase by touching an object on the screen, such as the cursor or an icon. In terms of HCI, we have devices which allow us to touch objects (touchscreens, touchpanels, touch tablets), and devices which allow us to move cursors towards objects. In recent years, we have seen a growth in the range of devices which allow movement in 3D, e.g., datagloves. One could propose a novel interface design which matches proximity of pointing with precision, such that touching an object on the screen will select it, pointing at a distance of between 2 and 10 cm could select objects within an area of the screen, say a window, pointing at a distance of between 15 and 30 cm could select the whole screen (e.g., to call the next screen on a database).

the < -s> command on the keyboard. While this appears to be a trivial problem, it illustrates an important point pertaining to the use of knowledge in interacting with a computer.

If we consider the selection of the wrong menu heading as an error, and then ask what caused the error, we can propose a number of candidate causes. However, the cause which strikes me as most obvious is the wrong *definition of* the action, which led to the choice of the wrong menu heading, i.e., defining "save" in terms of editing rather than in terms of file handling. This would imply that simply learning and remembering all the possible menu items in this particular package would not have eliminated this error. Draper (1984), in a study into the nature of expertise in skilled users of the UNIX operating system, found that even experts can rarely recall more than a small proportion of the total sum of commands which can be used in a particular software environment. When presented with a simple paper-based recall test, the experts fared very poorly, but when sitting in front of their computer carrying out work involving the commands that they had previously been unable to "recall", they were able to use the commands with few problems. What characterized their expertise was not so much their memory for commands as their ability to find appropriate information quickly and efficiently.

A study by Mayes et al. (1988) demonstrated that this phenomenon is also apparent in a WIMP environment. Experienced users of a Macintosh were poor at accurately recalling the information which appeared on the screen, even though they had little difficulty in actually finding and using this information for tasks performed on the computer. Mayes et al. (1988) suggest that, "Much of the 'knowledge' that underwrites [the] performance [of computer users] seems to be left in the world, which is thus used as a kind of extended memory." This implies a strategy by which memory demands can be minimized, and in which information is retained in the context in which it is useful. After all, there would seem little point in laboriously learning and remembering the information displayed on a computer screen if you knew that it would be displayed when you next used the computer.

These findings reflect similar outcomes in research into expert behavior. Recent research into the field of highly skilled performance has led to the suggestion that "experts" have some form of "skilled memory" (Ericsson and Polson, 1988). This theory implies that skilled individuals may be able to circumvent the problems of limited short-term memory by using a highly structured long-term memory which can be accessed rapidly, and that they can compensate attentional limitations by employing very efficient information encoding techniques. Thus, the nature of their expertise lies not so much in knowing a given item of information as in knowing how to find that piece of information. This would also lend support to the proposal that,

Rather than being based on "knowledge" consisting of mental models that replicate substantial aspects of the external world and support detailed advanced planning, human action may be organised around a flow of information picked up from the environment during execution.

[Mayes et al., 1988, p. 288]

This proposal bears a strong similarity to the model of tool use presented in Chapter 1. If human behavior is heavily influenced by the environment in which we act, then there will be characteristics of the environment which can be considered more conducive to fast, accurate performance than others. In Chapter 1, it was noted that the control of action could be considered in terms of a hierarchy of feedback mechanisms between different levels, that tools mediate human action in an environment, and that, in particular, the work environment can influence action. In Chapters 7 and 8, models of skilled behavior have been considered in these terms. Let us now turn our attention to the apparently simple sequence of actions involved in pointing to an object on a computer screen.

9.5 Pointing as a psychomotor skill

In Chapter 1, it was proposed that one of the principal determinants in the development of the mouse was the need to move a cursor around the computer screen in order to point to objects. However, is it necessary to use an intermediary object, i.e., a cursor, for selecting an object? It is possible to select objects directly, using a lightpen or a touchscreen, alternatively objects can be selected by typing, writing or speaking their name (see Chapter 5). Further, in the majority of empirical comparisons, object selection is performed more quickly using touch screens and light pens than mice or trackballs, although not always as accurately (see Chapter 3). Cursor positioning and moving can provide useful additional operations, such as leaving a trace of the cursor's path (which could be used for constructing pictures), or for moving objects by dragging. One could suggest, therefore, that pointing devices have been developed as multifunctional devices, capable of performing a range of actions based on cursor manipulation (where objects, once selected, could also function as cursors and be dragged across the screen). What behaviors are required to be performed by users in order to use pointing devices, and how can one model such behavior in order to gain a better understanding of the nature of HCI?

9.5.1 Fitts' law

Since the publication of Card et al.'s (1978) comparative study of interaction devices, there has been a significant level of interest, shown by the HCI community, in a "law" first expressed by Paul Fitts (Fitts, 1954).

Basically, Fitts' law describes the relationship between distance moved and target width in terms of movement time; it predicts that movement time will increase logarithmically with an increase in the distance:target width ratio. The assumption underlying this law was that highly skilled, i.e., well-practiced, fast and accurate, performance would be limited by the capacity of the human motor system to process information. Borrowing from information theory (Shannon and Weaver, 1949), Fitts (1954) proposed that the information used in controlling the movement of limbs would need to be communicated through a channel (drawing an analogy with an electronic system), and that this channel would have a limited bandwidth. As task difficulty increased, so the amount of information which needs to be processed will reach, and exceed, the bandwidth of the channel. Fitts sought to define the capacity of this channel, in terms of the information units, bits.

The most commonly referenced expression of Fitts' law is given in equation (9.1) (Fitts and Peterson, 1964).

$$MT = a + b \log_2 (2A/W) \qquad\qquad (9.1)$$

where

MT = movement time
a = a constant
b = a constant
A = amplitude of movement, i.e., distance from start point to target
W = target width.

In this formulation, the ratio of distance to the target to target width, i.e., $2A/W$, is defined as the index of difficulty (ID) of a particular task. This represents the notion that tasks involving movement to small objects and/or over large distances will be more difficult, i.e., take longer, than tasks involving optimal targets and distances.

In equation (9.1), a and b are presented as "constants". However, it is rare to find agreement between researchers as to the appropriate values for these figures (see, for example, Table 9.1). As these figures are the regression coefficients of intercept (a) and slope (b) of a line, they can be derived from data collected during experiments. This suggests that the "law" should be considered descriptive rather than predictive.

Glencross and Barrett (1989) demonstrate how Fitts' law can be generalized to cover performance of simple movement tasks by humans of all ages using any limb "possessing the necessary degrees of freedom" and by other species, such as monkeys. Thus, Fitts' law seems to capture an essential component of physical movement and would seem ideal for the study of manual actions at the computer interface. However, the status of the "law" has been the subject of controversy almost since its inception. We have already noted that *a* and *b* will vary across studies. This implies that, rather than being an unequivocal description of human performance, the principal function of Fitts' law is as a "data-fitter". Welford (1968), following this assumption, decided to reformulate the law (see equation (9.2)), in order to fit his data.

$$MT = b \log_2 (A/W + 0.5) \qquad (9.2)$$

where

MT = movement time
b = a constant
A = amplitude of movement, i.e., distance from start point to target
W = target width.

As a rule of thumb, one can use equation (9.2) in preference to equation (9.1) when *A/W* is less than 2 (Welford, 1968).

Crossman and Goodeve (1963) report that they were unable to find the derivation of the law from the original source material (Shannon and Weaver's, 1949, information theory). More recently, Mackenzie (1989), following the original information theory equations, derived a version of Fitts' law shown as equation (9.3).

$$MT = a + b \log_2 (A/W + 1) \qquad (9.3)$$

where

MT = movement time
a = a constant
b = a constant
A = amplitude of movement, i.e., distance from start point to target
W = target width.

9.5.2 Fitts' law as a model of movement

In order for Fitts' law to be viable as an explanation of human movement (as opposed to either an information theory model or a data-fitter), it must embody a theory of how the movements involved in the simple task of moving between two points are performed. Initial researchers proposed that movement consists of a series of sub-movements towards a target, each sub-movement bringing the movement closer to the target and each subsequent movement calculated to adjust the difference between current position and target position (Crossman and Goodeve, 1963; Keele, 1968). These proposals require us to make the following assumptions (Walker et al., 1993):

1. Positioning movements can be decomposed into one or more discrete sub-movements (termed "micro-corrections" by Card et al., 1978).
2. Each sub-movement travels a constant proportion of the remaining distance to the target.
3. Each sub-movement has a constant duration.
4. Sensory feedback (visual or kinesthetic) is used to guide sub-movements.
5. Sub-movement sequences terminate as soon as the positioning movement reaches the target.

One could argue that activity will be determined by the time it takes to plan the movement (Keele, 1968), or it could be influenced by additional factors beyond this intitial model of movement, e.g., noise in the channel, such as hand tremor or other antagonistic muscle activity (Meyer et al., 1982), characteristics of the instrument to be moved, such as the weight of the stylus (Fitts and Peterson, 1964), characteristics of the person performing the task, such as amount of practice and experience.

9.5.3   The application of Fitts' law to HCI

Having noted the derivation and some of the problems associated with Fitts' law, we will now consider some of the studies in which it has been used in the study of interaction devices. Table 9.1 gives values for a and b, and the index of performance, IP, for a selection of interaction devices drawn from a number of studies. (The index of performance is derived by dividing the tasks index of difficulty, ID, by the total movement time, MT.) It should be possible to derive figures for IP to allow interaction devices to be ranked; those exhibiting the highest IP ought to yield superior performance to devices with lower IPs.

Table 9.1 presents several different types of device discussed in Chapter 3. For instance, under the joystick heading, there are isometric, and displacement types, and under the touchpad, there are figures for absolute and relative position sensing. Further, the $C:D$ ratio is presented in terms of gain, either high (HG) or low (LG).

Clearly, and somewhat disconcertingly, there is a lack of agreement across studies as to appropriate values of IP; in some cases, it is difficult to even perceive a "ball-park" figure, e.g., compare the IPs presented for mice. One could help save face by examining relative differences, e.g., for both Card et al. (1978) and Epps (1986), the mouse has a higher IP than the isometric joystick and, as MacKenzie (1992) points out, the ratio between devices is similar across the studies: $10.4/4.5 = 2.3$ for Card et al. (1978), and $2.6/1.2 = 2.2$ for Epps (1986). Does this hold for other device comparisons? Consider the comparison of mice with trackballs. From the Epps (1986) data, the ratio of IP for trackball and mouse is $2.9/2.6 = 1.12$, and from the

Table 9.1 Summary data from studies using Fitts' law

Device	IP	a	b	%error	source
Hand					
	10.6	12.8	94.7	1.8	Fitts (1954)
Joysticks					
isometric	4.5	990	220	12	Card et al. (1978)
isometric (HG)	2.2	−846	449	25	Kantowitz & Elvers (1988)
isometric (LG)	2.2	−880	449	25	Kantowitz & Elvers (1988)
isometric	1.2	−587	861	0	Epps (1986)
isometric	5.0	−303	199	0	Jagacinski et al. (1980)
displacement	1.1	−560	919	0	Epps (1986)
Mice					
	10.4	1030	96	5	Card et al. (1978)
	2.6	108	392	0	Epps (1986)
	4.5	−107	223	3.5	MacKenzie et al. (1991)
Trackball					
	2.9	282	347	0	Epps (1986)
	3.3	75	300	3.9	MacKenzie et al. (1991)
Touchpad					
absolute	2.3	181	434	0	Epps (1986)
relative	1.6	−194	609	0	Epps (1986)
Tablet with stylus					
	4.9	−55	204	4	MacKenzie et al. (1991)

MacKenzie et al. (1991) data it is $3.3/4.5 = 0.7$. One reason for the discrepancy is simply that the index of performance for the trackball is higher than that for the mouse in the Epps (1986) study but lower in the MacKenzie et al. (1991) study. The magnitude of the difference between the devices is also larger in MacKenzie et al.'s (1991) study.

There are several plausible explanations for the differences in values of *IP* obtained. MacKenzie (1992) provides a detailed account of possible deficiencies in experimental design and analysis across the studies, noting in particular the alarmingly high proportion of negative intercept values. He points to factors such as differences in the manner in which errors are handled; the differences between devices; differences between the characteristics of the tasks used in the study.

Both MacKenzie et al. (1991) and Gillan et al. (1990) have found differences in performance for pointing and dragging tasks. Gillan et al. (1990) suggest that in object selection tasks, the cursor is moved onto the entire object to be selected. In this case, Fitts' law can be used to fit data as the task is influenced by target width and movement distance. However, for object-dragging tasks, the cursor is moved onto the left-hand edge of the target, and performance appears to be more sensitive to the height of the target rather than width.

There will be an interaction between IP and muscle grouping used to perform a device movement. Thus, there could be a relationship between IP and degrees of freedom of movement for a given limb segment. Thus, different operating requirements of the devices and the type of hand grips they support will have a bearing on what movements can be made and on how positional information is transmitted to the user, e.g., the relationship between the movement of the user and that of the cursor.

9.5.4 Problems with Fitts' law

While Fitts' law has been used to fit a wealth of data from different fields of study, it does not hold for movements where the target width exceeds movement amplitude, i.e., where $W > A$ (Klapp, 1981a), nor does it hold for very fast movements, i.e., movement speeds faster than 200 ms (Schmidt et al., 1979). Furthermore, the law requires assumptions concerning the relationship between target size and movement which may not always hold. Welford (1968) suggests that people use an effective target width (rather than the actual target width), and aim for an area around the center of the target. This suggests that rather than simply performing a physical action, people might be making some decisions about the most appropriate way to perform the action.

Fitts' law was developed to describe performance on discrete tapping tasks which involved little or no requirement for visual monitoring of performance. Keele (1968), used estimations of times for visual feedback to derive constant b in equation (9.1) and found a reasonable fit with the data. This suggests that Fitts' law describes a very broad aspect of human performance and would not provide sufficient detail to allow us to address the questions posed above. It is worth noting here that Card et al. (1983) substituted the calculation of Fitts' law for a constant of 1.10 seconds in their keystroke level model.

While Fitts' law assumes a relationship between movement speed and accuracy of performance, several studies have found a relationship between target size and on-target time, i.e., suggesting that accuracy cannot be related solely to movement time (Megaw, 1972). Furthermore, Megaw (1975) demonstrated that, while Fitts' law holds for movements between targets of equal width, it does not seem to hold for movements between different sized targets. For example, movement time from a large to a small target seems to correspond to that for a target of intermediate size. This suggests that movement time can be modified by users, rather than be a simple function of motor system activity.

MacKenzie (1992) notes that it is relatively easy to achieve high-performance levels of Fitts' tasks with short periods of training. Given this, one wonders how useful Fitts' paradigm would be for studying differences in performance between expert and novice users of different interaction devices, or for variations in performance due to different device characteristics. Thus, it is necessary to determine the psychomotor processes which underlie the mathematical description.

If we return to the five assumptions which underlie the iterative-corrections model on which Fitts' law is based, it becomes apparent that they over-simplify actual performance. While researchers accept that total movement time can be decomposed into sub-movements, there is a great deal of evidence to suggest that sub-movements are highly variable, both in terms of duration and amplitude (Carlton, 1983; Jagacinski et al., 1980; Meyer et al., 1982). Research by Walker et al. (1993), using electromechanical mice, also demonstrates the variability of these sub-movements. Furthermore, Megaw (1975) shows that positioning movements do not end precisely when a target is reached, but incorporate some "on target" phase, possibly involving verification of performance. Of course, it is in the nature of models to provide partial explanations of phenomena (by virtue of their tendency to concentrate on a subset of features of the phenomena). However, one should be concerned with the question of the details the model omits, and the possible value to be gained from considering these details. In the next section, alternative accounts of pointing behavior are considered, from the perspective of psychomotor skills research.

9.6 Psychomotor skills research

Psychomotor skills research can be traced back to a series of studies carried out at the end of the nineteenth century involving simple pointing and aiming tasks. These tasks can be grouped under the general heading of discrete movements. In Chapter 7, the complex motor skill of typing was decomposed, at least at the physical level, into the single discrete movements of reaching for, and striking, a key. The complexity (for skilled typists) arises from coordinating these movements such that they overlap in time, i.e., an action is being initiated before the termination of the preceding action. In this section, we will consider whether pointing is characterized by a single action, as one might suppose, or whether it contains several phases. If pointing does contain several phases, then it is important to understand how the phases are coordinated and controlled.

9.6.1   Phases of movement

One of the earliest empirical studies of single discrete movement was published by Woodworth (1899). In an ingenious and detailed series of experiments, Woodworth asked people to pace their movement to the beat of a metronome, with times between 20 and 200 beats per minute, and to perform aiming movements with and without vision. When vision was removed, performance appeared to be independent of speed and was similar to that produced with very fast movements (see Figure 9.2).

From this research, Woodworth proposed a simple classification of aiming movement which is still relevant to contemporary research. He suggested that an initial impulsive phase would take the movement towards a target, and a current control phase would lead to successively finer adjustments in terms of final accuracy. If target size is reduced, so the current control phase would need to increase to ensure accuracy, and if total time was limited so the control phase would be restricted.

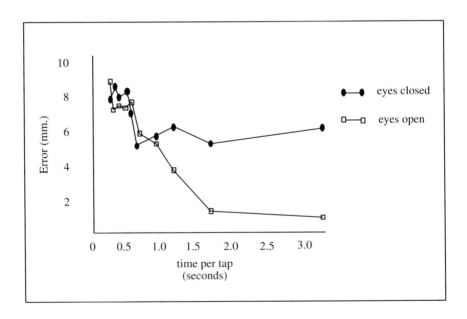

Figure 9.2   Data derived from Woodworth's research

The definition of two phases of activity was elaborated by Stetson and Bouman (1935), who demonstrated a relationship between muscle activity and phase of movement. During the initial impulsive phase, agonist and antagonist muscle groupings are used to start and stop movement; agonist activity will initiate movement and, as this activity decays, antagonist activity will act to halt the movement. Clearly this complex interplay of muscle activity needs to be carefully coordinated in order to achieve any accuracy. During the current control phase, the agonist and antagonist muscle groupings are continually working against each other to produce fine movements. Again there is a requirement for precision in the timing and control of such activity.

9.6.2   Levels of control

In order to make even the simplest of movements, it is necessary for the movement to be planned so that expenditure of effort is minimized in order for the movement to be performed as quickly and accurately as possible (Schmidt et al., 1979). At the simplest level of description, the planning of movement requires a set of instructions which will allow the appropriate limb, or part of a limb, to be moved to the correct place (Smyth and Wing, 1984). Some of the possible movements will be constrained by the physical characteristics of the environment in which one is moving (including the design and operational characteristics of different interaction devices) and by the structure and organization of the human body, i.e., the degrees of freedom problem. Taking this description as a starting point, we can say that the "instructions" will need to contain information relating to a number of factors: the place to where one wishes to move, i.e., its physical location in space, the relative distance between this place and the point from which the movement will start; the definition of the movement itself, i.e., how a movement will be made, which limb segment to use; any aspects of the environment which might have a bearing on the movement, i.e., any perceived obstacles, the use of tools to mediate the movement.

Several studies have been conducted into the order in which different aspects of movements are planned. In one paradigm, one asks someone to move either hand from a resting place to one of several end points, and precues one aspect of this movement, e.g., indicating which hand to move or in which direction to move. The time between a prompt and the start of the movement seems to depend on the type of precuing provided (Megaw, 1972; Meulenbroek et al., 1993), and suggests that the order of information used in the planning of movements is direction, arm, distance.

These findings lead to the proposal that on-target accuracy will relate to such factors as the relationship between target distance and correction of movement; the angular accuracy of aiming; the degree of tremor in a person's hand. This suggests that there will be a correlation between performance and skill. Skilled performance with interaction devices ought to exhibit fewer correction phases, have correction occur closer to the target, show greater accuracy in the initial angle of approach and less variation in movement due to tremor, when compared with "novice" performance.

9.6.3 Alternative models

There is some evidence to suggest that specifying direction is a key part of movement planning, in that even if the initial starting position of a limb is physically displaced or if kinesthetic information concerning limb position is removed, e.g., through blocking neural pathways, pointing accuracy can be maintained (Polit and Bizzi, 1978). The explanation of this phenomenon is that muscles can be considered in terms of springs, generating opposing forces. This is known as the mass–spring model. By varying the force exerted by agonist/antagonist muscle groupings, it would be possible to define movement in terms of its end-point, i.e., to say that, if the limb will finish in position x, it will have i force exerted on the agonist muscles and j force on the antagonist muscles. In this way, movement could be a simple matter of calculating the amount of force required.

These proposals would fit quite nicely into Woodworth's model, in that the initial movement plan would dictate the direction of a ballistic phase of movement, i.e., move to point x, followed by a more precise specification of how to make that movement, i.e., using limb segment y, and with some final specification of the intensity of the movement; with agonist in the ballistic phase and agonist/antagonist activity in the correction phase. Indeed, Schmidt et al. (1979) suggest that, for rapid arm movements taking less than 200 ms, nerve impulses trigger the arm muscle to exert a burst of activity throwing the arm towards a target.[9.2] The resulting forces vary during the course of the movement, both in terms of extent and in terms of their timing and coordination. In this model, the time and intensity of neural activity vary independently of each other, and so the principal task in planning movement is to calculate the precise magnitude of burst of activity prior to making the movement. This model seems to assume that the direction of the movement and the limb segment are given, and can account quite elegantly for the planning of the intensity of a movement. However, this model does not take into account the role of monitoring movement during its course, for instance through the use of visual and kinesthetic feedback.

[9.2] Recall that Fitts' law does not apply to movement of less than 200 ms. One explanation for this could relate to the fact that rapid movement is neither monitored nor corrected until after its completion.

Meyer et al. (1982) proposed an optimized initial impulse model of aimed movements. They suggest that such movements would tend to be made as quickly as possible. A person would make an initial, high-velocity movement towards the target. If, as a result of this movement, the target is hit, the task is completed. If the target is missed, then further movements are made from where the previous movement ended, i.e., one or several smaller movements will be made. Thus, one could suggest that movement planning should seek to minimize the number of movements in order to maximize movement time.

From the above, one can propose that movement plans will need to contain the following components:

- specify type of movement required;
- specify direction from start point to target;
- select appropriate limb segment to make movement;
- define required magnitude of burst of muscle activity;
- perform ballistic phase of movement;
- monitor progression of movement, using either visual or kinesthetic feedback;
- correct movement during current control phase, if required.

While it is still a matter of much debate as to whether this "plan" is completely written prior to action, or whether it might be "edited" during action, there are some general conclusions that can be drawn from this section. When we initiate any movement, we generate a series of units of activity which appear to be ordered in hierarchy. This means that a higher-order intention to act can call upon lower-level units of activity to fulfil specific parts of the intention. In Chapter 8, it was shown that simply describing a picture has a significant impact on the activity involved in copying it; although many of the basic units of activity remain the same, their coordination and combination changes with the higher-level definition of the outcome of the action.

9.6.4 Planning and correcting movement

Given the level of detail required in planning movement, one might ask whether humans had evolved some means of assimilating this information into executable units of code. One might also assume that as humans have a tendency to minimize cognitive and physical expenditure, people would seek ways of combining these units of code into larger units to permit graceful performance with minimal processing effort. From the discussion so far, it is apparent that people plan movement on the basis of an assessment of the situation and a definition of the appropriate type of action. To illustrate this point, consider the activity of mail-sorters putting packages into mailbags.

The sorter will read the label on the package and then throw it into the appropriate mailbag. Work by Pew (1974) shows that the accuracy of this throwing activity was very high, despite the variations in package size, shape and weight and despite that fact that the sorters were positioned several meters from 25 mailbags. Pew (1974) argued that it did not seem feasible to suggest that the sorters had learned the correct throwing activity for each size, shape and weight of parcel for all the possible distances. Rather, some generalized plan of action was required, which could be modified in the light of changing situational demands. Thus, the throw would need to be calculated on the basis of the parcel's characteristics and the distance to the mailbag. In other words, a general throwing movement would be planned within parameters set by these factors.

9.7   Interaction devices and psychomotor skills

In Chapter 5, a set of generic tasks was defined, of which object selection and dragging apply to pointing devices. In studies of the generic task of selecting an object, results tend to favor the touchscreen as the most efficient interaction device, followed by the mouse and the trackball. On the other hand, for the task of dragging objects, the mouse appears to be superior to trackball and touchscreen. In this section, we will consider the possible motor skills involved in using these devices and ask whether the type of errors which have been reported in the literature can be explained using the simple models developed. While attention is focused on only three devices, it is proposed that these devices represent, in some sense, the appropriate devices for the tasks.

9.7.1   Cursor positioning

Once a target has been selected, the user will define a path to the object; in effect, aiming the cursor and then, using the device at hand, moving it towards the object. One can expand this simple description by noting that movement needs to be verified and planned. Researchers have suggested that movement can be decomposed into several phases. If we concentrate on moving a cursor, using a mouse, we find that movement time can be divided into an initiation period, followed by a sub-movement, often followed by a pause, then another sub-movement and pause, and a ver-

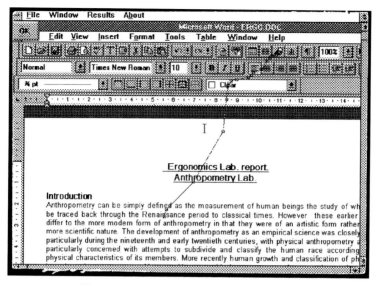

Figure 9.3 Phases of cursor movement

ification time (Barker et al., 1990; Walker et al., 1993). Figure 9.3 illustrates these phases.

It has been shown that positioning is faster with a mouse than a trackball (MacKenzie et al., 1991). There are two possible explanations for this finding: differences in device dynamics, and differences in movement. The mouse requires the user to move an artifact in space, while the trackball requires the user to move the artifact in its housing. Given the possibility of slippage between the trackball and its housing, it might be hypothesized that controlling cursor movement with the trackball could be more variable than control using the mouse, i.e., the user has to constantly correct the movement of the trackball in its housing in addition to moving the cursor.

The *C:D* ratio of the devices could also influence the control action, especially during a ballistic phase of movement, and lead to target over-shoot. This, in turn, introduces additional variability into the cursor positioning task. Finally, there might be a tendency for users to rely on the characteristics of the trackball to assist in cursor positioning movements, leading to problems of slip and roll, and to problems of loss of control when moving over large distances, i.e., by spinning the ball in its housing.

Baber (1996) demonstrates a relationship between spatial planning of movement and device use. He asked users of mice and trackballs to point to a series of numbers arranged in a grid. The series which the users had to follow were presented prior to movement. In some conditions, people were asked to remember the numbers, while in other conditions they were asked to determine the position of the numbers on the grid and to plan a route between the numbers. Performance was superior when people were asked to plan a route instead of learning the sequence, and a significant difference was found between mouse and trackball users in the route planning condition (differences in other conditions were not significant). The implications of these findings are that it is better to plan movement in space than as a sequence of steps and that the movement dynamics in the mouse were exploited in the route planning condition.

For the mouse, one could assume that movement will be effected using the forearm–wrist–hand combination, with large distances being traversed using movement about the elbow and shoulder and smaller, corrective movements, being made about the wrist. For the trackball, on the other hand, most of the action will be performed using the wrist–finger combination.

Having mastered the characteristics of the trackball, the user may need to rely more on visual feedback due to the lack of kinesthetic feedback. With the mouse, movement can be effected in space such that the user moves in a fashion similar to the cursor. For the trackball, movement is highly limited in space (an analogy would be to use a mouse on a quarter-size mouse mat), which requires continuous assessment of position and movement. This would be seen by the trackball exhibiting a larger number of correction phases than the mouse, and would influence performance time.

Hesse and Hahn (1994) show that interface layout also has a bearing on the execution of actions, and the subsequent stages of monitoring the effects of the action. Thus, different layouts of interfaces, and different ways in which an operator can interact with them, may require different forms of action planning and execution. While the layouts may fulfil a requirement to represent the objects in a fashion to which operators can relate, they may introduce additional action planning and execution tasks in the primary control task, which could lead to errors of extent, i.e., overshooting the target, or aiming errors.

Aiming errors could arise from selection of the wrong target, i.e., at a goal level. Such errors could also arise from premature onset of movement, i.e., initiating a movement before the final target position has been calculated. Suppose that, when using the trackball, people make their initial calculation based on hand movement, seeking to move the hand in a straight line towards the target, and that this serves as a model for their movement. If they fail to provide adequate compensation for the characteristics of the trackball, then their movement could be converted into a straight line tangential to the path of the ball in its holder, leading to a movement away from the target. The movement time would then consist of movements with erroneous aim, which require correction during ballistic movement.

9.7.2   Selecting objects

The selection of objects occurs when an additional action is performed, after cursor positioning. For the mouse and trackball this tends to be a button press, for the touchscreen it tends to be a touch with the finger on the screen (with selection being indicated either on touching the screen or on lifting the finger off the screen).

At first glance, the problem of cursor positioning does not appear to apply to using a touchscreen: there is no cursor. However, in touchscreen-based interaction, the user's finger is used to represent the cursor and problems can arise in the movement and positioning of the finger relative to the object, e.g., parallax errors. Furthermore, Sears and Shneiderman (1993) suggest that use of a "lift-off to select" touchscreen could be modelled using a variation on Fitts' law, with phases for finger movement and object movement. This variation is shown by equation (9.4). A constant (c) is used to multiply the distance to the screen (D) and width (w) components for the selection of the object. Presumably, the value of c will depend upon the experience and ability of the user. The second part of the equation describes the movement of the cursor on the screen.

$$T = a + b \left[\log_2 (cD/w)\right] + d \left[\log_2 (e/w)\right] \qquad (9.4)$$

9.7.3   Dragging objects

To a certain extent, dragging an object is similar to cursor positioning; once selected, the object functions as a large cursor. Comparisons of movement time for selecting and dragging objects, however suggest that dragging takes more time than selection (MacKenzie et al., 1991; Walker et al., 1993; Gillan et al., 1990). One can propose two possible explanations for this difference. As noted above, a number of studies have suggested that dragging objects using a trackball is less effective than when using a mouse. The principal factor in this finding seems to be the problem associated with manipulating the trackball and holding down a button on the housing (see Chapter 3). This would require a very difficult (and possibly uncomfortable) contortion of the hand about the wrist. It also reduces the possible locus of movement, from the wrist-finger to the finger. Obviously, there are simple solutions to this problem: either use the other hand to press the button, or allow the button to stay down during dragging. It is plausible to assume that the action of holding down a button on the mouse can also have an impact on the degrees of freedom about the wrist during movements, and reduces the possible locus of movement to the hand–forearm. Thus, one can posit a biomechanical explanation for these differences. Alternatively, one can propose that effectively increasing the size of the cursor will have a bearing on the effective width of the target to which one is aiming. If target width is, in some sense related to the size of the cursor, then one is reducing the size of target to which one can aim. Thus, one could propose some modification to Fitts' law to account for the relative difference in target size which, in turn, would lead to an increase in the predicted movement time.

9.7.4   Use of feedback

Movement can be decomposed into phases. Some of the phases will require information regarding the position of the cursor in order to check accuracy. This information is obtained primarily from the visual display. In recent years, researchers have been developing techniques which can supplement visual feedback when using interaction devices. If one removes information from one sensory modality, it is necessary to focus effort on interpreting information from the remaining modalities. In the case of HCI, one must focus almost exclusively on the visual modality.

From their studies, Walker et al. (1993) propose two main guidelines for designing visual displays to aid cursor positioning. Some menu-headings, such as that used in Word for Windows, have small objects with space above them. It is possible for users to overshoot such targets. Thus, when designing menu-headings, it is advisable to provide a line in the menu, perpendicular to the direction of movement, at which the user can aim. Also, current interface designs often provide poor visual cues as to whether the cursor has actually hit a target. This leads to extended verification times. If each object can be changed as the cursor hits, e.g., by the use of reverse video, verification time might be reduced. One might extend this idea by suggesting that each object can exhibit relative changes as the cursor approaches it, e.g., by gradually changing the intensity or color of the object as the cursor gets closer to it. However, this is probably not a good idea; how will the user know when to stop moving the cursor, when should the color intensity stop changing?

Kinesthetic feedback first relates to limb position and movement, and has been considered at length in this chapter. Broadly speaking, some devices provide the opportunity for users to monitor their physical actions and to relate these to cursor movement. Some forms of joystick can be operated on the basis of the amount of force exerted by a user, rather than on movement (isometric versus displacement). Thus, it is possible to design interaction devices which provide users with tactile feedback on the basis of general device activation.

Tactile feedback can be provided by the device itself. It is also possible to provide tactile feedback on the basis of specific actions, e.g., selecting different objects. As a cursor approaches an object on the computer screen, it is possible to alter the mouse's operating characteristics. For instance, one might increase the relative effort required to move the mouse by increasing the friction on its rolling ball, or one might provide some form of tactile feedback from the body of the mouse. In both cases, one is supplementing visual feedback with the type of feedback normally received when manipulating objects: tactile and kinesthetic feedback, which can provide useful information about the proximity of objects or about changes in force exerted. One could assume that the objects on a computer screen could be made to generate a "force field", such that when the cursor approached them its movement was altered (Gescheider et al., 1978).

Göbel et al. (1994) incorporated actuators into the mouse casing. A pair of actuators, one on either side of the casing, was used to adjust the relative horizontal position of small bars which rested against the user's thumb and little finger, and two actuators were placed in buttons on top of the mouse. Thus, by holding a mouse so that the thumb and little finger rested against the side buttons, and first and third fingers rested on buttons on top of the mouse, the user can be presented with tactile feedback. As the cursor approaches an object, i.e., as it enters the object's "force field", the appropriate actuator will change the position of a button and provide a tactile cue to one of the fingers. Data collected during experimental comparisons of conventional mice with this tactile mouse indicated performance improvements when tactile feedback was provided. For positioning objects, performance times were reduced by up to 14% when using the tactile mouse, and for object selection this improvement increased up to 25%.

There was, however, a slight tendency for users to overshoot targets when using the tactile mouse, and performance was less effective on a tracking task. Taken together, these results suggest that users can quickly accommodate to the use of tactile feedback, and that for many interaction tasks, the provision of tactile feedback can be beneficial. The results also suggest a change in strategy, with users being able to devote more effort to the ballistic phase (hence, improving acquisition times), with feedback being used continuously during movement, rather than sampled as is the case with visual feedback. The presence of overshoots suggests that, in some cases, users might be over-confident in this ability. Furthermore, when one considers the placement of the buttons on the modified mouse, it is clear that this design requires a specific type of grip. One might wonder whether this type of grip would limit the accuracy with which actions can be performed.

It can be suggested that providing tactile feedback in mice can improve cursor-positioning activity. One can consider this effect both in terms of sampling requirements for feedback, i.e., tactile feedback could be sampled more efficiently than visual feedback, and, in broader terms, with respect to the notion of compatibility (discussed in Chapter 6). Providing tactile feedback for a manual task could allow people to use information with minimal information translation requirements. This could also explain why isometric joysticks have been shown to produce superior performance to displacement joysticks. It would be interesting to see whether this concept could be applied to other manual interaction devices.

The preceding discussion illustrates how some researchers have given objects on the computer screen properties which can change as a cursor approaches them. Another means of presenting information pertaining to the changes in objects status can be via auditory feedback. Assume that each object on an interface can generate its own sound, and that some characteristic of the sound, e.g., intensity, changes as a cursor either approaches, or passes over, it.

Gaver (1986) has discussed the potential benefits to be gained from using auditory icons. He suggests that some sounds are highly meaningful, on the basis of everyday experience, and that it is possible for these sounds to be used to supplement information presented on the computer display. Gaver (1989) added auditory feedback to a Macintosh to produce the SonicFinder. In this system different sounds were associated with different user actions. For instance, the computer produced a "dragging" sound when an object was moved, or a "click" when the cursor passed the boundary of a window, or a "clunk" when a file was deposited in the dustbin.

Blattner et al. (1989) associated different sounds with different types of document, so that users could discern whether the documents contained text, graphics or spreadsheets. In their work, they have introduced the concept of "earcons", which are patterns of notes, to denote specific objects, which can be combined into families of earcons, on the basis of certain shared properties.

While Walker et al. (1993) suggest that the provision of additional visual feedback can be useful, and while studies using tactile feedback indicate some improvements in performance times, it is unlikely that such feedback will be useful for all users of all systems. Consider using auditory feedback to supplement cursor positioning. One can imagine that there might be benefits when it is used in situations when visual information is removed or degraded (see Chapter 11), or, possibly, to resolve ambiguity in object definition, e.g., in terms of attaching different sounds to files depending on what they contain. In this latter case, one could imagine a series of text files in a folder having similar icons but different sounds to indicate whether they incorporate graphs or pictures or tables, etc. However, the issue is surely one of user acceptance: to what extent will people become irritated by the auditory cues and attempt to remove them; much the same as happened with the "talking car" and "talking elevator".

9.8   Conclusions

Selecting objects on a computer screen can be considered as a motor skill. The movement activity is influenced by a number of factors, not least the characteristics of the device and the users' level of skill. Fitts' law has been found to be a useful, although very limited, description of device use. The limitations of Fitts' law can be overcome by considering the other factors which influence the use of pointing devices.

In Chapter 1, it was noted that one could not divorce interaction devices from the computer system on which they were used. This point is especially important when considering pointing devices. The principal determinants of performance with pointing devices appear to be less associated with the characteristics of the device, such as $C{:}D$ ratio, than with the design, layout and appearance of the display in which one is performing the pointing tasks.

One can further distinguish between devices and tasks on the basis of the biomechanical activity required of the user. Thus, for instance, one can determine a number of factors to predict why mice will produce superior performance to trackballs. There is an assumption among many of the people to whom I spoke when preparing this book that the trackball is better for high-stress environments than the mouse, or other pointing devices. This has not, to my knowledge, been empirically supported. I would suggest that the belief may be erroneous. Trackballs are designed to be controlled using discrete, fingertip corrections. This would lead to both slower positioning time and a tendency to spend a significant portion of time "hovering" over the target in final correction phase for the trackball. One could further argue that, as the control of movement is strongly influenced by factors such as workload and stress (Fleischer and Becker, 1986), either this pattern would be exacerbated by high workload or additional attention would need to be allocated to the control of the trackball during periods of high workload, thus leading to narrowing of attention on the target to be acquired. As noted in Chapter 1, a principal reason for choosing trackballs in preference to other interaction devices in high-stress domains may have less to do with human factors than with engineering considerations, e.g., reduced desk-space, lack of trailing wires, durability. While one ought not argue against the importance of these factors, I would hope that a reading of this chapter would lead to an appreciation of the wealth of human factors which will have a bearing on the successful use of pointing devices.

9.9   **Key points for practitioners**

- Consider the relationship between task requirements and biomechanical factors in device use: e.g., is there sufficient space to perform the actions? do users have sufficient capabilities to perform the action?
- Consider the relationship between pointing device and display design: e.g., are the objects of sufficient size and spacing to allow fast and accurate selection?
- Consider the potential physical problems which could arise from prolonged maintenance of specific postures required to use the device: e.g., holding the upper arm and elbow in tension when using a mouse.

9.10   **Key points for researchers**

- Extend the description of using mice, trackballs and touchscreens to the investigation of other pointing devices.
- Develop alternative models to replace Fitts' law as explanations of how people point to, select and drag objects using pointing devices.
- Consider the psychomotor skills involved in using pointing devices in novel domains, e.g., virtual reality or 3D.
- Develop new forms of interaction device to support human psychomotor skills.
- Consider the development of "direct manipulation" to allow reaching, grasping and holding objects in displays.

CHAPTER 10

Speaking

Abstract

There is an increasing range of products and applications being developed which utilize the capabilities of computers to recognize human speech. In order to appreciate the problems associated with speech technology, it is useful to have an understanding of how people produce, and communicate using, speech.

10.1 Introduction

In this chapter, speech will be considered in terms of making sounds which can be distinguished from "noise" and interpreted by a speech recognition system (either human or computer). Thinking about speech as sound provides an insight into the problems surrounding substitution errors in speech recognition (see Chapter 4), but also highlights some of the fundamental problems of getting a computer to recognize speech in the first place. Attention is also given to the planning involved in producing speech. This allows consideration of the factors which could lead to human error, partly in terms of slips of the tongue, and partly in terms of errors with a speech recognition system. This leads to a discussion of the nature of spoken dialogue between people and computers, and the similarities and differences between this form of dialogue and dialogue between two people.

10.2 Speech as sound

Human speech may be defined as a time-varying sound wave originating in a vocal mechanism in continuous movement during speech production.

Speaking involves coordinated movements to be performed on the muscles in the respiratory and vocal tracts. These movements need to achieve some degree of consistency for recognizable speech sounds to be produced (Pickett, 1980), and their coordination needs to exhibit a high degree of fluency in order for speech to be produced as a continuous stream of sound (Matthei and Roeper, 1983).

In everyday terminology, we tend to divide speech sounds into two classes: vowels and consonants. Vowels are the simplest type of speech sound to describe in acoustic terms, and are produced when there is no obstruction in the vocal tract to impede the airflow; rather the airflow is modulated by movement of the larynx and the position of the tongue. It is possible, in fact, to relate tongue position quite closely to vowel production, as shown in Figure 10.1.

The production of speech sounds can be explained using the source-filter theory (Müller, 1848, Fant, 1960). In this theory, the airflow from the lungs is modulated by the vocal cords in the larynx. This acts as the sound source for the production of speech. The vocal cords open and close very rapidly during speaking, causing a sound wave to be generated. The rate at which the vocal cords open and close determines the fundamental frequency of the voice, which is perceived by listeners as the pitch of the voice. For instance, the average fundamental frequencies for the speech of men is 120 Hz, while it is 225 Hz for women and about 265 Hz for children. The fundamental frequency changes during the production of speech.

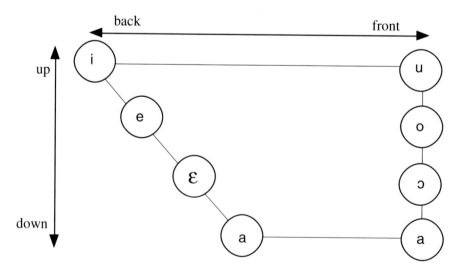

Figure 10.1   The "vowel quadrilateral" (reproduced with permission from Baber, 1993, in C. Baber and J.M. Noyes (eds), *Interactive Speech Technology*, published by Taylor & Francis)

The vocal tract (consisting of the pharynx, mouth, teeth, tongue, lips, nose, etc.) can be considered as the filter which modifies the sound wave. During speech production the dimensions of the filter will vary because the vocal tract is continually moving. Different shapes of the vocal tract can be considered as filters with different transfer characteristics: allowing maximum energy for some frequencies to pass and suppressing other frequencies. However, these frequencies are harmonics of the fundamental frequency, and the vocal tract produces sound energy with peaks at certain of these harmonics (known as formants). The fact that the harmonics are based on the fundamental frequency ensures that the speech signal has some similarity over time, even though the fundamental frequency is constantly changing. In addition to changes in the frequencies of speech as a consequence of alterations in the vocal tract, there are also changes in the quality of the signals produced. For instance, one can distinguish periodic sounds, such as vowels, from aperiodic sounds, such as consonants.

Stop consonants are produced by blocking the flow of air completely, usually with the lips or tongue, and then releasing the air which has built up, e.g., the "b" in the word "bus". Fricative consonants are produced when the airflow is partially impeded, causing a hissing sound, e.g., the "s" in "bus". Finally, some of the consonants are produced with overtones in the nasal cavity. While it is possible to classify the different speech sounds in terms of their production, it is important to note that the articulations tend to overlap each other. This means that the sound patterns are in transition much of the time. The approximate consonants, or glides, are produced by partial constriction of the vocal tract (as with affricates and fricatives), which is gradually released as the vowel sound is formed.

Vowels are often produced when the vocal tract is moving towards or away from the production of consonants. Thus, as the vocal tract is in continuous motion, it is unlikely that precisely the same muscular configuration is used to produce the same sound on two occasions. Many of our speech sounds are produced as approximations, influenced by the context in which they are uttered, e.g., the voiced stop consonant "t" has a different sound in "bat" than its sound in "table". This suggests that one aspect of speaking is the coordination of the muscle movements, within the constraints imposed by the context of the other speech sounds. Similarities between points of constriction could suggest that some speech sounds will have similar properties, i.e., that under certain listening conditions it might be possible to confuse "p" with "d" (Clark and Clark, 1977). In addition to the physical aspects of producing speech, there are also cognitive aspects involved in determining what to say and how to say it.

10.3   Levels of control in speech production

In constructing and speaking a series of words, a speaker must make a number of decisions. Initially, the information to be communicated must be planned and selected in terms of the appropriate linguistic and social contexts of the conversation. Obviously, words cannot be spoken in a random order, but must adhere to a recognizable syntax. Three influential theories concerning how humans produce speech have been proposed in recent years. Garrett (1984) analyzed the types of errors that people make in producing speech. From this analysis, a four-stage model of speech production is proposed. Mackay (1983) and Dell (1986) approach the problem from the viewpoint of "spreading activation theory" (cf. Rumelhart and Norman's, 1982, model of typing discussed in Chapter 7). Dell (1986) proposes a four-stage model, while Mackay's (1982) model contains a number of nodes at approximately four levels. The models of Mackay (1983), Garrett (1984) and Dell (1986) are sufficiently similar, for the purposes of this book, to allow them to be collapsed into a single, four-stage model. At the highest level, the meaning of the message to be communicated is generated. This semantic level employs the speaker's knowledge of the language, the context of the conversation and the goals of the speaker to develop a basic intention to utter a message with a specific meaning. At the next level, the broad outline of the utterance is generated. In very simple terms, this syntactic level can be considered analogous to the construction of a set of "slots" which need to be filled by certain types of words.

Following the syntactic level comes the morphological level at which the words selected to fill the "slots" are constructed from the appropriate morphemes of the language, i.e., the basic units of meaning. Finally, an articulatory program needs to be constructed and run to produce the utterance. At each level a set of "rules" need to be invoked to govern the fluent performance of the activity at that level and the smooth transition to the next level. Some idea of the rules and knowledge required by the speaker is indicated by Figure 10.2.

In Figure 10.2, the process of planning a message (drawing on appropriate knowledge sources) involves both the generation of the message and the monitoring of the ongoing utterance. The message is encoded grammatically, i.e., drawing on the appropriate rules of syntax and selection of words, and then encoding phonologically, i.e., bringing together the appropriate speech sounds which are required to articulate the message, and the process concludes with the production of the utterance. However, speakers monitor what they say for any speech errors. Indeed, there is good evidence to suggest that correction can occur prior to articulation, suggesting that,

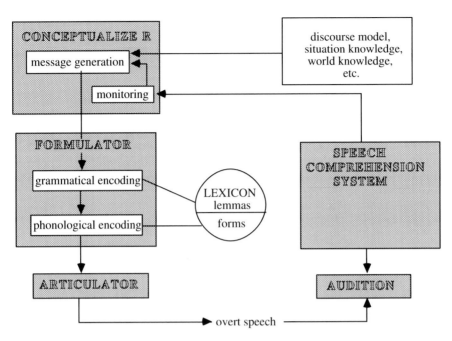

Figure 10.2 Schematic diagram of speech production (from Levelt, 1989, *Speaking: From Intention to Articulation*, MIT Press)

like typing, there is some facility for the speaker to be able to perform some pre-checking prior to utterance.

10.4 Dialogue

The use of the term "dialogue" to describe HCI suggests that the relationship between user and computer involves the communication of information according to sets of rules. The process by which people and computers communicate has been termed dialogue since the 1960s. So ubiquitous is the term that researchers in HCI tend to take it for granted. However, a number of writers have pointed out that "dialogue" may be a misleading term to describe HCI (Smith, 1980; Sheehy, 1987). One reason to suppose that HCI may not be a "dialogue" is that there is seldom shared knowledge between user and computer. This means that, rather than being based on a symmetrical relationship of knowledge, understanding and language use, HCI is asymmetrical (Pinsky, 1983). The asymmetry can be seen in two ways: first, the rules held by the user and computer as to what constitutes appropriate turn taking might differ; second, the knowledge of the language and context held by the user and the computer may differ. Traditionally, these problems have been resolved by efforts to bring the human down to the level of the computer, i.e., using languages which the computer can understand and structuring the interaction so that the computer maintains some degree of control.

The success of "dialogue" in HCI depends on how well the interaction is scripted. Providing the script is simple and unambiguous, the interaction can progress with little problem. However, Wilensky (1978) has pointed out that the majority of human communication is not well scripted. Rather people have powerful strategies for inferring their dialogue partners' intentions through their partner's words and actions and adapting their own plans to fit the changes in situation.

Consequently, it is possible to define dialogue in terms of its style, structure and content (Barnard and Hammond, 1983). Style refers to the medium through which the dialogue is performed, structure refers to its syntax and content refers to the semantics of the message. Some writers, notably Buxton (1983), have proposed that it is also necessary to understand the pragmatics of the interaction, i.e., the relationship between what is said and what is understood. HCI has often circumvented problems associated with the different aspects of dialogue by prescribing highly limited domains of interaction. However, with the introduction of speech comes the possibility of creating domains which are similar to other forms of speech use.

10.5 Rules for interaction?

Communication requires the use of a sequence of speakers (Longacre, 1983). If all parties were to speak at once, or if all parties waited for each other to speak, there would be little chance of effective verbal communication. People employ a variety of strategies to define who will speak next. These strategies have been termed "turn taking" (Sacks et al., 1978), and draw on a wide range of linguistic and extralinguistic cues (Duncan, 1972, 1973, 1974). Grice (1975) defined a set of maxims, for human communication, under the general rubric of a "cooperative principle" (Table 10.1). Grice argued that in order for a conversation to function effectively it was necessary for speakers to obey these maxims.

It might be possible to employ these maxims in the design of human–computer interfaces (Pinsky, 1983; Baber, 1993). Sperber and Wilson (1986) collapse the four maxims of the "cooperative principle" into the single principle of relevance. Relevance assumes that a speaker should try to express information which is most relevant to the auditor. This suggests

Table 10.1   Maxims derived from the cooperative principle

Quantity		
	Qni	Make your contribution as informative as required (for the current purposes of the exchange)
	Qnii	Do not make your contribution more informative than is required
Quality		
	Qli	Do not say what you believe to be false
	Qlii	Do not say that for which you lack adequate evidence
Relation		
	R	Be relevant
Manner		
	Mi	Be perspicuous
	Mii	Avoid obscurity of expression
	Miii	Avoid ambiguity
	Miv	Be brief (avoid unnecessary prolixity)
	Mv	Be orderly

that, on hearing an utterance, the auditor will make inferences relating the content of the utterance to the situation in which it is uttered and to the characteristics of the listener. Baber and Stammers (1989) found differences in utterance between people who believed that they were speaking to a computer and those who believed they were speaking to a person. When people knew that they were speaking to a person, many of their commands included the words "please", or "would you", and "thank you". In none of the cases when people believed that they were speaking to a computer did these utterance types occur. Thus, people speaking to a person retained a degree of social contact in their communication. In the cases where people believed that they were speaking to a computer, there did not appear to be a necessity for establishing and maintaining a "social contact" through the use of expressives.

Table 10.2 illustrates possible approaches to dialogue management, based on speech act theory of Austin (1962) and Searle (1969) and applied to speech recognition research by Bunt et al. (1978), Waterworth (1984) and Baber (1993). The speakers will mark the start and termination of the interaction, such as greetings/farewell, and also the start and termination of each individual utterance within that interaction, such as prompts from the computer to signal the user to speak, or a signal from the computer to indicate that something has been recognized. Within the interaction, there will be both some form of protocol to ensure that the interaction is

Table 10.2 Speech acts in speech-based HCI (Baber, 1993)

Boundaries	Dialogue acts	
	Goal directed	Interaction management
• Start		
	• Greeting	
		• [Enrolment/speech sampling]
• Prologue		
		• Preamble
		• Explanation
	• Instructions	
		• Vocabulary items
• Interaction		
	• Speaker → auditor	• Grunt
		• Yes/no
		• Direct
		• Command
		• Request
		• Recovery/repair
	• Auditor → speaker	• Confirm
		• Acknowledge
		• Accept
		• Reply
		• No response
		• Recovery/repair
		• Provide extra information
• Termination	• Quit	
	• Sign off etc.	

progressing smoothly, and "goal directed" acts. Waterworth (1984) suggests that the primary use of such protocols is to prevent and correct mistakes. Baber (1993) suggests that they can also serve to maintain the principle of relevance in the interaction. Human conversation uses a number of protocols to reduce the size of the required vocabulary, e.g., the development of a shared terminology, based on common knowledge (Krauss and Glucksberg, 1977; Falzon, 1984), and the use of short feedback phrases which control the amount and rate of information exchanged (Oviatt and Cohen, 1989). This latter form of control is often performed using paralinguistic devices, known as "backchannelling", e.g. "mm-hmm" or "huh?" (Schoeber and Clark, 1989).

In Table 10.2, there are a number of "acts" which are placed between the "goal directed" and "interaction management" columns, this is to illustrate that there will be several acts which are used to link parts of the interaction. For instance, the "greeting" will be partly an "interaction management" act, in that it will serve to initiate the interaction, and it will be partly goal directed in that it will be performed with the twin goals of providing specific introductory information and establishing the appropriate interaction style. This latter point is based on the observation (discussed below), that the feedback from the computer can help to shape both the user's perceptions of, and attitudes towards, the computer, and the manner in which the user will speak to the computer. From Table 10.2 it is conceivable that we can begin to define certain stereotypical structures, e.g. greetings/farewells which can be used as building blocks for the design of interactions.

The reader will note that, while Table 10.2 provides an idealized conception of the flow of a "dialogue", there is little indication of what sort of vocabulary or syntax would be used in the interaction. A number of writers have proposed that one can apply some of the findings from conversation analysis to the design of HCI (see Luff et al., 1990 for a collection of papers on this topic). From this perspective, one can take naturally occurring, i.e., spontaneous, fragments of human conversation and attempt to match this to the dialogue requirements in HCI. For instance, if one compares the way in which people correct misrecognitions in their conversations over the telephone, one might require users of a speech recognition system to repeat the misrecognized portion of the phrase. Unfortunately, while repetition can be an effective means of error-correction, people may attempt to repeat words with added embellishment, perhaps by emphasizing the misrecognized portion of the phrase. While this latter strategy can be beneficial in human conversation, there is a possibility that the added emphasis might distort the speech signal to a sufficient extent to lead to further misrecognition. Consequently, Button (1990) has argued against the straightforward application of principles and findings from conversation analysis and its associated approaches to the design of HCI. A problem lies in one's definition of "rules": should they be considered as routines (which will "fire" under the right conditions), or as resources (from which participants in a conversation can select, depending on their perceptions of appropriateness)?

There has been some interest recently in whether it is possible to use the feedback from a computer to shape the user's speech. In human communication, people often, and presumably without being aware that they are doing so, imitate mannerisms and forms of expression of the interlocutor. This is a phenomenon known as convergence (see for example Giles and Powisland, 1975), and affects such properties of a human dialogue as pause length, and use of particular linguistic structures (Schenkein, 1980).

A number of studies have found that, given unrestricted speech input, subjects would often adapt to the "linguistic style" of the computer (Zoltan

Ford, 1984; Leiser, 1989a, 1989b), and, in some instances, the intonation of the speech synthesis device. Thus, when users are free to employ whatever commands and vocabulary they thought necessary, they often used terms and structures that the computer used in its responses. This does indeed suggest that it might be possible to use feedback to shape, and constrain, users' speech. However, it is worth asking whether these findings result from the linguistic phenomenon of convergence, or whether there may be another explanation?

Baber (1991) reports studies investigating the use of speech for a simple task in which people were provided with either "verbose" or "limited" feedback, on the assumption that feedback type would influence performance in a manner predicted from the notion of convergence. While feedback type did influence performance, it was actually in the opposite direction to that expected. When feedback length increased, i.e., was verbose, subjects' responses became shorter.

Falzon (1984) identified specific communication strategies used by experienced medical secretaries. These strategies allow the secretary to obtain relevant information quickly and efficiently, often involving pre-empting questions and comments from the caller. The pre-emption is performed on the basis of formulating hypotheses concerning the nature of the callers' request and the possible courses of action which constitute appropriate responses to the request. This implies that the process of communication can be simplified by the judicious use of a model of one's conversation partner. However, in HCI it is often difficult to determine the appropriate model of the computer as conversational partner (Baber, 1993). From these studies, one can propose that "convergence" might, in fact, be a deliberate strategy on the part of the speaker; either as a means of reducing uncertainty in the interaction or as a result of a specific dialogue model.

10.6 Errors and speech recognition systems

In Chapter 4, it was noted that the errors made by speech recognition systems can be classified as rejection; insertion; substitution. Rejection errors occur when a legal vocabulary item is spoken by the user and the device does not respond. Insertion errors occur when spurious noise is recognized as a legal vocabulary item. Substitution errors occur when an incorrect item is substituted for the spoken one.

Ringle and Bruce (1982) define three types of "failure", on the part of listeners, which could lead to mistakes in recognizing speech:

1. perceptual failure: in which words are not clearly perceived, or are misperceived, or are misinterpreted;
2. lexical failure: in which the listener perceives a word correctly, but fails to interpret it correctly;
3. syntactic failure: in which all words are correctly perceived and interpreted, but the intended meaning of the utterance is misconstrued.

Baber and Hone (1993) propose that almost all errors made by speech recognition systems are a result of "perceptual failure". This means that errors arise because words will be incorrectly "perceived" by the speech recognition device. Maintaining this anthropomorphism, one could suggest that rejection errors result from a form of deafness, in which a speech sound transmitted by the user is not received by the speech recognition system; insertion errors result from competing sound signals, in which environmental "noises" are mistakenly recognized as speech; substitution errors arise when the transmitted sound signal is sufficiently similar to another sound for the device to "hear" the alternative sound. It is fair to say that the majority of insertion and rejection errors can be readily dealt with by careful setting up of the speech recognition equipment, including microphone placement and enrolment of speech samples. Substitution errors pose the biggest problem.

Sometimes speech recognition devices make errors which can be predicted from analysis of the sounds in the speech signal. Indeed, Moore (1977) has proposed that performance of speech recognition systems can be considered analogous to the performance of human speech perception in different levels of background noise. The human equivalent noise ratio (HENR) approach allows one to predict possible confusions within a specified vocabulary set. While this approach can work well, it cannot capture all errors because some of the recognition errors arise due to similarity between other characteristics of the speech signal. For instance, suppose that during the enrolment of a speech template for the word "four", I took a deep breath prior to saying the word, and that I took a similar deep breath prior to saying the word "process". It is quite plausible that the sound made by the deep breaths in each of the templates would be sufficiently similar for the speech recognition device to "mistake" one word for the other. The suggestion, therefore, is that speech recognition devices tend to make errors in the matching of one sound pattern to another. Recent research has been aimed at either developing more robust sound patterns and matching algorithms (see Ainsworth, 1988 for a review), or using additional sources of information to differentiate speech sounds in a given linguistic context (Allerhand, 1987).

10.6.1   User errors

Reason (1990) defines errors of intention as "mistakes" and errors of execution as "slips". Mistakes can be defined as errors at the planning level of action, specifically in terms of interpreting the situation. It is suggested that mistakes could result from a number of factors when people speak to computers. Users can have difficulties when faced with the restrictions imposed on their style of speech by some speech recognition devices; the user might repeatedly attempt to use an illegal word to issue a command; the user's response might be adversely affected by the feedback provided by the device.

The simplest type of slip would occur when words are mispronounced due to users introducing spurious noise, such as yawning, etc., into their speech, or due to environmental factors influencing their speaking, such as extreme levels of vibration. Alternatively, users could introduce pauses into their commands, as a result of being distracted by another task. The inability to pause appropriately between words can cause problems, particularly when the user is under stress and might reduce inter-word pausing (Simpson, 1986). Finally, there is an extensive literature concerned with speech errors known as "slips of the tongue" (Fromkin, 1980). Users of speech recognition devices could mispronounce items while speaking, although this has not been studied to date.

Garrett (1984) estimates that approximately 1 word in every 1000 will be distorted by some form of speech error. Examples taken from speech-based interaction with machines are classified into possible error types in Table 10.3.

Given the limited vocabularies used in speech recognition devices, it is unlikely that one would see as many types of error as would be seen in everyday conversation. However, the peculiarities of speech recognition means that some speech sounds which are perfectly acceptable in human communication can be problematic when speaking to a computer. In Chapter 11, various forms of stress are shown to have a number of effects on human performance, and one of the most commonly observed psycho-

Table 10.3   Examples of speech errors in speech-based HCI

Spoken	Required	Type of error
"John F. Kennedy"	Juliet. Foxtrot. Kilo	Illegal vocabulary
"Plus"	One	Illegal item
"Withdraw_cash"	Cash_with_receipt	Substitution of legal items
"Open_V_two"	V_2_open	Transposition
"Ten"	Ten pounds	Truncation of item

logical effects is regression to well-learned behaviors. Furthermore, speech errors can increase in frequency when the speaker is under some form of stress. For instance, Graham and Baber (1993) recorded a number of speech errors during a time-paced data entry task. The task involved entering information using the ICAO alphabet (A = alpha, B = bravo, etc.). Many of the errors took of the form of substitution of other words for individual letters, e.g., "Beta" for "Bravo", or for letter sequences, e.g., "John F Kennedy" for "Juliet Foxtrot Kilo". This suggests that speech errors, which involve violation of vocabulary constraints in using speech recognition systems, could arise because users revert to more familiar words and phrases.

It is also probable that the location and conspicuity of information on the display could influence speech errors. For instance, in one application that we were developing, it was noted that people had a tendency to say "quit" instead of "next". This was thought a little odd, until it was realized that the "quit' item was placed higher and to the left of the "next" item; it appeared that users were reading the first word on the screen. Another case of device design influencing user behavior can be found from the use of synthesized speech displays. Researchers have found that some users attempt to "mimic" the speech of the display, presumably in the expectation that this will aid in recognition (Leiser, 1989b). Thus, the feedback provided to users can influence their behavior.

When a speech recognition device has failed to correctly recognize a word spoken by the user, it is necessary to inform the user. However, there is a possibility that the user may, in turn, misinterpret the feedback supplied by the device. For instance, Usher and Baber (1989) noted that, on some occasions, users appeared to regard textual feedback as a *general* indication that something had been recognized rather than as evidence of the recognition of a *specific* item. In other words, the users failed to monitor the meaning of the word and only responded to its presence. Subsequent studies suggested that one of the reasons for the failure to monitor feedback appropriately could be due to the lack of integration between task performance and feedback monitoring. Consequently, if feedback was incorporated into the primary task display (Baber et al., 1992) or if feedback was presented in such a way as to interrupt primary task performance, e.g., through the use of synthesized speech (Frankish and Noyes, 1990), then monitoring errors could be reduced to a negligible level. These findings suggest that appropriate feedback has to be designed into the dialogue.

10.7   Conclusions

This chapter has focused on two aspects of speaking to computers: the production of speech and the process of speech-based interaction. It is proposed that an understanding of how speech is produced can lead to an appreciation of why speech recognizers make mistakes and why people often exacerbate these mistakes when they try to "help" the recognizer, e.g., by speaking the word in a different fashion. The production of speech was also considered as a form of psychomotor skill, which led to discussion of how users of speech recognition devices monitor and check the performance of the recognizer. One common form of user error is to mistake the presence of a response from the recognizer as indication that a word has been correctly recognized; in actual fact, the response only indicates that something has been recognized and the user is still required to confirm that this word is correct.

From a discussion of the nature of speech-based HCI, one can make a number of proposals as to how to engineer effective "dialogue". The notion of turn-taking and rules for interaction would lead one to conclude that it might be possible to engineer appropriate loci of turns, i.e., opportunities when a person can speak to the computer (Frohlich and Luff, 1990). However, it was noted that the application of rules could be problematic. An alternative solution would be to consider turn-taking, etc., as resources for the partners in an interaction. From the work on convergence, it is possible to move some way towards defining the most appropriate subset of possible resources from which to draw when speaking to a computer.

Following the general trend in this book, it would be very useful to begin to examine context effects of using speech technology. For instance, while research has studied how people converse with other people, there has been less work on how people converse with computers (although see, for example, Foster et al., 1993). Thus, studying the language and behavior of users of speech technology would yield answers to many of the questions that still irk system engineers, such as how will untrained users attempt to deal with misrecognitions, how will they structure queries, how much flexibility is needed in the speech system to deal with variations in the user population, etc. Finally, it was noted in Chapter 4 that human conversation need not be the most appropriate model for speech-based interaction with computers. This raises the question, what would be an appropriate model and how does such interaction occur?

10.8 Key points for practitioners

- Consider the use of speech in applications which are currently performed by other means.
- Define dialogues and vocabularies to be habitable.

- Define systems to support convergence.
- Consider the possible sources of error in the dialogue (both human and computer) and design dialogues to include error handling.

10.9   Key points for researchers

- Develop models of speech-based dialogue with computers on the basis of field studies.
- Consider the definition of rules for interaction and define how these rules will be applied in different fashions on the basis of contextual requirements.
- Consider the potential for combining speech with other devices.

Part III
Further Topics

Chapter 11   Devices for restricted environments
Chapter 12   Physical aspects of interaction device use
Chapter 13   Interaction devices at work
Chapter 14   Multimodal human–computer interaction

CHAPTER 11

Devices for restricted environments

Abstract

In this chapter, we consider the use of interaction devices in less than optimal situations. Such situations can be characterized by either permanent or temporary impairment of a person's ability to control and use specific devices. From this, we can consider ways in which task performance can be supported, through either redesign of the device, or replacement with another type of device, or redesign of the task.

11.1   Introduction

For most of the discussion in this book I have implicitly assumed that interaction devices are used for office-based applications. This is a common assumption in the HCI literature. While this assumption might reflect the majority of applications of interaction devices (at present), it does exclude two very important application domains: those in which operation is limited due to some physical constraint, and those in which operation is limited due to psychological constraint. For example, the pilot of a modern fighter aircraft, flying at speeds in excess of Mach, needs to change the radio frequency on the communications systems as new flight-zones are entered. In such a domain, operation of many interaction devices will be particularly difficult as the pilot has to cope with acceleration and vibration forces, with limited visibility and possibly with bulky clothing. Clearly, in this context, device operation is physically limited. To take another example, a person with severely limited use of the arms is effectively prevented from using a keyboard and mouse; what form of interaction device can be used to enable the use of a computer? Again, the operation of some interaction devices is physically limited. However, in both examples the physical limitations which prevent the use of some devices does not preclude the use of computers; it simply means that one needs to consider alternative technologies. While physical limitations can often be overcome through the use of appropriate technologies, there will also be situations in which psychological limitations can reduce effective use of interaction devices. I am thinking, in particular, of high levels of user stress or workload and their implications for degradations in performance, and of the problems associated with human error. As noted in Chapter 1, if one wishes to expand the range of applications of computers, it is important to consider how the applications will be used, e.g., for what tasks will the application be used? who will use it? where will it be used?

Finally, it should be noted that I have decided to exclude two significant forms of disability, visual and auditory impairment. One could argue that without vision or hearing, many users will have problems with interaction devices. However, the exclusion of these factors is an extension of the focus on interaction devices as distinct from displays. Of course, one needs some form of display to determine the success of using an interaction device and impairment to either vision or hearing can have a bearing on the choice of appropriate display, but my concern is primarily with the use of the interaction devices themselves.

11.2 Restrictions of movement

In this section two forms of restriction of movement will be considered, these will be termed permanent and temporary restriction. Temporary restrictions will arise when the person performing a task is required to wear special clothing which can limit their range of movement. For instance, large gloves can make it difficult to perform precise control actions using small controls. Permanent restrictions arise due to physical disability, and this will be the first area discussed. For the purposes of this discussion, permanent restrictions can give rise to two classes of problem: communication and psychomotor problems.

There are clearly people who may not be able to talk, gesticulate or write due to reduced motor control. Even when they are able to control some motor functions, communication can still be impaired, either frustratingly slow for the speaker or confusingly noisy for the hearer. The problems can lead to all manner of difficulties and frustration in everyday life. Darragh and Witten (1992) distinguish two categories of communication difficulties: reduction in the ability to speak, and reduction in the ability to exert motor control over physical movements, specifically with respect to writing. They propose that computer technology can be developed to serve as communication aids.

11.2.1 Communication aids

Computer equipment often seems to contain an implicit model of the user as possessing a full complement of fully functioning limbs and an unimpaired visual system (Shein et al., 1992). If there is loss, damage or difficulty in using any part of the body, then access to computer technology will be restricted. Consequently, research in this area has examined ways of using existing physical abilities of users to operate computers. However, this immediately raises a problem: there is not a single, homogeneous group of people which can be labelled "disabled" and for whom one can design and build a separate range of computers to those people labelled "normal". In order to navigate this problem, I have decided simply to consider a range of interaction devices which have been developed for use by people whose communication is restricted and plan to leave consideration of the appropriateness of the different devices to researchers and practitioners with more insight and experience than I have into the particular needs of people with different types of disability. In the context of human–computer interaction, communication will be considered in terms of issuing commands to the computer or entering (or otherwise manipulating) text which can then be used as the basis for messages transmitted by the computer.

Speech recognition systems can offer significant benefits to disabled people (Damper, 1984; Noyes et al., 1989). At quite a simple level, a speech controlled telephone dialling system could prove useful for people who normally have difficulty using the numeric keypad on the telephone (Fisher, 1986). At a higher level of complexity, speech recognizers could be used to control domestic appliances. Haigh and Clark (1988) described a system called VADAS (Voice Activated Domestic Appliance System), which uses a speaker-dependent, isolated word recognizer. VADAS has a vocabulary of 7 command words which could be extended to control up to 16 appliances. Initial trials, however, were disappointing, due mainly to the effects of noise on the signal received by a desk-mounted microphone. While a headset could have reduced many of these problems, it is difficult to imagine that all potential users would be happy to wear such a device.

In addition to using speech to issue commands, there have been proposals to produce "speech training assistance". A speech recognizer can be used as a front end to an intelligent speech trainer (Damper, 1984). Users are prompted to speak a word, and the matching process of the device will compare this with a stored set of "acceptable" pronunciations. An example of this is the "Star" system developed by the Speech Research Unit at DRA, Malvern. In a similar vein, the development of combined speech recognition and lip reading devices could provide support for speech therapy. For instance, an image processing system, with the ability to interpret variations in lip movement, has been reported by Petajan et al. (1988). This system combines a lip reading system with a speech recognizer, so that the lip reading can supplement speech recognition. While the performance was not very high (at around 90%), the concept is interesting.

The use of speech to control a "talkwriter" (see Chapter 4) could prove useful for people with restricted mobility (Stephens et al., 1988). However, the use of speech systems for prolonged periods of time could lead to problems of fatigue, particularly for disabled users (Newell, 1986). Obviously, some users of computers will be unable to articulate spoken commands with sufficient consistency to produce the appropriate computer response (although it is possible to define a vocabulary of utterances which are based on vocal sounds rather than on words *per se*). In this case, some other means of issuing commands could be used, such as entering text or pointing to objects on the visual display unit.

For users with a degree of motor control in both hands, it might be possible to effect quite minor changes to conventional keyboards in order to make them easier to use, e.g., changing the physical dimensions and operation of keys, or increasing inter-key spaces, or using guards over some sections of the keyboard. The first two proposals would simplify key pressing for users with limited targeting ability (Shein et al., 1992), while the latter is intended to minimize inadvertent key operation. At this level of design, the keyboards can also be used by primary school children, e.g., expanding key size and spacing to make key pressing easier. However, there ought to be a trade-off between what makes a device easy to use and what type of device respects a user's intelligence, i.e., if you were given what could be perceived to be a child's keyboard, how would you react?

An alternative approach to the design and development of "hard" keyboards comes in the form of "concept" keyboards, i.e., reconfigurable overlays which can be used with touch tablets (see Chapter 3). An example of this device is the "Intellikeys" keyboard (developed by Unicorn Engineering). Each user is able to reconfigure the keyboard to their requirements by modifying such features as key press duration (to prevent inadvertent operation, the user must press down a key for a specified duration in order for the character to be registered), repeat features (specifying the time period between repeated pressing of a key, to prevent inadvertent repeated keying), sequential key substitutes for dual key functions, e.g., CTRL-ALT-DEL replaced by a single keypress.

The system also incorporates a degree of predictive capability, e.g., if the user types "q" the computer will automatically add a "u". (cf. the Reactive keyboard of Darragh and Witten, 1993). Finally, the keyboard can be used to emulate a mouse, with cursor positioning using cursor keys and single and double clicking using specified keys.

Some users might be unable to use both hands, and researchers have been examining the possibility of using one-handed keyboards. The one-handed QWERTY and chord keyboards were discussed in Chapter 2. Starkson (1992) reports a seven-key chord keyboard specifically for use by people with visual and physical problems. The operation is much the same as a conventional chord keyboard; the main difference appears to lie in the color and texture of keys (five white, smooth keys for text entry, one red textured key and one blue textured key for issuing commands).

While some researchers have focused on redesigning the keyboard, others have focused on redesigning the act of typing. There are a number of products on the market for people who, although unable to move their arms, are able to exert control of their neck and head. In these products, the users have to either wear a head band on which is attached a long stick, or hold a stick in their mouth. The stick is used to press keys on a keyboard. In Chapter 4, some of the wide range of alternative pointing devices were reviewed. One thing that strikes me is how potentially time consuming and tiring it is to use devices like the head-mounted stick. One user I spoke to told me that it could take around three hours to type a couple of pages of A4, with much of the time spent either resting or trying to correct mistakes which arose from hitting the wrong key.

11.2.2 Temporary physical restrictions

I once met a human factors specialist, who works for the UK Defence Research Agency, who told me that he takes a large, padded mitten to demonstrations of new technology. When the equipment designers have put the kit through its paces, he hands them the glove and tells them to use the kit wearing the glove. The point is that "normal" operational environments for many items of military equipment are far removed from the benign surroundings of the laboratory, and normal operation is often conducted with operators whose physical performance is restricted in some fashion. By far the most common form of restriction will be produced by clothing, although different forms of restraint, such as harnesses, will also have an effect.

In Chapter 3, a taxonomy of hand–device coupling was presented. When gloves are worn, the range of grips and precision of movement is impaired. There is general agreement in the literature that wearing gloves leads to a reduction in grip strength (Sanders and McCormick, 1992). Research also tends to suggest that wearing gloves can reduce performance time and precision of movement (Oborne, 1988). However, these findings should be considered in the light of the finding that the performance decrement is related to glove type, material, resistance to slip and "snugness of fit" (Bradley, 1969).

The question of how people perform manual tasks when wearing full protective clothing has become an important issue, with the increasing number of missions to space, and with the increasing threat of chemical warfare. On one level, the human factors issues could be seen as an extension of the discussion of gloves. However, there are some additional

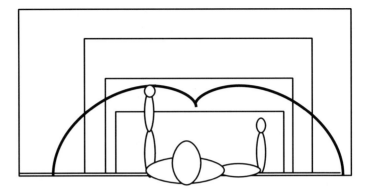

Figure 11.1   Example of a "reach envelope"

factors which need to be considered when discussing full suits, such as mobility, movement of limbs, sensation of movement, etc. As with gloves, the kinesthetic feedback that the wearer receives from moving a limb could be reduced, perhaps leading to additional demands in terms of monitoring and controlling actions.

The most obvious form of restraint which can affect performance will be a variation of the theme of seat belt or harness. Human factors specialists speak of the "reach envelope" which can be said to surround someone in a typical working posture. An example of a reach envelope is shown in Figure 11.1. Notice that there are different regions within the envelope (indicated by the four rectangles), and that reach to these regions will depend upon movement of the person. The solid black lines indicate full arm reach without movement (i.e., shoulder to finger-tip), and the rectangles illustrate regions for primary, secondary and tertiary controls. If movement is restricted then the reach envelope will be reduced.

Lovesey (1989) points out that restraints can also limit head movement, e.g., in a cockpit, and that this restriction can be exacerbated when wearing a helmet and an oxygen mask. Furthermore, the use of oxygen masks can lead to problems of reduced visibility and to disruption to speech. This latter factor has implications for the use of speech recognition systems in particular (Poock, 1980).

11.3   The effects of environmental factors on performance

When considering the relationship between the use of interaction devices and hostile environments, one can assume two broad classes of human factors issues: those pertaining to physical performance involved in holding and manipulating the devices, and those pertaining to cognitive performance involved in planning actions and interpreting feedback. In reviewing the effects of stress on pilot performance, Baber (1995) suggests that there are six broad categories of human performance which can be affected by hostile environmental factors, ranging from life-threat to physical stressors, such as noise and acceleration, and these are: psychomotor skills, memory functions, situational awareness, attention, planning, and judgement. The only one of these items which might require expansion beyond a common-sense definition of the terms is "situational awareness", which means the ability to integrate a wide range of information, from different sources, into a unified depiction of the current state of the environment.

Driskell and Salas (1991) provide a detailed review of the effects that environmental stressors have on human performance, with particular reference to military applications. Table 11.1 lists some of the principal physiological, physical, affective and psychological effects induced by adverse environmental factors.

While the issues raised in the following sections will undoubtedly gain in prominence as the number of "outdoor" computer applications increases, it must be realized that published research into the effects of environmental stressors on the use of interaction devices is scarce. Thus, much of the following is, of necessity, speculative and involves drawing inferences from published studies which can be considered analogous to the activities discussed in this book.

It is very difficult to clearly separate the effects of the different stressors on physical and cognitive performance, i.e., it is not always possible to determine whether impaired performance is related to physical effects, such as

Table 11.1   Effects of environmental factors on people

Physiological	*Physical*
● Increased heart rate	● Trembling
● Laboured breathing	● Reduced manual dexterity
● Muscular contraction	
Affective	*Psychological*
● Loss of motivation	● Increased reaction time
● Inability to act	● Reduced search efficiency
	● Fewer cues selected
	● Decreased vigilance
	● Reduction in problem solving ability
	● Performance rigidity
	● Increased errors in following procedures
	● Disruption of memory

increased tremor, or to cognitive effects, such as over compensating for the tremor.

11.3.1 Mud and snow

As computers move off the desk, out of the office and into the outside world, they are going to encounter a severe change in operating environments. Imagine that you are surveying the building of a road, that the ground is very muddy and slippery and that you have to use a portable computer to collect and process data. In addition to the computer, you are also carrying a theodolite tape measure etc. Alternatively, imagine that you are cataloguing saplings in an area of newly planted forest, once again the ground is muddy and once again you are carrying other equipment, perhaps requiring you to handle the trees as well. Finally, imagine that you are involved in conducting an ordinance survey of part of a battlefield, say in very swampy terrain.

In each of the examples, the environment will be extremely hostile to the use of computers. Of course, there are some portable computers which have acquired a reputation for their ruggedness in use in these types of terrains, such as the Husky Hunter. However, my point in proposing these scenarios is as much to do with the tasks for which the computer will be used as how well it will withstand the mud, etc. If the portable computer employs a keyboard for data entry, then it is feasible that, within a very short space of time, the keys will become clogged with mud. Of course, this risk could be minimized with some form of protective cover, but that will influence keying performance. Furthermore, the computer will need to be positioned to allow typing, perhaps the user will have to engage in the frustrating business of using a QWERTY keyboard one-handed (although as we saw in Chapter 2, there have been some efforts to develop a one-handed QWERTY keyboard). System designers might decide on an alternative, for example speech, or a pen-based system. They might decide to go one step further and remove the need for an interaction device, e.g., using some form of intelligent measuring and sensing equipment which is pointed at the item of interest and some data presented to users. However, despite the possibility of "automatic devices", in all of the examples given, one would assume that there would be a need for the user to amend the data or to add comments to it. Thus, it does not appear plausible to eliminate the human entirely from the process.

The properties of the environment can also have an impact on performance. These properties include noise and vibration levels, temperature, etc. In general, the impact of these variables will be greater on the human than the device. However, a basic assumption in this book is that one should consider the total human–device system within the context of operation in order to understand the effects of such variables.

11.3.2   Noise

The effects of noise on human performance have been a subject which has perennially exercised human factors specialists and psychologists. It is worth noting that there are several characteristics of noise which can have a bearing on performance, e.g., whether the noise is regular and predictable or whether it is sporadic and unpredictable, whether the noise results from impact (such as in a drop-forge press) or whether it is impulsive (such as a gunshot), the frequency spectrum of the noise, the duration of exposure, etc. Much of the research on noise has tended to focus on the intensity of the noise. Broadly speaking, early research suggested that high-intensity noise, i.e., in excess of 100 dBA, tended to impair performance. However, subsequent studies demonstrate either no effect or the opposite effect (Kryter, 1994). One popular explanation for these results employs the Yerkes–Dodson law, as shown in Figure 11.2.

The graph in Figure 11.2 shows that performance is related to arousal in such a fashion as to allow the prediction that, if arousal shifts from optimal levels then performance will deteriorate. Thus, if a person is under-aroused, e.g., bored, then performance will decrease, and likewise if the person is

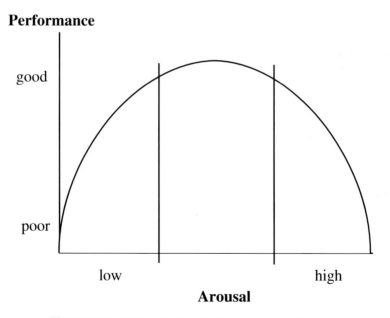

Figure 11.2   Yerkes–Dodson Performance Arousal curve

over-aroused, e.g., under very high workload or stress, then performance will also decrease. The effects of workload and stress on performance will be discussed in Section 11.4. For the purposes of this section, it is necessary to appreciate that arousal can be caused by environmental properties, such as noise or temperature. From Figure 11.2, one can propose that there will be "optimal" levels of noise for performance. Stokes (1993) reports a study in which participants were asked to track a moving target using a rate-controlled joystick and perform a memory task, while being exposed to white noise at an intensity of 90 dBA. The results showed that, in noise, tracking accuracy was reduced by 15%, when compared with performance in quiet. Lévy-Leboyer (1989) showed that noise tended to impair performance on fine motor tasks, while leading to improvements in performance on tasks requiring physical effort.

The results of these studies can be interpreted in terms of the performance–arousal hypothesis. However, there is a major problem with this hypothesis; it is difficult to falsify, in that all results can find an interpretation from the Yerkes–Dodson law. This means that, although one can provide a hypothesis prior to the experiment, if the results do not fit the hypothesis advanced they could fit the opposing hypothesis, depending on how one reads the relationship in Figure 11.2. Furthermore, while one can find evidence to support this effect when considering high intensities of noise, it is more difficult to find evidence for low levels of noise. For example, while decreasing intensity from a high to moderate level (e.g., 108 dBA to 89 dBA) can lead to improvement in performance, there is little reason to suppose that reducing from a moderate level to a low level (e.g., 73 dBA to 59 dBA) will also lead to a change in performance.

In recent years, the effects of noise have been considered in terms of the coping strategy that people adopt (Smith, 1989). People deal with noise through the adoption of specific task-performance strategies. Noise seems to encourage people to concentrate on surface aspects of information rather than deeper aspects (Hockey, 1979). Noise tends to encourage dominant responses, rather than the appropriate ones (Broadbent, 1971). Noise tends to lead to a reduction in flexibility of response (Smith, 1989). However, appropriate strategies can be developed which act as buffers to the detrimental effects of noise, e.g., well-learned tasks do not seem to be as badly affected by noise as tasks which are either very complex or very new to the performer. Often, it is the "new" tasks, encountered for the first time for instance during battle conditions, which would be most susceptible to noise effects, and yet which would require immediate and appropriate response.

A final point to note in this section is the effect of noise on communication and the production of speech. Communication in noise can be made difficult due to masking of the speech signal by other auditory signals, or due to loss in hearing sensitivity on the part of listeners. It is possible to determine the relationship between noise level and communication efficiency using the articulation index, which basically indicates the relationship between the spectra of the speech signal, thresholds of hearing and the presence of competing noise.

Noise can affect the production of speech via the Lombard effect, which basically describes the phenomena by which people raise their voice levels in response to increases in ambient noise (Junqua, 1995). The Lombard effect is of particular concern to the design of speech recognition systems in that it might cause speech patterns to deviate markedly from the stored representations.

11.3.3 Vibration

As with noise, there are several factors which can influence the relationship between vibration and performance, such as the direction of motion which causes the vibration (horizontal, vertical, etc.), the frequency and intensity of the vibration, the duration, etc. In this section, in order to simplify matters, I shall use the general term vibration without giving any information regarding the properties of the vibration. Interested readers are advised to consult the excellent handbook by Griffin (1990).

One would anticipate that vibration will affect physical performance, and there is reasonable evidence to support this view. Motor performance will deteriorate under vibration (Lewis and Griffin, 1980). This leads to, amongst other things, a decrement in pointing activity when using pointing devices in tanks (Jensen, 1989). However, the decrement can be reduced by stabilizing the arm, using an armrest, or changing the design of the device used (Parsons, 1994).

One might further suppose that vibration will influence visual performance, and this seems to be the case (Lewis and Griffin, 1980; Furnass and Lewis, 1978), although the decrements relate to a complex combination of object size, vibration direction and whether it is the object, viewer or both which is vibrated.

It is more difficult to determine whether cognitive performance is affected by vibration. Reaction time appears to be relatively unaffected by vibration (Hornick, 1962; Schoenberger, 1974), although the perceptual component of tasks might be affected as noted above. Thus, despite ongoing research it is fair to say that broad theories of how vibration affects human performance are somewhat less forthcoming in this area than for noise research.

The effects of vibration on speech have been reviewed by Baber and Noyes (1996). Basically, the principal effects can be related to the displacement of the speech production apparatus under vibration, which leads to a "shakiness" in the speech and to changes in the frequency characteristics of the speech. It does appear that vibration (within limits) can be accommodated by current speech technology.

11.3.4 Heat

As one might expect, there is much variation in the results of research into the effects of heat on performance (Kobrick and Fine, 1983). Much of the research into the effects of heat on human performance has tended to reach the conclusion that heat will only have a significant effect on performance if it results in a change in body temperature. For instance, Colquhoun and Goldman (1972) found that performance on a signal detection task (i.e., detecting auditory signals against "noise") was affected when ambient temperature was increased to 38°C. The main effect was the increase in confidence of detection, with little effect on detection rate, i.e., the participants were more confident that they had detected a signal even when they had not improved their rate of detection. In another study, Wyon (1974) found that an increase in temperature led to a decrease in keying rate for typing activity. These findings suggest that heat can act as an arouser, modifying people's performance around optimal levels (see Figure 11.2 above). However, as with the noise research reported above, there is some evidence that the effects of the arousal can be mediated by the strategy people adopt. This is especially evident when considering the effects of cold on performance. Meese et al. (1989) have shown that when ambient temperature falls to 6°C, reaction time slows down, hesitation increases and performance is less risky than in warmer conditions. However, this finding only occurs when people are not trained in the task. If people have been trained prior to exposure, their performance does not appear to be affected. Thus, training can be used to limit the effects of variation in temperature on performance. Obviously, in order for training to be effective it is necessary to know in advance the various task demands which will be made on individuals during their work. It is a problem with high stress work domains that, by definition, the task demands will remain unpredictable.

11.3.5 Acceleration

Human performance seems to deteriorate under high acceleration (von Gierke et al., 1991). The principal problems seem to arise in situations in excess of 5 Gz. Manual control, particularly in terms of fine motor activity, requires an increase in effort to perform manual activity. This also leads to an increase in subjective ratings of workload. Reaction time performance also seems to be affected at these levels, although it is possible for individuals to adapt over time.

There will also be problems in terms of visual perception, particularly in tasks requiring fast and accurate reading of displays. Furthermore, in excess of 5 Gz, there is a greater possibility for pilots to black out, and in excess of 6 Gz there are disruptions to memory, particularly to immediate recall, and the ability to retain and follow procedures.

11.3.6 Conclusions

Even a cursory tour of the literature on the effects of environmental stressors upon human performance illustrates that the research contains some contradictions. This makes the provision of ready-made solutions very difficult. There are, of course, good reasons for the problems, e.g., the relationship between task demands and individual performance will be as much a function of individual characteristics as the environment in which the task is to be performed. However, the main point in raising these issues in this chapter was to extend the notion of operating context on interaction devices to encompass domains such as aviation, military, maritime and transport systems. If interaction devices are to continue moving off the desk and into other working environments, then designers need to consider the potential hazards of these "other environments". It is proposed that this consideration should lead not simply to making devices more rugged and able to withstand the environmental stresses, but also to a greater awareness of the relationship between person and device and the extent to which the performance of this "system" can be supported.

Table 11.2 summarizes some of the conclusions which can be drawn from this review. Table 11.2 shows three data entry devices and three pointing devices. In general, the effects of the environmental stressors are to reduce performance (—). However, in many cases there is insufficient evidence to draw a conclusion (?), and in one case there is probably no effect (0).

Table 11.2 Interaction devices and environmental factors

Device	Noise	Vibration	Acceleration	Heat	Mud/snow
Keyboard	?	?	?	—	—
Pen	?	?	?	?	—
Speech	—	—	—	?	0
Mouse	?	—	?	?	—
Trackball	?	—	?	?	—
Joystick	—	—	?	?	—

11.4   Psychological restrictions

Some aspects of psychological limitations have been considered in relation
to the effects of environmental factors, such as effects involving memory
and perception. In this section, attention is turned to the broader issues of
stress and workload, and how these can impact on device use and performance. There is growing evidence to link work-related upper limb disorders to occupational stress (see Chapter 12). This link has been recognized
in recent regulations on work with computers, and has led to a requirement
that all computer-based work should involve adequate rest breaks and
should allow an adequate range of tasks for workers. This is discussed
further in Chapter 13, together with the implications for managing
computer-based work.

In addition to stress resulting from the demands and pressures of work,
there are also forms of stress which result from perceived or actual threats
to the individual. Rather than attempting to define stress in this section, I
will focus on research and evidence which relates various forms of stress to
performance.

11.4.1   Stress and performance

Marshall (1947) notes that anecdotes from World War II suggest that
during combat a percentage of soldiers failed to discharge their weapons.
As is the case with anecdotal evidence, although this may be an over-
statement, it does contain an element of truth. Extreme stress would
seem to disrupt performance of manual tasks.

Davies and Parasuraman (1982) have shown how even quite moderate
levels of anxiety can impair performance on tasks requiring short term
memory. Naturally the applicability of such research is limited by requirements to obey ethical codes of practice in the conduct of psychological
experiments. However, a series of studies conducted by Berkun (1964) for
the US Army seems to have circumvented such issues of ethical experi-
mentation. Berkun (1964) placed soldiers in a number of "threatening"
situations while they were completing specific tasks. For example, soldiers
were asked to complete an insurance form while flying in an aircraft, and
were then led to believe that the plane was about to crash. The effect of
such stress was to reduce performance on tasks utilizing short-term memory, or which required the soldiers to follow procedures. However, Berkun's
(1964) data also revealed that the effects of stress were far less pronounced
on soldiers who had several years of experience. Wickens et al. (1991) found
that judgements requiring retrieval of information from long-term memory
were relatively unimpaired by stress. Thus, stress seems to result in impair-

ments in performance for inexperienced people (for that task domain) drawing on relatively recently acquired information. Fitts and Seeger (1953) have suggested that a characteristic of behavior under stress is a reversion to well-learned behavior patterns which are compatible with the situation in which one finds oneself. This implies that while some of the key problems resulting from stress can be reduced through the use of adequate training and the design of systems, one may not be able to deal with reversion to well-learned behaviors under stress.

11.4.2   Workload and performance

There are many definitions of workload, each definition emphasizing the particular theoretical and methodological perspective of its author. A popular approach to the study of mental workload is to consider mental capacity in terms of a limited pool of resources from which information processing can draw (see Figure 11.3). If too many demands are placed on the pool then there will be negative consequences for the distribution of the resources. This supports the common-sense view of workload as having too many things to do at once or not being able to attend to all task demands at a time. In contrast to this notion, however, is the finding that people can often perform several tasks at once, e.g., consider the multiple tasks involved in driving a car. Thus, some tasks compete for resources, while other combinations of tasks can share resources. This suggests that there is

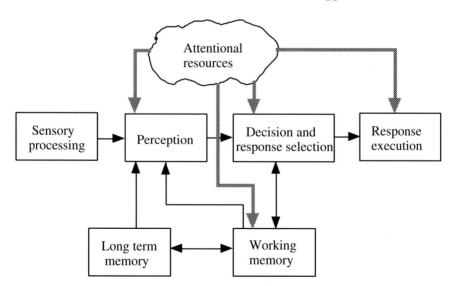

Figure 11.3 Attentional resources and stages of processing (from Wickens, 1992, *Engineering Psychology and Human Performance*, p. 17, Harper Collins)

some mechanism which determines the allocation of resource to particular information-processing tasks. Wickens (1992) proposes three principles of resource allocation: cooperation, confusion and conflict.

In general, tasks which use similar information-processing routines can cooperate in the performance of a task. For instance, a common finding is that simultaneous performance of two tasks involving tapping rhythms can be achieved relatively easily if the tasks share a common rhythm, but are more difficult to combine if they employ different rhythms (Klapp, 1981b). However, it is also evident that cooperation can be enhanced through training and practice. For instance, a skilled drummer can combine several rhythms played with hands and feet.

While pairing similar tasks can lead to cooperation, it can also lead to increasing demands on a particular resource. If one accepts the proposal that different types of information are processed using different processing codes, e.g., verbal and spatial (Baddeley, 1986), then it is possible to predict that two tasks requiring the same processing code will lead to either confusion or conflict. In the case of confusion, consider listening to two spoken messages; not only is this a difficult task, but also some of the information in one message might be interpreted as belonging to the other message.

There is some agreement that compatibility can reduce the detrimental effects of workload. For instance, in tasks involving a high level of visual activity, it might be possible to reduce demands by using the "free" speech channel to "off-load" some of the demands (Baber, 1991). In terms of interaction devices, one can offer two conclusions from this brief review. First, judicious pairing of devices can lead to the possibility of multi-task performance. This proposal is explored in Chapter 14. Second, appropriate pairing of devices can allow workload to be reduced. In practice, this often leads to calls for the introduction of speech technology into the operating environment, e.g., the cockpit. However, without full exploration of the task demands in the environment and without full consideration of alternative solutions to the problem of workload, one might make matters worse rather than better. For example, there might already be a high level of verbal communication in the environment, and introducing speech to reduce spatial demands may only shift the locus of demands to verbal tasks.

11.5 Discussion

As with the results of the research into environmental factors and performance, there is not a clear-cut picture which describes stress and workload and their effects on performance. However, it is possible to propose a few tentative conclusions. For instance, the capacity of working memory appears to be reduced by stress and this might explain why people tend to concentrate on a few items of information rather than the total available information. If this is the case, then one might anticipate a narrowing of attention onto information which the person deems "important". This can also lead to people focusing their attention on some of the tasks they are supposed to perform. Such a strategy can, of course, lead to the person missing important information or failing to perform certain tasks. In addition to reduced capacity of working memory and narrowing of attention, there appears to be a tendency for people to become more "risky" in their response to stimuli, i.e., trading speed of performance for accuracy in many situations.

As far as the use of interaction devices is concerned it is proposed that one needs to consider how best to integrate devices into the range of tasks being performed. This will involve not only the integration of the device into the total system, but also consideration of feedback to users. For instance, Baber et al. (1992) show that, for an application using speech to navigate through a series of pages of information, feedback could be most effectively presented via the use of highlighting within the overview diagrams than through the use of textual feedback.

11.6 Key points for practitioners

- Consider the environment in which the system will eventually be used: who will be using it, under what conditions and for what purpose.
- Consider the capacities and capabilities of the users, in terms of possible temporary and/or permanent restrictions.
- Design to exploit compatibility and to allow well-learned responses to equipment (rather than assuming that humans are infinitely adaptable).

11.7 Key points for researchers

- Define and consider the possible stressors which will have a bearing on user performance.
- Develop models of human performance with interaction devices under different types of stress.
- Consider whether the effects of these stressors can be compensated, by training or by redesign of the system.
- Consider the requirements of the different users who will have access to the system.

CHAPTER 12

Physical aspects of interaction device use

Abstract

There have been many reports of problems relating to the use of computers in the workplace, with a growing number of law suits being taken by individuals over work-related strains and injuries and an increasing amount of legislation to counter these problems. In this chapter, consideration is given to the problems and their possible causes, with attention given to the possible role of interaction devices as causative factors.

12.1 Introduction

One of the main domains in which the introduction of computers has been widespread is the office. Computers have revolutionized the ways in which information is collected, stored and processed. Landauer (1995) noted that, during the 1960s, the comparative increases in productivity for industry was over 80% but less than 5% for office work. Thus, efforts have been made to improve the performance and productivity of office work. However, it is becoming increasingly apparent that computerization of office work is not delivering a return on investment to the extent that had been hoped (Forester, 1989). Not only do there appear to be problems associated with productivity, there is also growing concern over the potential health problems associated with using computers. These problems range from occupational stress to visual fatigue and discomfort to musculoskeletal problems. This chapter will focus exclusively on the latter class. Readers interested in discovering the broader issues involved in health problems associated with computer-based work are advised to consult Grandjean (1987) or Cakir et al. (1980).

12.2   Musculoskeletal problems and office work

Work-related injuries, stemming from poor working conditions and posture, have been scientifically studied since the mid-nineteenth century. In recent years, there has been widespread interest in the possible relationships between work posture and musculoskeletal problems of keyboard operators. Early research found that people whose work involved keyboard operation and who remained in the same position for prolonged periods of time concentrating on a single activity, tended to present a higher incidence of reports of tiredness than operators whose work involved movement and variety (Dainoff, 1982). The earliest reports of physical, or musculoskeletal, discomfort experienced by computer operators came in the mid-1970s. For instance, Duncan and Ferguson (1974) demonstrated that the constrained postures required in computer operation led to an increase in reports of discomfort.

During the 1980s, a consensus of opinion began to emerge concerning possible relationships between keyboard operation and musculoskeletal problems, with a range of definable symptoms linking work posture to specific parts of the body, i.e., neck, shoulders, arms and wrists, and the lower back (Hünting et al., 1981; Carter and Banister, 1994; Dainoff, 1982). However, the causes of these problems are still the subject of a great deal of debate. There appear to be three groups of contributory factors for these injuries (Jeyeratnam et al., 1989):

1. Task-related factors: these factors include aspects of workstation and furniture design and use, work posture, task design and factors related to workload and movement.
2. Non-task-related factors: in some instances musculoskeletal problems can have roots in physical factors outside the task domain, for example arising from injuries from sports and accidents, or from the general physical condition of the operator (with age and biological factors contributing to the symptoms), or from some source of current emotional stress outside of the work environment.
3. Psycho-social factors: certain social factors, e.g., media campaigns on the topic of "repetitive strain injury", may validate or help to identify existing symptoms or lead to the creation of spurious symptoms.

While these three areas appear to represent quite different phenomena, it is important to bear in mind that musculoskeletal problems are more likely the result of a combination of contributory factors rather than be traceable to a single cause (Pheasant, 1995). Thus, although there are definable symptoms relating work to musculoskeletal problems, it is no easy matter to determine which are causative factors and which are contributory factors. This problem is further compounded by the continued problems related to labeling the condition, e.g., using the term "RSI".

12.2.1 Does repetitive strain injury exist?

Over the past few years, compensation for work-related injuries has risen dramatically, both in the US and in the UK. For instance, in 1992, the US Bureau of Labor Statistics estimated that reports of work-related injuries in the office had more than doubled each year from 1989 to 1991. Recent court cases in the UK have seen well-respected companies such as Ford and British Telecom (BT) paying compensation running to many thousands of pounds to employees suffering the consequences of poor working conditions and practices. However, some people question whether RSI exists as a physical condition or whether it is a convenient fiction with which to cover all manner of work-related discontent and grievances.[12.1] To a certain extent, this attitude is shared by both doctors and ergonomists, e.g., many ergonomists would share the claim that RSI is an acronym that describes a phenomenon rather than a medical condition.

The key problem with the term "RSI" is that many of the symptoms associated with the conditions rely solely on subjective reports with no clinical signs of abnormality. Thus, it is often impossible to define RSI as distinct from stress, fatigue, musculoskeletal injury or discomfort. While the status of the term RSI is still highly contentious, the symptoms which people describe under its aegis are very real, as is illustrated by the following quotation.

> I started getting RSI symptoms when I was industrial editor in the autumn of 1989 . . . tremendously sharp pains in my shoulder as though I had pulled a muscle. It was difficult to do things like put my coat on, but it was mainly awful when I was using the keyboard or writing. Then it spread into my back, a throbbing ache over my right shoulder blades. The pain travelled down my left side, into my wrists, thumbs, the ridges of flesh on my hands.
>
> [Dodsworth, 1992]

While an increasing number of people question whether we should use the term "RSI", the problems described in the above quotation must strike even the most unsympathetic of readers as being particularly debilitating for the person involved. The question, therefore, is can one provide a more explicit and acceptable set of terms to describe the musculoskeletal problems which could be associated with work with computers?

[12.1] In the UK, an infamous case involving claims for compensation for "RSI" was dismissed by the judge, who argued that the claimant was imagining the symptoms, that the problems were all in the mind.

12.3   Work-related upper limb disorder

The ergonomics literature has tended to use the term work-related upper limb disorder to describe the sort of problems raised by Dodsworth (1992) quoted above. In very broad terms, we can say that work-related upper limb disorder might occur when forces placed on a tissue, while not large enough to cause sudden failure of the tissue, can potentially produce some functional impairment or trauma in the tissue, providing the forces are exerted with sufficiently high frequency of repetition. From this definition, one can see that such disorders may be caused by almost any activity involving repeated, rapid movement, be it from work, sport or leisure.

With reference to office work, the repetitive action of touchtyping with little or no rest breaks, coupled with an uncomfortable posture, could lead to an increased risk of injury to wrists, hands, arms and shoulders (Grandjean, 1987). The injury would be likely to manifest itself as inflammation in the tendons and muscles of the limb grouping (Kurpa et al., 1980); specifically, in typing this may be trauma to tendons, nerves and muscles in hands, wrists, arms and shoulders.

12.4   Surveys of computer operators

In this section, a selection of some of the growing number of field surveys of computer users will be presented in order to discuss some of the major causes of problems related to computer-based work. The surveys cover a range of computer use, i.e., programming, data entry and word processing.

12.4.1   Cakir et al. (1980)

Cakir et al. (1980) surveyed 250 computer users in offices in Berlin. The operations considered were data acquisition, programming, editing and supervision. Data was also reported for staff who did not use computers. The first set of questions in the survey concerned current medical treatment. Cakir et al. (1980) report that while 18% of the editors were receiving treatment for back problems, this figure rose to 25% for programmers, 35% for supervisors and 47% for data acquisition operators. Furthermore, length of service seemed to have a bearing on treatment, e.g., of the operators with less than 2 years experience some 27% were receiving treatment, but of those with over 5 years experience this figure rose to 51%.

Respondents were also asked to complete a work stress questionnaire. While less than 20% of the programmers reported problems, this figure rose to 50% for the supervisors and to 70% for the data acquisition operators. The most common symptoms were back and neck problems. These figures should be considered in terms of the staff who did not use computers, around 50% of whom reported back problems and 25% reported neck problems. However, the study also suggests that data acquisition operators, whose work was repetitive and intensive, were around 20% more likely to report musculoskeletal problems than programmers or editors, and 10% more likely than clerical workers to report these symptoms.

In addition to musculoskeletal problems, the study also indicated a high prevalence of headaches as a generalized response to working conditions. Around 45% of the data acquisition operators reported headaches, with 30% of supervisors and less than 10% for the programmers.

12.4.2   Hünting et al. (1981)

Hünting et al. (1981) surveyed 295 people. 53 data-entry operators, 109 word-processor operators, 78 typists and 55 "traditional office" staff. The survey comprised a postural pain questionnaire, medical examinations, postural recording, work satisfaction questionnaire and measurement of skin temperature while working.

The results suggest that the traditional office staff have the lowest incidence of problems, less than 2% reported problems. The data-entry staff reported the highest number of problems, especially in the back, the upper arm, shoulder and right arm. The word-processing operators reported similar problems (although at a lower incidence) and the type-writer users reported problems with the left arm and the back.

Following the survey results, the medical examination suggested that people whose work involved the use of a keyboard, either for a typewriter or a computer, reported far higher occurrence of pain in the neck–arm–shoulder regions and also reported problems associated with pain and discomfort when moving the head. Furthermore, data-entry operators had the lowest skin temperature (and the highest sensitivity to neck–arm–shoulder pain). One can assume a relationship between hand temperature and blood flow, compression of the arteries and nerve tracks in the neck and shoulder regions leading to reduced blood-flow and to increased sensitivity.

Hünting et al. (1981) conclude that their results are related to the work activity performed and to the "unnatural" posture which the work setting requires of the operators. For instance, the incidence of reports of pain (from both survey and medical examination) rose steeply when the angle of ulnar abduction exceeded 20° (i.e., when the hand bends upward to reach the keyboard, rather than having the fingers rest on or about the keys). The main finding was that work involving keyboard use tends to lead to constrained posture, which, in turn, leads to reports of pain. Equipment design and lack of rest breaks exacerbates these problems.

The authors suggest that the problems could be reduced using a three prong attack: ensure that the equipment is fully adjustable; ensure that appropriate physical support is provided; ensure that work is designed to permit diversity of movement and rest-breaks.

12.4.3 Jeyeratnam et al. (1989)

In this study, 694 users were surveyed at three different sites (with 672 actually returning the questionnaire). All respondents were classified as computer operators and no indication was given of the type of work they performed. The study indicates that discomfort is experienced in three regions of the body: 60% of respondents reported discomfort in the neck, 54% reported discomfort in the low back, and 43% reported discomfort in the shoulders.

There was evidence to suggest that the amount of time spent working with computers had a bearing on reports of discomfort. Significant differences were found between operators who worked 2 to 3 hours per day at a computer and those who worked in excess of 4 hours per day.

A significant difference was observed between the three ethnic groups comprising the study, with Chinese operators reporting lower incidences of back and neck pain than the Malay and Indian respondents. The authors conclude that this latter finding is predictable as most of the equipment used was designed for western workers rather than the people who were using it.

12.4.4 Conclusions

From these surveys one can see that musculoskeletal complaints are common among computer users. A notable minority, i.e., 25% to 35% of computer users experience some form of discomfort during their work. However, it is important to maintain a sense of perspective and note that such complaints are found in other types of work (Carter and Banister, 1994) so the reported problems are not necessarily peculiar to computer design. Further, pain or discomfort do not, of themselves, constitute disability (Waddell, 1987), i.e., while people report the symptoms they do not necessarily seek to remove themselves from the workplace or complain that the pain prevents them from working (although see Dodsworth, 1992 above). Finally, computer operators are generally more likely to report pain rather than disability arising from musculoskeletal disorders. From the surveys discussed above, the most common sites of pain are the back, shoulders, and neck, with problems in the wrists, arms and hands being of lower frequency. From the growing ergonomics literature pertaining to these problems, it is possible to suggest a set of factors which could contribute to the reports of pain.

Suboptimal working postures have been shown to be a significant causative factor in such problems as myalgia and occupational cramp. The postures that people adopt when working can be related to the equipment that they use and the work environment in which they perform their tasks.

> keyboard design and work height lead to ill advantaged postures, repeated adoption of which gives rise in some operators to recurrent symptoms of incoordination and muscle pain.
>
> [Duncan and Ferguson, 1974]

Consider the "typical" posture shown in Figure 12.1. The typist is sitting on an inappropriate chair (see below), and is leaning to one side as he types. The spine is clearly not straight, but slightly curved and the right shoulder is lower than the left shoulder. Continued sitting in this posture can lead to discomfort in a number of regions, notably the lower back and shoulders.

It is known that, while it can provide a relatively stable posture, sitting can lead to an increase in the force applied to the intervertebral disks of the spine (Sauter, 1984). This increases the tension on the ligaments and muscles of the back, especially in the lumbar region. Thus, prolonged

Figure 12.1   Poor posture

periods of seated work can be related to reports of aches and pain in the lower back; these aches and pains can be exacerbated if the lumbar region is not adequately supported.

It is often assumed that people need to keep a straight back while using keyboards. However, there is little ergonomic, orthopedic or physiological evidence to support this assertion and little reason to believe that people naturally adopt this posture (Mandal, 1981). Recent research tends to fall into at least two camps: one espouses that chairs should be designed to allow people to adopt a backward leaning posture (Dainoff and Mark, 1987), the other argues that the chair should be designed to slope forward and down (Mandal, 1981). Indeed, this latter proposal has led to the design of the Balans chair, on which people effectively adopt a kneeling posture, although many people report that this posture is uncomfortable (Life and Pheasant, 1984). Broadly speaking, the advice tends to be for chairs to be adjustable, to allow individuals to sit comfortably and place their feet squarely on the floor, and for chairs to provide adequate lumbar support. Pheasant (1988), for instance, provides data on the optimal limits for height, adjustment, lumbar support, arm rests, etc.

The relationship between chair, desk and other equipment can lead to people adopting awkward or uncomfortable postures (Duncan and Ferguson, 1974). Combining such postures with the relative lack of movement associated with computer-based work can exacerbate musculoskeletal problems (Kilbom, 1987) and lead to physiological problems such as those related to reduced blood circulation. Many of these problems can be dealt with effectively through repositioning of equipment, through adjustment of furniture, e.g., chair height, and through ensuring that breaks are taken at regular intervals (Grandjean, 1987).

Figure 12.2 captures some of the complexity of the relationship between factors which could contribute to "stress" at work. There will be a number of different stresses arising from deadlines, quality standards, task complexity, supervisory practices, etc., which are mediated by the individual. It is, of course, important to note that the manner in which these "pressures" are dealt with varies tremendously between individuals. Figure 12.2 is used, in this context, to provide an overview of the factors. While the various task, performance and environment factors contribute to the perceived work demands (and will be discussed further in Chapter 13), there are also objective work demands, such as the quantity of work and its duration, which can create the potential for muscular and psychological demands on the individual. While this is not the place to debate the relative merits of different models of stress, it is plausible to assume that when these demands exceed certain thresholds the individual will experience some form of stress. The muscular demands, which are of interest in this chapter, can be exacerbated by poor workplace design (as discussed above), poor equipment design, and poor equipment use. These latter factors will be

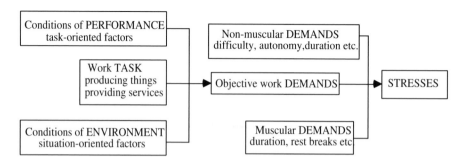

Figure 12.2 Work analysis description of factors contributing to stress (reproduced with permission from Rohmert, 1985, *Ergonomics* **28**, 1115–1134, Taylor & Francis)

considered in the remainder of this chapter, with reference to a range of interaction devices.

12.5 Keyboard-related problems

Even cursory observation of groups of people involved in typing will suggest that the "typical" typing posture involves a rotation of the forearms and wrists towards the center of the body with a corresponding lateral deviation of the hands (Carter and Banister, 1994). This is partly because the linear arrangement of the keys requires the hands to be placed closer together than the elbows (Ilg, 1987). From this observation, it is possible to propose that the wrists will be placed in ulnar deviation, placing strain on wrists, forearms and the shoulders. If we add to these possible problems the fact that people have a tendency to sit below optimal height, i.e., assuming that optimal height places the elbows level with the center row of the keyboard, then a further complication will arise from the extenstion of the wrists to allow hands to reach the keyboard (see Figure 12.3). Thus, in order to reduce complaints of pain, it is necessary to reposition the upper body relative to the keyboard, firstly by ensuring that the seated elbow height equals the center row height, and secondly by placing the forearms perpendicular to the keyboard (Grandjean, 1987). While the first proposal might only require a simple adjustment in chair height, the second requires a radical rethink of keyboard design.

12.5.1 Keyboard design

In Chapter 2, some of the alternatives to standard linear keyboards were discussed; many of the alternatives involve splitting the keyboard into two

Figure 12.3 Wrist extension during typing

halves and rotating these halves at an angle to each other (see, for example, Figure 2.3). The obvious questions are, does such a radical redesign have any benefits for the well-being of the user, and will the benefits related to well-being have consequences for typing performance?

Grandjean (1987) reports the relative levels of electrical activity in the muscles of the shoulder (using electromyography), when working in different postures. The postures are related primarily to the position of the keyboard's center row relative to the typist's seated elbow height. From these EMG studies, it would appear that ulnar abduction of the hand (related to different postures) can lead to an increase in muscle activity.

Using a keyboard which reduces ulnar abduction might, therefore, reduce muscle activity. Keyboards like the one shown in Figure 2.3 reduce ulnar abduction from around 20° to around 10° (Grandjean, 1987). This, in turn, leads to a reduction in muscle activity (Zipp et al., 1983). Thus, the current crop of "ergonomic keyboards", which split the keyboard and angle the two halves, would appear to offer benefits over standard keyboards in terms of reduction in muscle activity.

It was noted in Chapter 2 that not only have keyboards been split, but some have also been contoured to follow the shape of the human hand (Klockenberg, 1926). Gerard et al. (1994) evaluated a keyboard produced by the Kinesis Corporation. They found that use of the contoured keyboard led to significant reductions in muscle activity during typing, relative to a standard keyboard. While they found similar levels of accuracy for the two keyboard types, they found a lower level of typing speed for the Kinesis (e.g., mean typing speed for the standard keyboard was 73 words per minute whereas mean typing speed for the Kinesis keyboard was 53 words per minute). However, it should be noted that this study employed a relatively small sample, i.e., six people, and drew the sample from a biased population, i.e., professional typists who had an average of 26 years' typing experience using keyboards with a conventional QWERTY layout and design. Given the relationship between keyboard arrangement and typing skill, discussed in Chapter 7, it would not be surprising to find performance differences, especially when one considers the possibility of negative transfer of training (when training and experience in using one product interferes with performance when using another product). Furthermore, given that typing is a skill which requires a considerable period of training, e.g., in the order of 40 hours, and Gerard et al.'s (1994) study lasted only 2 hours, it is, perhaps, interesting that typists could reach almost three-quarters of their normal typing speed when using the alternative design. Finally, it might be that the alternative design, by altering the spatial relationship between keys, requires more travel between keypresses and would result in slower typing performance.

12.5.2   Keyboard layout

It was noted in Chapter 2 that there are numerous problems associated with the QWERTY layout, and that Dvorak (1943) claimed that the QWERTY keyboard was the worst possible. In order to appreciate why Dvorak made such a claim, it is necessary to consider the relative loading on each hand while typing. From Table 12.1, one can see that the QWERTY layout overloads the typist's left hand, even though most people are right-handed. It also overloads the weakest fingers, presumably due to the need to operate the shift, shift lock, and backspace keys. Furthermore, much of the typing activity performed on the QWERTY layout is performed using the left-hand. In Chapter 7, it was noted that keying speeds are faster if one can alternate between two hands.

In Chapter 2, some of the alternatives to the QWERTY layout were considered. However, many of the musculoskeletal problems relating to typing are probably due more to work regime and posture than specifically to do with the force required to press keys. Nevertheless, the QWERTY layout coupled with the traditional linear arrangement of keys can be assumed to encourage certain postures, and these postures have been related to musculoskeletal discomfort in the preceding sections.

Table 12.1 Relative loadings on hands when typing with different keyboard arrangements (given as percentages) (data from Oborne, 1988)

Finger	Keyboard arrangement	
	QWERTY	DVORAK
Left hand		
Index	37	14.2
Middle	33	12.8
Ring	16	8.8
Little	14	8.1
Total load on left hand	54	44
Right hand		
Index	46	18.5
Middle	18	15.3
Ring	32	13.4
Little	4	8.9
Total load on right hand	46	56

12.6 Mouse-related problems

Many writers have suggested that mice are trouble free, as far as musculoskeletal problems are concerned, suggesting that working with the mouse allows users to change posture easily (Foley et al., 1990; Dix et al., 1993). These assumptions have passed into computer-lore with little or no questioning. However, in recent surveys of office staff who are using windows-based software, we have noted a high incidence of reports of musculoskeletal problems relating to the right wrist and shoulder; in many of these cases the mouse is positioned at a distance from the keyboard (Noyes et al., 1994). Furthermore, Newsome (1995) has suggested that the average user of a mouse will make in the region of 8000 to 10000 button clicks per year when using a windows-based package. Thus, prolonged mouse usage could, potentially, lead to problems.

Martin (1993) proposes that the position of the mouse should be considered using the ergonomic notion of a reach envelope (see Figure 11.1), which he terms the "immediate reach zone", and which is defined as the horizontal distance between elbows at seated elbow height, i.e., sitting with the forearms perpendicular to the upper about the elbow. Moving the mouse outside the immediate reach zone inevitably leads to shoulder abduction, and the further the mouse is moved from this zone, the greater the abduction. Martin (1993) suggests either substituting another device for the mouse, or positioning the mouse within the immediate reach zone. This is difficult because of the position of the keyboard, but Martin (1993) suggests that one solution would be to place the mouse on a platform above the keyboard.

For large movements, across the screen or to large targets, it is possible to move the mouse using full arm movement, but for small movements, either across small distances or to small targets, more precise control will be had from using wrist movements, often with the fourth and fifth fingers resting on the table surface. As screens become both larger and more cluttered, with an increase in small targets, there may well be a mismatch between these different task requirements.

The mouse is often controlled using the forearm/wrist muscle (White-field, 1983). It is probably for this reason that users rest the heel of the hand or their forearm on the desk while using the mouse (see Figure 12.4). However, some evidence is beginning to accumulate in the literature relating extensive mouse use to specific injuries. Davie et al. (1991) report the case of a progressive weakening of the right hand over a period of five months of mouse use. Examination of the patient indicated that there was some muscle wastage, which led to an inability to fully extend the ring and little fingers. The authors suggest that the injury was consistent with ulnar nerve compression. This probably arose from an operating posture in which the forearm rests along the desk surface, with the little finger lying along the desk and the hand held slightly off-center on the mouse. Franco et al. (1992) report a case of tenosynivitis occurring at the base of the right

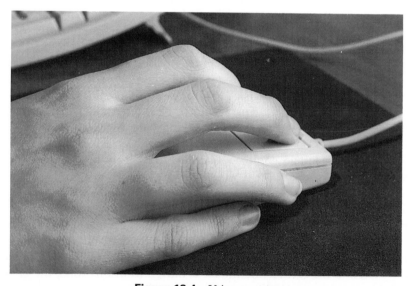

Figure 12.4 Using a mouse

wrist, specifically where the wrist rests on the work surface. The injury seems to arise from the combined friction and pressure on the wrist tendon caused by moving the wrist against the desk surface. As with the Davie et al. (1991) report, the problem seemed to be exacerbated by the ulnar deviation of the right hand.

In both cases, the problems could have been minimized by adoption of an appropriate posture, i.e., one in which the fatty pads at the base of the palm rest on the desk surface and the hand curves over the mouse. Mice are generally placed an appreciable distance to the right of the keyboard (Noyes et al., 1994). If this is the case, then the right hand will need to reach away from the perpendicular. Given that to hold the hand in such a way may obstruct mouse movement, it becomes apparent that the resting posture of the right hand for a mouse user will more than likely involve ulnar deviation, with the little finger resting on the desk surface. A walk around the computer laboratory in the building in which I work suggested that this posture was by far the most common. Consequently, as suggested in Chapter 1, the mouse seems to have been designed for a specific operating posture which differs from that in general use. In general, the mouse is located to the right of the keyboard. This leads to an increase in the likelihood of prolonged muscle activity in the shoulder and upper arm, in order to reach for and operate the mouse, and an increase in the possibility of discomfort associated with ulnar nerve compression in the wrist.

12.7   Problems associated with other devices

Several papers which discuss touchscreens or lightpens cite musculoskeletal fatigue as a limiting factor in their effective use. In other words, the very directness of these devices for pointing to objects can lead to reports of fatigue and discomfort from prolonged activity requiring the arm to be held raised. Several authors suggest that the problems can be dealt with by simply adjusting the angle of the screen from near vertical to near horizontal. The participants in the studies reported by Albert (1982) were asked to rate devices on a number of dimensions. In Figure 12.5, a selection of the devices have been ranked on two dimensions: discomfort and fatigue.

It is interesting to note in Figure 12.5 that the indirect pointing devices, i.e., trackball and joystick, fared poorly in this study. One would have expected the postural requirements involved in holding the arm horizontal to the screen (for touchscreen and lightpen) to have a bearing on perceived fatigue. The fact that both trackball and joystick were rated as being less

Subjective ranking
of devices

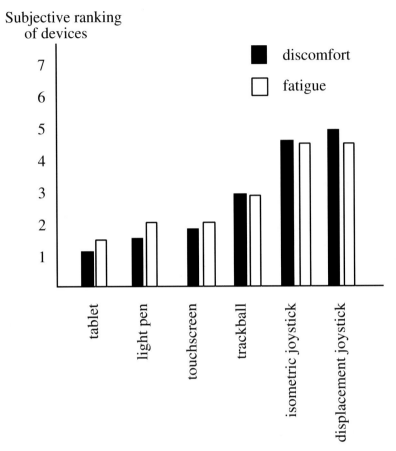

Figure 12.5 Classification of interaction devices in terms of discomfort and fatigue (adapted from Albert, 1982, with permission)

comfortable and more tiring to use than touchscreen, lightpen or tablet requires some comment. Fatigue and discomfort would have been factors if the posture was held for prolonged periods of times. If the users were selecting objects with discrete movements, and moving the arm to a rest position between selection, then the effects of fatigue may not be so apparent. Alternatively, users' perceptions of comfort and fatigue may be linked to their task performance. From this argument, devices which yield suboptimal performance may be seen as more frustrating to use and this frustration could have a bearing on perceptions of other factors.

From Chapter 3, one might assume that the isometric joystick might be slightly more fatiguing to use than the displacement joystick, if only because of the differences in force required to effect change in cursor movement. By the same token, one might assume an equivalence between displacement joystick and trackball in terms of force required. However, this does not appear to be borne out by Figure 12.5. Rather the two joystick types have an equally poor showing. The figure represents ranking of devices, and all one can sensibly say is that the joysticks were the least preferred. This probably colored users' ranking on the other dimensions. As far as the trackball is concerned, the interesting point to note is that while this is the preferred device for all manner of high workload domains, it is not particularly well received in this study.

12.8 Conclusions

As the use of windows-based software continues to increase, one will probably find an increase in the number of reports of problems relating to the use of mice. Thus, the conventional pairing of QWERTY keyboard and mouse can be seen to be a major factor in the cause of musculoskeletal problems for its users. However, it should be clear from much of the discussion in this chapter that simply apportioning blame to the interaction device is both misguided and foolish. Rather, the problems experienced by people using computers relate to the complex combination of working posture and work regime, as well as work equipment. However, given that interaction devices are the artifacts with which people physically interact with the computer, it seems logical to consider their design, use and placement in the work environment.

Some of the problems can be overcome by redesigning the workplace or by changing the work regime. For example, problems relating to discomfort while typing can be reduced by changing posture, and the problems relating to discomfort while using mice could be reduced by moving the mouse closer to the keyboard (Martin, 1993). Furthermore, a number of these problems arise as a result of the combination of poor posture and prolonged activity. Thus, introducing rest breaks will reduce some of the problems (indeed, recent legislation in the UK and Europe holds that rest breaks are important aspects of job design and lack of adequate rest breaks contributes to work-related upper limb disorder). However, there is still scope for reconsidering the nature of HCI in many aspects of computer-related work and, from this reconsideration, to develop new forms of interaction using new forms of interaction device. This point is illustrated by the modifications to keyboards and the resulting reductions in muscle activity when using the new designs. It is possible to consider the design of pointing devices from a similar perspective.

12.9   Key points for practitioners

- Canvass users as to their musculoskeletal complaints.
- Consider the possible causes of the complaints, in terms of work demands, work regime, workplace and equipment.
- Effect changes in the work to overcome the musculoskeletal problems.
- When buying new equipment, think beyond the demands of the software, to the requirements of the user.
- Consider the layout of the workplace and placement of interaction devices.

12.10   Key points for researchers

- Consider the design of interaction devices in terms of postural demands made on prospective users.
- Evaluate new designs of interaction devices in terms of musculoskeletal demands as well as performance.
- Develop new forms of interaction, supported by new forms of interaction device to meet the changing needs of HCI in modern workplaces.

CHAPTER 13

Interaction devices at work

Abstract

In Chapter 1, the relationship between the use of interaction devices and the context in which work is performed was highlighted. This relationship is explored further in this chapter by considering work activity and device use in different work domains.

13.1   Introduction

In Chapter 1, a simple framework for the use of interaction devices as tools was proposed. This framework implies that it is not possible to isolate a device from the context of its use. In subsequent chapters the context of device use has been defined in terms of human skill, i.e., at the level of user activity. In Chapter 11, it was argued that user activity is itself bounded by contextual factors, such as the environment in which the activity is being performed.

Traditionally, HCI has tended to focus on the interaction between an individual and a computer. While this is still the dominant focus of research, there is a growing awareness of the need to consider wider issues of the domain in which the person is working. In this chapter, the notion of the context of interaction device use is extended to include the work domain in which the user activity is performed. I am using the term "work" with as broad a meaning as possible, along the lines of purposeful activity directed towards the attainment of a goal and/or making of a "product" (a book chapter, an architectural drawing, etc.).

It is further assumed that work is, predominantly, performed in an organizational setting, and the goals of the worker will be strongly influenced by the prevailing culture in the organization. From this point of view, the organizational setting will influence use of interaction devices by setting the agenda for the work activity that a person performs (and equally, the devices used will affect the work activity).

13.1.1 Work activity

The impact of computer technology can be illustrated with the mundane example of filing a new piece of information, using a traditional office system (i.e., comprising a typewriter and a filing cabinet), and a computer-based office system. Figures 13.1 and 13.2 present possible descriptions of the activities in the two office systems.

While the diagrams have been drawn as if the activity proceeds from left to right, it does not necessarily follow that the activities have to obey this sequence. This is illustrated by the "plans", which indicate the various choices open to the person performing this task, i.e., to alternate tasks 2.0 and 3.0.

In practice, the plans may become fixed and the sequence performed in a set order, either due to training or to other work-related factors. Another point at which some discretion could be exercised by the person performing the work is in terms of the overlap between activities, for instance, if the new information is being collected over the telephone or by face-to-face interview, the person might decide to perform task 2.0 in parallel with task 1.2.

As one might expect, the computer-based office system (Figure 13.2) has kept most of the "top-level" tasks, but has changed the operations required to perform these tasks. In one instance, the computer-based office system has pre-empted a task and hence, removed this from the activity (i.e., task 5.0 is contained in task 4.0). At first glance this might appear to be a good thing, in that by reducing the number of tasks, the work can be faster to perform. However, consider the role of task 5.0 in performing this task; performing the physical task of placing the folder in the correct place would lend what psychologists term a sense of closure to the task (i.e., task 5.0

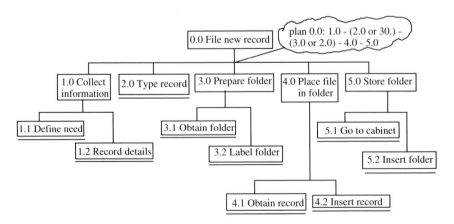

Figure 13.1   Filing a new record in a traditional office system

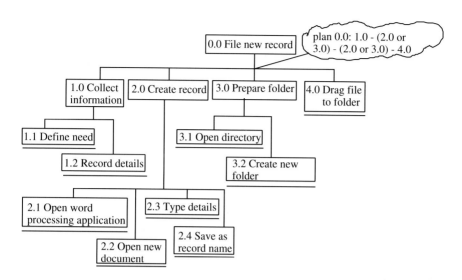

Figure 13.2   Filing a new record in the computer-based office system

confirms that the task has finished). Simply removing the need for this task will not guarantee that it will not be performed, e.g., the user might perform some additional (unnecessary) activity, such as manipulating the file in the folder or saving the file again, "just to be on the safe side". Thus, simply removing the need for a task need not guarantee that the user will omit that step in the performance of the activity, rather an additional task might be introduced into that step for the sake of closure.

In addition to changes in task activity, there are also obvious changes in the equipment used, e.g., while the traditional system uses a filing cabinet the computer-based system uses a directory. If one looks beyond the obvious, one can see that this also leads to two important consequences. The environment in which the work is performed has been altered. In the traditional system, the work required the operator to move from the desk to the filing cabinet, while in the computer-based system, all the work was performed on the computer while seated at a workstation. The implications for prolonged adoption of a specific posture have been discussed in Chapter 12, suffice it to say, that the workstation requires minimal changes of posture and movement which might lead to musculoskeletal problems.

While the traditional system used physical artifacts, i.e., paper, files, folders, etc., the computer-based system uses representations of these artifacts. Furthermore, the replacement of physical artifacts with representations also changes the manner in which people can interact with the artifacts, i.e., from direct, physical manipulation (picking things up, carrying them, opening and closing them, etc.) to partial manipulation (dragging and selecting icons, clicking on icons to open and close them, etc.). These latter aspects have implications for the way in which people conceive of task activity.

One can compare the two systems shown in Figures 13.1 and 13.2, in terms of the generic actions involved in performing the activities and in terms of the cognitive loads placed on the people working with the different systems. Office work, in general, can be described in terms of a small number of high-level generic actions, e.g., information capture, information processing, information storage and information retrieval. Each of these high-level generic actions can be performed using traditional methods or new technology, e.g., information capture can be performed using personal communication or electronic mail. As one switches between different methods for performing these actions, so the cognitive load on the people in the office system can be said to change. One can propose that it is possible to distinguish between levels of memory and reasoning load across different actions. For instance, word-processing activity will involve relatively high levels of memory load (both recall and recognition), high levels of deductive reasoning (e.g., deciding on the appropriate menu option or command to use), and low levels of inductive reasoning (i.e., defining the "rules" to use). One can aim to reduce some of the memory and deductive reasoning loads by defining routines which the user should follow. In this way, one can propose standard approaches to the performance of the task. It is here that one moves beyond computing as simply the provision of enabling technology towards computing as a medium for organizing and controlling work. I would suggest that many of the people who work in the development of computing systems would object to the insinuation that they are producing technology which, rather than having the positive benefits of enabling and liberating people, only serve to make work mundane, boring, repetitive and restricting. However, simplification is a double-edged sword; reducing cognitive load can also lead to a reduction of autonomy and decision latitude, which can have an impact on job satisfaction (Ivanevich, 1979).

13.1.2   Goals, tools and work activity

The goals that I have in writing this particular chapter would be very different from the goals of a typist to whom I gave a dictated version of the material, even though the end-product may be the same. Furthermore, my use of a word-processing package and keyboard will probably differ from that of a trained clerical assistant. Equally, my assumptions regarding page layout and formatting are different from those of the production editor working on this book. Consequently, our approach to the task of producing a page of text will be quite different.

This notion has been developed in several research and development projects. In one study, Bødker (1989) reports the development of computer-based aids for page-setting in the newspaper industry. She notes that different people involved in page-setting have different goals and different requirements of the technology, e.g., an editor might be interested in producing an eye-catching headline, a typesetter might be interested in producing a well-balanced layout. Thus, the person's job influences the uses to which they will expect to put the technology.

In an earlier study, Cockburn (1983) considered the transition from "hot metal" page-setting to linotype machines to computer-based systems. At each transition from one method to the next, the compositors felt increasingly deprived of the ability to use and practice traditional skills. Indeed, while some of the more pragmatic workers felt that learning to type was a transferable skill, the workers felt that the work was changing such that it no longer depended on their abilities but upon the practices chosen by management. The transition to computer-based printing was seen as a process of erosion of traditional skills, knowledge and abilities and the substitution of skilled workers with "semi-responsible computer-operators".

Bødker (1989) argues that the traditional skills used in composition have much to offer in terms of the work performed, and suggests that it might be possible to design an interface to exploit these skills. In recent years, there has been much emphasis placed on the notion of human-centered work, with calls for the utilization of traditional skills and abilities (Cooley, 1981). Typically, the shift towards new (i.e., computer-based) technology involves the transition from "physical" skills to "cognitive" skills (Scarborough and Corbett, 1992). The example which is described by Bødker (1989) is no exception. She notes that the traditional, i.e., manual, approach to the activity of page-setting involved the use of tangible artifacts manipulated by the workers, e.g., paper, scissors, composing stick, etc., while the computer-based versions use representations of these artifacts. The design she describes is based on the provision of adequate information on the display to aid arrangement of material on the screen. This is interesting in that, while it can capture some of the page-setting skills, it omits many of the skills involved in physically manipulating the artifacts (in the new design, the system uses a mouse as the interaction device). This means that the representations on the new system will not only stand for artifacts, but also the functions performed by those artifacts.

Returning to the discussion of hammering in Chapter 1, recall that it is possible to consider this activity at two levels: the use of a tool, and the performance of a task. While one can separate these (and use something other than a hammer), in using the tool we often lose sight of the distinction, i.e., we are hammering rather than using a hammer. It is only when things go wrong that we become aware of the distinction. In HCI, there is a tendency to design systems which have been based on the task performance level. This tendency sacrifices the tool level. Consider any WIMP-based word processing package; the functions "cut" and "paste" exist as commands and as symbols which stand for the artifacts of scissors and glue pot. As with many of the metaphors used in HCI, we do not tend to imagine the artifacts when we use these commands (the use of a "scissors icon" probably strikes the readers as particularly passé). Indeed, for a number of writers, the term "tool" can be used interchangeably for a physical artifact or for the symbolic representation of the function of the artifact in a computer system (Greenberg, 1993). This begs the questions, what is the role of physical artifacts in our conceptualization of work activity? how is this influenced by the work setting? what happens when one uses symbols rather than tools?

In Chapter 1, reference was made to the concept of "mediation" (Vygotsky, 1978). Recall that mediation refers to the phenomenon by which the tool shapes the users knowledge of the task and work activity, i.e., the requirements of using a particular tool have an impact on the way in which a task is approached. One can raise a number of questions pertaining to the relationship between tools and knowledge. Sometimes tool use can be defined in terms of a verbal description. For HCI, this means that a particular function of a tool can be translated into an iconic or a verbal sign, e.g., the use of a "scissors icon" or a "cut" command in a drawing package as mentioned above. This would appear to be the general direction in which metaphors have been adapted by HCI, with physical actions becoming represented by symbols (icons or verbal descriptors, i.e., from tool use to representation of the function of a tool). However, it is equally plausible, though perhaps not so explicitly stated, that the development of interaction devices can be considered in terms of symbols becoming tools. By this I mean that the particular ways of representing or organizing knowledge in the world can become established through work practices, and that subsequently tools can be developed to support this praxis. For instance, the layout of print trays used by printers was proposed to arise primarily from work practice (Chapter 2), and the UTOPIA project has been looking at ways in which traditional compositor skills can be retained in a computer system to support the layout of pages.

Mayes et al. (1988) have suggested that the knowledge used in HCI resides less in the user's head than in objects being used to perform a task (see Chapter 9). This is particularly relevant when one considers that use of external memory aids is likely to increase as task complexity increases, i.e., people attempt to recruit more information from the world when the task is perceived as complex. The search for "knowledge in the world" calls to mind the concept of compatibility, in which the design of an artifact could be said to "suggest" its use (see Chapter 5). Combining these notions with the concept of mediation suggests that interaction devices shape our expectations of how they ought to be used (cf. Carroll's task–artifact cycle, in Chapter 1).

In order to explore this point, consider the design of a three-button mouse. There are possible problems with the labeling and use of the buttons. It might be that if users are uncertain as to the functions of the buttons, they may be reluctant to use the computer system. This is exactly what happened on a computer system used in the control of a complex production process. A new condition monitoring system had been introduced to the plant. This system offered a wide range of facilities previously not available and management and designers were equally concerned to find that the system was not being used. While there were many factors contributing to the lack of use, one of the most widely cited was the fact that the operators were unsure which of the buttons on the mouse could be used to perform which function. In reality, all three buttons offered equal functionality and it did not matter which button was used. My interpretation of this example is twofold. The new system was perceived by the operators as "complicated", and this perception of complexity was supported by the three-button mouse. Thus, the operators were reluctant to try to use the mouse because they felt that it would be difficult to know which button to press. The new system, as far as the designers and management were concerned, was simple. This led them to assume that training could be minimized and that operators would explore the system by using it. Thus, no one explained the fact that the mouse buttons all did the same thing. After some modifications to the design of the interface and a change of mouse (to a single-button mouse), the operators have been using the system with some success. The point of this anecdote is to illustrate that the interaction device supplied with a system can often carry additional interpretations beyond those originally assumed, even to the point of being seen as the focus for complaint, e.g., a student complained to me that the word-processing package he was using was too slow (after cleaning the mouse, he found that it ran much faster).

Norman (1988) has suggested a simple, seven-stage model of human action. Prior to any action, the user of a computer will both formulate a goal and plan a set of actions to achieve that goal (see also Figure 6.10). This model can be paraphrased for the purposes of this chapter as follows:

1. Form goal.
2. Form intention.
3. Specify action.
4. Execute action.
5. Perceive results of action.
6. Interpret results of action.
7. Evaluate outcome.

The stage of goal formation can be influenced by a number of factors. Assume that the goal is to write a letter. This goal will be influenced by the contents of the letter, i.e., whether it is a job application or a letter to a friend. This goal will also be influenced by the originator of the letter, e.g., whether the letter is requested by your boss or is written by yourself. Furthermore, the goal might be affected by time pressure (does it need to be written to catch this evening's post or is it written because you have not written to your friend for a while?), and possibly by quality considerations, i.e., you would probably use more expressions of a formal nature in a job application than in letters to a friend, and might also be more concerned about spelling mistakes in the job application. Thus, although the overall goals might appear similar, there are distinct differences which will arise due to the requirements which constrain the task. It is proposed that the work domain will contain a great deal of such requirements.

The goal will be decomposed into an intention (which can, in turn be influenced by a number of work-related factors, such as equipment availability, time pressures, competing tasks, etc.) and to specifications for action. Action will be influenced by the demands of the task; the characteristics of the user interface; the knowledge, skills and abilities of the operator; the work domain in which the action is performed. The task will obviously depend on the work domain. It is assumed that the work domain will set an agenda to which work will be performed, e.g., in terms of deadlines and acceptable quality levels. In order to consider this, it is necessary to recruit a framework to organize the discussion of the relationship between technology and the work domains in which it is used. In this chapter, that framework will be sociotechnical systems.

13.2 Sociotechnical systems

The idea underlying the sociotechnical systems approach is quite simply that one should place equal emphasis on the social and technical components of a work system. The term "social aspect" refers to the communication networks and management practices in the organization. The technical aspect covers not simply the hardware but also the manner in which the workplace is laid out and the ways of working within an organization. For instance, the use of a word processor may well be quite different for an operator in a "word-processing pool" than for a clerical assistant in an individual office.

Sociotechnical systems research has its roots in a number of projects carried out by members of the Tavistock Institute in London in the 1950s (Trist and Bamforth, 1951; Emery, 1959). In much of this work, the researchers were able to demonstrate that the social components had been overlooked in the introduction of new technology, and that it was possible to improve overall performance by addressing the social components.

In recent years, human factors researchers in the UK and Europe have been reconsidering the use of sociotechnical systems as an approach to the study of working with new technology (Mumford, 1987; Eason, 1987; Daniellou and Garigou, 1992). These recent developments have begun to extend the limited notion of technology in the earlier versions of the theory, in order to demonstrate that technology is not "neutral" or a given (Sharifi and Baber, 1992). Rather, the ways in which an organization will use technology will be influenced by the "design" of the organization, i.e., its culture, management structure, etc., and by the way in which technology itself has been represented (Scarborough and Corbett, 1992). Two examples will illustrate these points.

Noble (1985) has suggested that, in the 1950s, there were two alternative approaches to the computer-based machining of metal. One approach used a "record/playback" method, in which the operator performed a sequence of tasks and the task sequence was recorded on magnetic tape to be played back to the machine. The other approach used a program written to tape, which could be played on the machine, i.e., numerical control (NC). Noble (1985) suggests that the reason why NC machines proved to be popular was simply a matter of opportunity for management control of the use of the machines; the NC machines allowed skilled workers to be replaced by programs, and the programs could be written away from the shop-floor. Thus, the organization of work shifted to allow a greater degree of control of the manufacturing process.

The second example concerns the introduction of a CAD system into a white goods manufacturer. The manager of the drawing office (who, incidentally, had little experience of design work) was shown a demonstration of a new CAD package. He asked the salesperson whether the package could be used to draw cookers. The salesperson called up a cooker picture from the pre-drawn library and the office manager introduced the system on the understanding that the design could be a simple matter of editing the pre-drawn image. In Section 13.2.1, further examples will be used to illustrate that this anecdote is not as far-fetched as it might at first appear.

13.2.1 Computer-aided design or drafting?

In Chapter 8, drawing and computer-aided design were contrasted in terms of a shift in requirements due to changes in the manner in which the drawing is represented and constructed, and changes in the artifacts used. In terms of the artifacts, the shift is from pen, paper and T squares to mouse or puck, screen and objects; in terms of the manipulation of artifacts, the shift is from drawing with a pencil to controlling a cursor, selecting options and, in some packages, entering coordinates. With the shift in skill requirements, it appears that the activities of conceptualization and consideration of options have been superseded by the appropriate specification of a drawing routine. With the use of "standard" solutions, the role of sketching is reduced. Finally, the creation of drawings in CAD is radically different from those in paper-based design. While the relative advantages of the two approaches can be debated, it should be clear that CAD requires a different sort of planning and specification of the activity than the use of a pencil; we have separated the use of a tool from the performance of the task. This leads to the further requirement of learning and understanding the capabilities of the CAD software which is being used.

Some writers have proposed that this latter requirement constitutes "reskilling". However, if one considers the general pattern of managerial response to the technology, one will see that the sociotechnics of CAD tends towards deskilling. In broad terms, the shift in terms of worker skills involves transition from the combination of physical skills and accumulated experience of design, to the search for and use of solutions contained in the software. This is not to deny that the software could be used creatively, but to suggest that many organizations might prefer to limit this aspect of CAD use. Löwstedt (1988), in a survey of CAD installations, suggests that the principal reasons for investing in CAD is the assumed reduction in "drawing" time when using these systems, compared to conventional drawing practices, primarily through the use of "standard" solutions. A survey of CAD offices in Scotland found that managers tended to view the introduction of CAD in terms of scientific management. The systems were introduced with the idea of deskilling drawing room staff. This involved a decrease in the autonomy of designers with an increase in the use of machine pacing to produce more work in the same time periods, with standardized, routine work in a drawing pool, to maintain high volume. In order to achieve this, there was a reduction in detailed design work (McLoughlin, 1989). Cooley (1981) has argued that the use of "standard" solutions leads to an increase in managerial control and a reduction in the opportunity for CAD users to exercise their design skills; in effect, the CAD users move from designers to drafters, whose job it is to produce rather than create drawings, i.e., to create a "drafting pool" along the lines of a typing pool.

CAD systems can serve as a means to Taylorize work in the drawing office (Cooley, 1981; Löwstedt, 1988). McLoughlin (1989) shares this fear, but argues that the utilization of the CAD system will depend on management attitudes towards the work. Thus, CAD applications can be used to remove tacit skills from drawing work, and result in a transition to drafting work. From the point of view of interaction devices, one can argue that the trend in the use of pointing devices for object selection and manipulation supports the view of CAD operation as the selection and manipulation of standard solutions, whereas the alternative designs, which supported sketching, could be seen as recruiting traditional design and drawing skills back into CAD.

13.2.2 Job redesign

There have been numerous efforts to design the way in which job redesign is performed. Some of the early attempts used "scientific management" to determine the most efficient number, sequence and timing of operations. In the 1920s, the limitations of these approaches were becoming apparent and over the years efforts have been made to produce job designs which can lead to "human work". Several of these approaches emphasize the importance of fundamental characteristics of jobs, such as the opportunity to use a variety of skills, to perform meaningful work, to have a degree of autonomy, to feel that one's work is making a contribution to the organization (Hackman and Oldham, 1980).

It is clear that computerization does not, of itself, humanize work. The examples of the possible use and abuse of CAD presented above illustrate the role of managerial choice in the application and use of technology. Furthermore, it is equally plausible that the nature of the organization will have an impact on the design of the technology, especially, as we move towards bespoke system design. This means that technology may reinforce existing organizational structures, rather than offering an opportunity to develop more efficient or appropriate structures. For instance, while physical workload has a bearing on work-related upper limb problems (see Chapter 12), there are organizations which record the keying rate of data entry clerks for performance monitoring. In this instance, the computers are used to support the control of work activity.

Table 13.1 presents a number of factors which will influence the use of computer systems. Several of the topics have already been mentioned and I will illustrate three of them further.

If one considers users' attitudes to mainframe and personal computers (PCs), it is likely that they will feel more ownership of the PC than the mainframe. This will be influenced by a number of factors beyond the simple fact of possession. Access to software and other material will be under the control of the user and at the discretion of the user of a PC, but may be influenced by central computing and other authorities on the mainframe. Access will also be influenced by organizational factors, such as training. For instance, two clerical assistants might have access to the same word-processing package, but one might be able to use the full range

Table 13.1 Factors influencing the use of office automation (adapted with permission from Eason, 1989, in A. Sutcliffe and L. Macauley (eds), *People and Computers V,* Cambridge University Press)

Organization level	Organization issues	Technical requirements
Organization structures	Power structures, control, monitoring, accountability, values	Monitoring, access, authorization
Multi-user cooperation	Shared access, role definition, cooperation, control	"Read access", "write access", change control
Individual work role	Responsibility, ownership, autonomy, information, reward, tools	Privacy, reliability, flexibility, personalization

of functions as a result of training and experience, whereas the other might have rote-learned a set of procedures. In this instance, the latter clerical assistant can be said to have a lower level of access than the former.

Ownership and access will influence the level of responsibility a person feels for the work being performed and the use of the package. Responsibility will also be influenced by the level of autonomy and by the value that is placed on the individual's work by the organization. The issue of multi-user working will be considered in the next section.

13.3   Organizational computing

Malone (1987) coined the term "organizational interface" to describe computers which allowed several users to work on shared work. This notion can be illustrated with three examples: electronic mail, project management tools and collaborative writing.

There are a number of approaches to computer-supported communication, and the most well-known is electronic mail. What is interesting about the use of email, from an organizational perspective, is that it appears to break down traditional barriers. For instance, email messages tend to be less inhibited and more spontaneous than hand-written memos, and the style of writing email tends to be similar regardless of position in the organization (Sproul and Kiesler, 1986). The lack of inhibition has been proposed to support the activities of "brain-storming" over email (Kerr and Hiltz, 1982).

Email also has the advantage of reducing the problem of "telephone tag" in organizations (Kenney, 1985). Rather than leaving a trail of messages on answer phones, email can allow people to leave messages for response as soon as the receiver is able to access their email. Coupled with the changes in communication style, this has led some organizations to modify their communication protocols. For instance, General Motors Environmental Activities Division have found that the use of email has increased the amount of task-related communication between individuals and also increased the amount of personal contact between people in the organization (Foster and Flynn, 1984). While email tends to use keyboard for text entry, there is an increasing range of products which use voice mail systems, such as voice store and forward (Erlich and Akiba, 1985). In this case, the spoken message can be sent to a sophisticated answerphone for storing, editing or relaying. Having said this, the protocols associated with the use of answerphones are still somewhat poorly developed and many people either refuse, or are reluctant, to use them. Finally, while email can be used for verbal messages (either spoken or textual) it is often more difficult to send either formatted documents or graphics through the email. Of course, the technology solutions to these problems already exist and are being used by many organizations. The potential to communicate with graphics in real time can be useful not only for design projects but also for project management and document creation.

In Chapter 8, the use of graphics packages to support project management was proposed. If one extends this notion to a project management system which can be accessed by all members of the project team, then it is possible to see the software as being a planning aid, a forum for negotiation and a record of project progress. However, one might find that automatic diaries are resisted if people are unable to retain the right to arrange and agree appointments for themselves. Thus, one can see that the technology can offer the potential to support democratic project management, but can also be used to support more coercive styles of management.

There are clearly a number of areas in which the joint writing of reports, etc. require the collaboration between a number of "authors". In paper-based systems, this collaboration required the production of a manuscript for circulation, comment and revision. Although the initial production could have involved more than one person, the process of reviewing and editing the document could be time-consuming. In recent years, the technology has developed which allows several people to work on the same document on a computer network. In comparison with paper, word processing is often deemed more useful once the initial draft of a piece of writing has been produced, i.e., when the document can be revised and edited (Bridwell et al., 1984). From this one could argue that word processing tends to focus on the production of a product, rather than the creation of a document, and that often the focus of the "writer" is on the surface aspects rather than the overall structure. It strikes me that using collaborative writing to revise a document would miss a major opportunity to capitalize upon collaboration in the first place. If people could collaborate at the initial stages of document planning, then more benefits may accrue. In Chapter 8 some products were discussed which can be used to support the writing process, and which can be applied to collaborative writing. One such product is a form of shared whiteboard which allows participants to construct and amend mind maps for project management or document creation. An extension of this notion takes the form of cards which can have ideas added to them and filed or linked. In both cases, the emphasis is on the overall structure of the document, allowing users to add information and link pieces into appropriate sections. At this stage in the production process, one would anticipate negotiation and collaboration to be most fruitful, whereas, when discussing a finished product, comments may be directed either by the choice of words in a specific section or possibly at the level of moving parts of the document around.

In order to perform these tasks, it becomes apparent that the provision of a keyboard alone will not allow sufficient support for the sketching activities. One might suggest that the use of a pointing device, such as a mouse, would be useful. However, it seems that the concepts owe more to paper than to computer and that a pen-based system could provide even more benefits. Furthermore, the size of the screen and the manner in which users can access the document requires careful consideration. Malone (1987) cites work which allows each contributor a separate "voice", e.g., in terms of the color of the text, etc., used for each person. The structure of people's interaction through the computer now becomes an issue. Finally, if one is to enter text to be edited at a later date, one might feel that a speech-based system would offer more benefits than a keyboard (although see Chapter 4).

In many work domains, the "flow of information" can be achieved through non-verbal channels, e.g., by the use of gesture and also by observing the actions of other people. One way in which interaction devices can contribute to the social aspects of work is through the visible signs of their operation. If a pilot of an aircraft pulls back his control joystick, the co-pilot's joystick also moves. From this, the pilot's action has been communicated to the co-pilot. The implications of changing the nature of the interaction devices used in this domain can be illustrated by an example. Norman (1993) points out that in Boeing's Airbus, pilot and co-pilot are provided with joysticks for entering control commands. He notes that not only can the yoking of control now be effectively removed, with pilot and co-pilot able to enter different commands simultaneously, but also the communication component of operating a control is removed on two levels: the co-pilot cannot feel the control move, nor see the pilot performing an action. From this discussion, it is proposed that "traditional" controls offered additional work-related information to people in some work domains. The development of more compact, multifunctional controls can remove some of this information.

13.4   Conclusions

The focus of this chapter has been on the social aspects of interaction devices. This notion can extend beyond the workplace to the realms of "public technology" (Baber and Parker, 1994), i.e., to consider interaction with ticket vending machines and public information systems. It is argued that the way in which people use computers for their work and everyday activities influences their expectations and use of interaction devices, and that, in many cases, the design of interaction devices has an impact on how people think about their interaction with a computer.

HCI research has tended to distance itself from physical activity to focus instead on cognitive activity. In Chapter 1, this focus on cognitive activity was felt to be the result of the emphasis on information processing in both the cognitive psychology and software engineering perspectives on HCI. However, it is felt that this focus has led to a shifting of the concept of tools from physical artifacts to cognitive artifacts. While I do not object to the notion of cognitive artifacts (Norman, 1991), I do feel that the current trend ignores physical devices and physical activity. This rather throws the baby out with the bath water, and we may well be missing important factors of work and task activity by failing to consider the ramifications of physical activity. For instance, the simple action of placing a file in a folder and closing the drawer of a filing cabinet contains quite different information, feedback and opportunities for action than the version of the task performed using a windows-based package. It is not an issue of which is better, but of how the task requirements and information are altered.

Furthermore, the work domain provides a number of constraints on the type of activity and tasks which can be performed by individuals. Taking the example of CAD, it was proposed that the management requirements were supported by contemporary HCI design, and that the interaction devices used supported the object selection and manipulation approach in contrast to sketching and design approaches. The thrust of this argument is that, rather than being peripheral in HCI, interaction devices represent the tools by which people respond to and act upon computers. From this, one can say that the design and use of interaction devices reflects both the manner in which people expect to use the computers and the manner in which their work domain permits them to interact with computers.

13.5   Key points for practitioners

- Consider the organization setting in which the computer systems are used.

- Consider the manner in which work is performed. Rather than attempting to "automate" current practice, consider ways in which better practice can be introduced.
- Consider the trade-off between managerial control and individual autonomy. How can technology best serve the interests of one without impairing the requirements of the other?

13.6   Key points for researchers

- Design systems for work-domains rather than tasks, i.e., either build bespoke systems or provide advice on how best to tailor applications and systems to organizational requirements.
- Consider the potential role of interaction devices in the way in which work is performed, i.e., do interaction devices constrain user activity or lead to specific task requirements?

CHAPTER 14

Multimodal human–computer interaction

Abstract

As new computer products are developed, there is an increasing level of interest in the possibility of combining several devices, i.e., multimodal HCI. In this chapter, the notion of multimodal HCI is discussed and some of the human factors issues are considered.

14.1 Introduction

As computers become applied to an ever wider range of operations, so the environment in which they are used will impact on usability. For instance, the communications and surveillance systems in high-performance aircraft will utilize computer support and require operation while pilots are flying at high speed; on-board car diagnostics and navigation equipment will not only supply information to the driver but could also capture information from the driver while the vehicle is being driven; a maintenance engineer could have a head-mounted display, showing circuit diagrams, which could be accessed while the repair work is being undertaken. Contemporary computer technology often appears to be based on the assumption that computer use is manual and visual; the user receives information from a display screen and interacts with the computer using a keyboard or a mouse (Buxton, 1986; 1990a; Jacob et al., 1993). This ties the user to a workstation, and recent efforts have been directed at permitting some mobility on the part of the user and some portability on the part of the computer.

Not only do the conceptions and definitions of HCI need to be rethought, but it is also necessary to modify ideas of how people will use such products. For instance, the activity of entering information into a computer, whether by typing or speaking, may be superseded by techniques which allow documents to be constructed through sophisticated "cut and paste" techniques. This will reduce the amount of effort spent in entering information, and increase the amount of effort spent "browsing" through electronic documents, selecting information and constructing new documents. Using conventional, serial HCI, "browsing" through large documents can become a matter of tedious pointing and clicking, or could lead to disorientation. In order to capitalize on their potential, it is necessary to take the notion of direct manipulation in large documents and make interaction more direct (Stanton and Baber, 1994).

One way in which direct manipulation can be made more direct is to allow the user recourse to more than one interaction device. However, rather than using these devices in serial, as is currently the case with keyboard and mouse, it is necessary to combine devices in parallel. For example, in order to move a cursor to issue a command from the menu bar, I need to stop typing, reach for the mouse, move the cursor to the menu bar, select the menu heading, drag the cursor down and release on the appropriate menu item. I sometimes use command keys as a short cut, but this still involves stopping the main task of typing, remembering the correct command and entering it. Suppose I could simply issue the command while continuing with the main activity of typing, e.g., by speaking a command to "save" the document. This brings us into the realm of the multimodal interface, and in this chapter we shall examine the growing research in this area.

14.2 Combining tasks

When using pointing devices, users have the opportunity to combine discrete components of generic tasks into single actions: for instance, moving the cursor while holding down a button. This will strike the reader as a trivial example. However, if one recalls the relative ease of performing the dragging task using a mouse versus a trackball, one will begin to appreciate that combining component activities into single tasks can depend on several factors, not least of which will be the design of the device and the capabilities of the user. For instance, when using the key combination <Ctrl-Alt-Del> to reboot a computer, some users may have difficulty reaching all three keys and will use two hands.

Thus, a simple solution to the problem of one-handed operation would be to use two hands. In the example of dragging an object using a trackball, one could simply use one hand to operate the trackball and the other to press a button. This notion can be extended further in the selection of large sections of text. For instance, while I can select a paragraph of text in a word processing package by dragging through it, I can also click at the start of the paragraph, hold down the <shift> on the keyboard, scroll to the end of the paragraph and click again to select the whole paragraph. In this case I am using a pointing device and a button on the keyboard. The purpose of using the <shift> is to extend the functionality of the pointing device. In these examples, the second, i.e., key pressing, tasks are not particularly demanding. However, humans are capable of performing quite complex sequences of actions using two hands (typing is an obvious example), and can also combine actions using hands and feet (for example, using the pedals while playing a piano).

Buxton (1986) has taken the notion that much of HCI appears to be one-handed (or at least, does not exploit the possibility of two-handed operation to any great extent), and developed a range of applications which can capitalize upon two-handed operation. For instance, when using a graphics package one should be able to position objects with one hand and scale the drawing or objects with the other, or in a word processing package one should be able to scroll a document while moving the cursor to a line of text.

This notion of using two hands raises several issues for HCI (beyond the technical problems of having several, possibly, competing inputs to the computer). The first and fundamental issue is the implied shift in design philosophy from single, multifunctional devices to a collection of discrete, single function devices. Taking the analogy with using hands and feet while driving a car, notice that the control devices tend to perform specific actions, such as depressing the clutch, selecting the gear setting, etc. One could imagine quite complex workstations with all manner of novel inter-action devices being used to control the movement of objects on the screen, while resizing and editing the images using some of the devices considered in Chapter 4. In contemporary HCI, the functionality of the computer tends to lie in the objects on the screen, with icons representing specific functions or "tools". Interaction devices are considered simply as the means by which these "tools" are operated, and one reaches the paradox that contemporary HCI is based on the notion of using physical tools (i.e., interaction devices) to operate virtual tools (i.e., objects on the screen) to perform functions in order to satisfy user goals. In order to effect all of the operations which the virtual tools permit, it is necessary to incorporate an increasing level of functionality into the physical tools, e.g., rather than simply allowing an interaction device to move a cursor, it is now used to signal state changes or issue commands through button presses. The analogy with car driving leads to a change of direction, from multiple virtual tools to multiple physical tools.

This raises the second question of whether users can combine activities. Smyth et al. (1987) use the homely example of rubbing one's head while patting one's stomach. When children first attempt this activity, they tend to either pat both head and stomach or rub both head and stomach. With a little practice, however, they can adapt to the correct combination. This example suggests that two-handed operation requires deliberate control of the type and timing of actions required (as one might anticipate from a consideration of typing, see Chapter 7). However, unless people are highly skilled, their actions tend to share similar timing for both hands, although the forces applied or movements made can differ (Schmidt et al., 1979). Thus, simultaneous movements made with more than one limb appear to be subject to various rules of coordination. It appears, further, that coordination tends to favor the dominant hand over the non-dominant hand and both hands over the feet (Gunkel, 1962). Finally, it would appear that highly skilled musicians are able to decouple the coordination rules and produce movements which are relatively independent (Ibbotson and Morton, 1981). This would suggest that, unless one was prepared to engage in lengthy training of users, it is likely that combinations of movements would need to be kept relatively simple and that the timing of sequences of movements would need to be sufficiently clear to allow people to coordinate them, e.g., when changing gear in a car the biggest problem faced by novice drivers is the sequence of depressing the clutch, moving the gear shift, increasing the revs and releasing the clutch. There is an alternative to the combining of manual tasks, and that is to combine manual tasks with speech.

14.3   Combining speech with other activities

A number of writers have proposed that the use of speech adds a second channel through which information can be communicated from user to computer (Lea, 1980; Baber, 1991). This implies that a first channel will be used for ongoing activities. As noted above, the first channel of HCI is typically manual response to visually presented information. Thus, one might anticipate that speech could be combined with manual activity. In Chapter 4, the role of speech recognition for object selection and entering commands and/or information was considered. In this section, the combination of speech with other interaction devices will be discussed.

One way in which speech could be combined with another interaction device would be simply to duplicate functions between the two devices. Bekker et al. (1994) found that around one third of participants in a document annotation study preferred to use a combination of speech and mouse for issuing commands. It appears that speech was perceived as faster, (although this was not supported statistically), but was more prone to error than mouse. In this example, speech was used for its speed, but the mouse was used as a back-up, to compensate for recognition problems. This implies that, should speech recognition have near perfect performance, the use of the mouse will be redundant. In another study, Schmandt et al. (1990) allowed people to use mouse and speech in a windows management task. They found that if the user's hand was on the mouse then people used speech less than 25% of the time. However, the percentage of total actions in which speech was used was over 60%. Speech was seen as particularly useful when windows were stacked; the user could speak the name of a "hidden" window and it would come to the front of the stack. While this might appear useful, it overlooks the window management strategies that people adopt when using windows systems (Shneiderman, 1992), such as limiting the number of windows which are open. What is interesting in the Schmandt et al. (1990) study is the fact that people would continue using the mouse if their hand was already holding it, rather than use speech, but would use speech in preference to reaching for the mouse.

This adds a second factor to the proposal that speech is used for speed and a mouse for back-up, that users will attempt to minimize effort, with speaking being perceived as less effortful than using a mouse. From this idea, the usefulness of pairing speech with another device will be influenced by the task context, i.e., the requirements of preceding and succeeding tasks. Providing duplication of the same functions can offer some benefit to computer users. However, if the task context involves activity which is primarily focused on the use of a mouse, then duplication of function might not be useful. Of more interest to this chapter is the notion of using two devices to perform distinct tasks.

In a number of papers, speech has been combined with direct manipulation of objects as a means of entering commands or information. In most of these applications, objects are selected physically and speech can be used to enter information, etc., pertaining to the objects (Martin, 1989; Cohen et al., 1989; Weiner and Ganapathy, 1989). Biermann et al. (1992) found that participants performed an editing task as well with a combination of speech and touchscreen as with mouse and keyboard. Hauptmann and McAvinney (1993) found that users preferred to combine speech and gesture in their transactions, i.e., while gesture alone was used in 14% of the transactions, where a choice was possible in their study, and speech alone was used in 16% of transactions, gesture and speech combined was used for 70% of the transactions.

Bolt (1980; 1984) reports on part of the MIT Media Room project. The best way to introduce this work is by example. Imagine that you are sitting in a chair facing a large (i.e., wall-sized) screen, on which is displayed a map of the Pacific Ocean. Your task is to monitor and control the movement of a fleet of ships. On the basis of incoming information, you decide to order the movement of one of the ships in the fleet. You point at the ship on the map and say "put that . . ." (the ship becomes highlighted to indicate that it has been selected), you then point to the new location and complete the command, ". . . there". The picture of the ship then moves to the new location. The gesture recognition part of this project has been discussed already, in Chapter 4. In the "Put that there" system, it is possible to issue commands which allow users to create shapes of different colours and sizes, which can be positioned to different places (i.e., point to a place and say "there"). The objects can be copied ("copy") and their properties altered ("make the blue square big"). In these examples, the interaction takes the simple form of pointing at an object and speaking a command.

Thorisson et al. (1992), in what could be seen as an extension of the "Put that there" concept, developed a system which combined speech with hand gestures (using a data glove) and eye tracking. The tasks they were examining required a small vocabulary of actions {move, delete, name, create, request information}, and one of the claimed advantages of the system was that, "By allowing for multimodal interaction, people can use their social skills in interacting with the computer" (p. 654). In Chapter 10, the differences between communicating with other people and with computers using speech were discussed. One would expect users of multimodal systems to need to develop new "social skills" in their interaction with semi-intelligent technology, rather than simply to be able to adapt conventional skills which have proved useful in human communication. In the Thorisson et al. (1992) paper, the notion of "social skills" is exemplified by the relatively simple task of resolving deictic ambiguity, e.g., the expression "delete that object" could be ambiguous if the user does not indicate which object to delete. The use of multiple interaction devices permits the computer to take the user's action and command, and then guess the intended object. I am not sure what happens if the computer's guess is wrong; hopefully, there will be an undo facility.

Multimodal HCI raises the interesting question of timing in interaction. If a speech recognizer takes 250 ms to process a spoken word and a touchscreen takes 25 ms to respond to a touch, then one might find that a combined spoken command and touch, used to signal an object, could be ordered incorrectly (see Figure 14.1).

This could simply be a matter of defining an appropriate syntax for ordering user actions. However, it raises the further question of when two actions belong together and when they are separate. Should the system incorporate detailed and sophisticated knowledge of the task domain and likely combinations of actions? Should the user be forced to perform actions to strict timing? Or are there other solutions? Given the relative novelty of multimodal HCI, it is unlikely that this debate will be resolved in the near future.

In addition to the use of gestures as a means of locating objects in space, people use gestures to describe objects, e.g., to indicate how large an object is. Taking this idea further, Weiner and Ganapathy (1992) have proposed a system which combines speech and gesture to allow designers to commu-

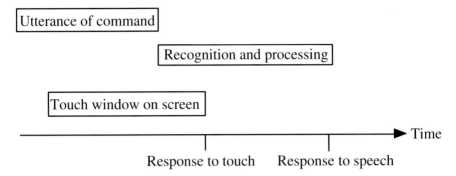

Figure 14.1 Sequencing problems for multimodal HCI (after Bellik *et al.*, 1995)

nicate design ideas via a computer. The gesture can be used to trace hand movement, for example in the drawing of curves, and speech recognition is used to enter commands and instructions.

It would appear that combining speech with manual interaction is both popular and useful. In addition to the benefits suggested above, it is possible that part of the utility of combining manual and spoken inter- action arises from the appropriate use of the modalities for interaction, i.e., where movement, pointing, manipulation and other physical actions are performed manually, and actions involving alphanumeric data entry are performed using speech. Taylor (1989) has noted that in high-performance military aircraft, pilots' hands and feet are fully occupied with controls, vision is fully occupied with displays and with surveying the visual environ- ment outside the aircraft, and both reach and field of vision are severaly limited. Consequently, efforts have been made to provide a means by which the pilot can communicate with on-board computers using the potentially spare speech modality. However, as Baber (1991) has pointed out, speech is not always a "spare" modality in the cockpit, with requirements for spoken communications between the pilot and a number of other people.

14.4   Multiple resource theory

Cognitive psychologists have debated the codes used in information pro- cessing for decades. One of the popular notions in contemporary cognitive psychology is that there are several codes in which information is processed. Typically, psychologists speak of visuo-spatial and verbal codes (Baddeley, 1986). The notion of information codes allows one to classify objects in the world in terms of the code by which they can present information to the observer, e.g., via words or graphics, and to define the manner by which the information will be processed, and to define the type of response that an individual can make, e.g., verbally or manually (where manual response can be considered as a movement in space). While the first and third forms of classification are difficult to refute, there has been much debate concerning the nature of the information-processing stage, with some writers arguing that all information is processed in a similar fashion (Pylyshyn, 1984) and others arguing that information is processed using distinct codes (Paivio, 1982). For the purposes of multiple resource theory, assume that each type of information code has its own processing capability and its own processing resources (Allport, 1980; Wickens, 1992). From these assumptions, one can propose a model of human information processing which has several stages and uses several codes (Figure 14.2).

In the first (encoding) stage, information from the world is presented using one of the information-processing codes and perceived via the appropriate sensory modality, e.g., a spoken message is transmitted using the verbal code and received by the auditory modality. The second (central processing) stage involves the interpretation of the information, again using the appropriate code (in this case, it will be the verbal code). The final stage involves defining an appropriate response to the information. Following the notions of compatibility, one can predict that verbal information should be responded to vocally, and spatial information should be responded to manually.

Given the notion of separate codes and resources, it is possible to make the further hypothesis that the information-processing demands on a particular code would increase if more information was presented using

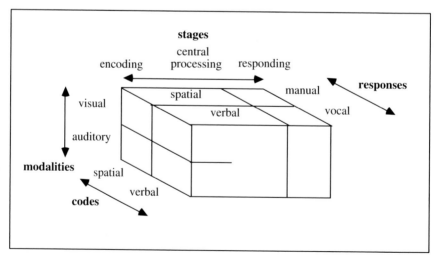

Figure 14.2 The structure of multiple resources (from Wickens, 1992, *Engineering Psychology and Human Performance*, p. 375, Harper Collins)

that code, e.g., if a large number of objects on a display started flashing at once the visual modality would be overloaded. Consequently, it is felt that combining more than one information code can utilize "spare" resources. In Chapter 11, some of the issues surrounding the conflict and competition between processing codes and demands were discussed.

The main support for multiple resource theory comes from secondary task experiments. Participants are required to perform a primary task, such as controlling the movement of a cursor on the screen or "flying" in a flight simulator, and then asked to perform a secondary task, such as entering specific information during the performance of the task. The manner in which the tasks are performed and information is presented to participants is varied across conditions in order to determine which combinations of spatial or auditory display and manual or spoken response leads to best performance. In general, the results tend to support the argument that performance on a verbal secondary task, when paired with a spatial primary task such as tracking, is best when spoken responses are paired with auditory displays (Harris et al., 1978; Wickens, 1980; Wickens et al., 1983; Wickens et al., 1984). Further, performance on a spatial secondary task, when paired with a spatial primary task, is best when manual responses are made to visual displays (Wickens et al., 1983; Wickens et al., 1984). Performance on a verbal secondary task is better than that on a spatial secondary task, when paired with a spatial primary task (Wickens and Liu, 1988).

From the study of Wickens et al. (1983) one can conclude that visual competition at input disrupts performance, especially if participants are required to perform visual scanning with tracking tasks. Spatial tasks show far more interference than combinations of verbal and spatial tasks (Baddeley and Lieberman, 1980). Further, interference between tasks can be related to the timing of demands, as well as the code used (Damos, 1986). Thus, one could argue that competition for resources can be scheduled, depending on the relative urgency of the tasks (Navon and Gopher, 1979). These studies support the notion that human information processing involves a limited attentional resource, employing discrete sensory modalities. Compatibility can be achieved by appropriate pairing of information with response.

There are a number of problems with multiple resource theory which need to be considered. The first problem lies at a conceptual level; multiple resource theory allows one to explain competitions for resources between similar tasks. However, the theory also allows one to predict compatibility between similar tasks. Thus, the mechanism by which tasks compete or combine is difficult to define. While one can argue that this is a matter of competition for resources across codes, i.e., how much attentional effort is given to each task, one could also argue that it is a matter of scheduling of resource allocation (Vidulich, 1986). This makes it difficult to use multiple resource theory to predict performance instead of describing performance *post hoc*.

The second problem lies in the methodology most often used in multiple resource theory research, the secondary task approach. Secondary tasks can disrupt primary task performance. This means that results from secondary task studies may not reflect performance on one task or the other, but may reflect the performance on a combined task, i.e., in which performance on the tasks interacts. As Duncan (1979) has pointed out, when two tasks are performed concurrently, there will exist a number of relationships that are not present in single task conditions. This further complicates the problems of deciding whether the results arise due to competition, compatibility or scheduling of attentional demands across the tasks.

The third problem relates to the definition of codes for information presentation. While it is clear that text is verbal, and maps are spatial, it is less clear how one should define numbers, for instance, or how one should define coordinates on a map. This means that specifying the combinations of tasks can be more of an art than a science.

The fourth problem is one of scope. At present, multiple resource theory only considers visual and auditory modalities for perception. However, it is equally feasible to employ tactile or kinesthetic feedback from computers to the user. In Chapter 9, for instance, several recent developments were discussed with reference to the design of mice. The use of tactile and kinesthetic feedback was proposed to be beneficial for spatial tasks due to compatibility across information codes. This can be further illustrated with the following example; imagine a plane has suddenly gone into a stall. In a "traditional" cockpit, the stick would judder and shake in the pilot's hands, giving immediate and clear indication of the emergency. In a modern cockpit, a stall warning might be presented using an auditory alarm, such as an auditory warning or a synthesized speech message. In this instance, the tactile feedback of previous generations has been replaced by another presentation medium, which might require some degree of translation on the part of the pilot, thus introducing a time penalty.

While one can offer criticisms of the current state of multiple resource theory, it does offer a very useful framework for considering multimodal HCI. From multiple resource theory, one might anticipate that using manual devices for spatial tasks (such as drawing) can be effectively paired with speech recognition for entering commands (such as changing color or resizing the drawing). Martin (1989) has shown that combining speech with pointing devices is an effective means of drawing using CAD.

While this section has briefly considered the separation of modalities, and the implications for system design and human performance, there is a final area which is of interest: cross-modality perception. Most of us are familiar with the concept that certain sounds can be associated with colors, e.g., low pitch tones are perceived as darker and high pitch tones are perceived as lighter (Marks, 1975). One might anticipate that the association between colors and temperature is related to this notion (Crozier, 1994). As far as HCI is concerned, the use of auditory cues to "describe" actions and objects has been used for some time (see Chapter 9). Gaver (1986) has proposed that people tend to have associations between sounds and events which can be used to support task performance in HCI and to support organizational computing (see Chapter 13), e.g., one could use specific auditory cues to indicate when a visitor has arrived or when it is time for a meeting.

14.5 Conclusions

HCI, by definition, sees the task of interacting with a computer as its principal area of concern. However, this can omit consideration of other relationships in the workplace which could influence task performance and does not account for the wide range of tasks in which computers are used while the user is engaged in another activity. This other activity could be relatively demanding, such as driving a car or piloting a high-performance jet, or could be relatively mundane, such as watching the television. The point to note is that in all of these situations, the use of the computer ought to be secondary to the primary task.

There are some environments in which this distinction has become blurred in recent years, the most obvious being in the control rooms of large-scale industrial process plants. A number of writers have noted that, with the increase in the use of computers in these control rooms, operators are faced with the tasks of monitoring and controlling the process and controlling the computer (Edwards and Lees, 1974; Rasmussen, 1974; Ivergard, 1989). In some instances, the computer begins to act as a barrier to the smooth performance of the primary task of process control, requiring the operator to engage in lengthy and confusing dialogues to obtain specific items of information. In this instance, it is clear that operating the computer becomes a task in its own right.

The notion of HCI as a secondary task simply strengthens the arguments that computers should be usable, etc. However, I feel that there is another benefit to considering HCI as a secondary task: the need to consider the context of HCI. In the preceding chapters, the notion of context has been developed to cover a number of topics. From the arguments concerning compatibility, comes the notion of task-fit in which appropriate devices are used to perform specific tasks. This led to the discussion of the design of generic devices for generic actions. Taking this argument further, it is possible to envisage combinations of devices which can be used to allow users to focus on their primary tasks and goals. The notion of direct manipulation has gone some way to achieving this aim. If appropriate devices are to be fitted to computers, to allow focus on primary tasks at work, then the issue of multimodal HCI will become increasingly important. Multiple resource theory has been presented as a possible framework for considering the effects and benefits of combining interaction devices in future systems.

In this book, it has been proposed that, in addition to cognitive aspects of HCI, one should consider interaction in terms of the physical activities performed by users of a computer. From this perspective, the design of interaction devices becomes central to the development of new computer systems. It is becoming apparent that the devices with which we interact with computers are becoming less adaptable and less useful; the interest in designing and marketing new forms of interaction device supports this hypothesis. On the one hand, this raises a simple question of whether one ought to strive to develop more physical tools for HCI, rather than simply develop more virtual tools. In a number of places in the book, the arguments imply a shift of focus from seeing "tools" as objects on computer screens (i.e., icons, menus, etc.) to physical artifacts (i.e., interaction devices). However, this proposal founders on the recognition that one may well require a veritable toolkit filled with a number of discrete, single function tools; the *reductio ad absurdum* of this position is the image of the computer as a small, light portable artifact but the interaction devices requiring a large bag to carry around. On the other hand (and more importantly), comes the need to recognize that HCI has a physical component, that the physical activities involved in using computers are important and that these activities can be helped or hindered by the design and operation of interaction devices. This suggests that interaction devices can be developed as significant components of the computer system, not only acting as transducers to convert user action to computer response, but communicating all manner of feedback to the user and support a greater variety of physical activity. By considering the nature of interaction devices and the ways in which people use them it will be possible to inform the design of a new generation of interaction devices.

14.6 Key points for practitioners

- Consider the various task demands on computer users, e.g., to what extent do manual tasks interfere with each other?
- Consider the extent to which the computer acts as a barrier to the performance of primary tasks.

- Consider whether the use of additional devices will help to unload task demands by utilizing other modalities.

14.7   Key points for researchers

- Develop multiple resource theory as a framework for investigating multimodal HCI.
- Consider the design of interaction devices in terms of their compatibility with information processing demands.
- Consider the design of combinations of limited function devices rather than single, multifunctional devices.

References

Ainsworth, W.A. (1988). *Speech Recognition by Machine.* London: Peter Peregrinus.

Albert, A.E. (1982). The effect of graphic input devices on performance in a cursor positioning task. In *Proceedings of the 26th. Annual Meeting of the Human Factors Society.* Santa Monica, CA: Human Factors Society, pp. 54–58.

Alden, D.G., Daniels, R.W., & Kanarick, A.F. (1972). Keyboard design and operations: a review of the major issues. *Human Factors* **14**, 275–293.

Allard, F., & Starkes, J.L. (1991). Motor-skill experts in sports, dance and other domains. In K.A. Ericsson and J. Smith (Eds), *Toward a General Theory of Expertise.* Cambridge: Cambridge University Press.

Allerhand, M. (1987). *Knowledge-based Speech Pattern Recognition.* London: Kogan Page.

Allport, D.A. (1980). Attention. In G.L. Glaxton (Ed.), *New Directions in Cognitive Psychology.* London: Routledge and Kegan Paul.

Anderson, J.R. (1990). *Cognitive Psychology and its Implications.* New York: W.H. Freeman and Co.

Anderson, N.S., Sobiloff, B., White, P., & Pearson, G. (1993) A foot operated PC pointing device. In *Proceedings of the 37th. Annual Meeting of the Human Factors Society.* Santa Monica, CA: Human Factors Society, pp. 314–317.

Annett, J., Duncan, K.D., Stammers, R.B., & Gray, M.J. (1971). *Task Analysis.* London: HMSO.

Anson, J.G. (1982). Memory drum theory: alternative tests and explanations for the complexity effects on reaction time. *Journal of Motor Behaviour,* **14**, 228–246.

Aretz, A.J. (1983) A comparison of manual and vocal response modes for the control of aircraft systems. In *Proceedings of the 27th. Annual Meeting of the Human Factors Society.* Santa Monica, CA: Human Factors Society.

Austin, J.L. (1962). *How to Do Things with Words.* Oxford: Oxford University Press.

Baber, C. (1991). *Speech Technology in Control Room Systems: a Human Factors Perspective.* Chichester: Ellis Horwood Ltd.

Baber, C. (1993). Developing interactive speech technology. In C. Baber and J.M. Noyes (Eds), *Interactive Speech Technology.* London: Taylor and Francis, pp. 1–18.

Baber, C. (1995). The effects of workload on the use of speech recognition systems. In *Proceedings of the NATO/ESCA Workshop on Speech under Stress.* Lisbon: INESC, pp. 75–82.

Baber, C. (1996). The psychology of pointing. First International Conference of Engineering Psychology and Cognitive Ergonomics. Stratford-upon-Avon, October 23–25, 1996.

Baber, C., & Hone, K.S. (1993). Modelling error recovery and repair in automatic speech recognition. *International Journal of Man Machine Studies,* **39**, 495–515.

Baber, C., & Noyes, J.M. (1996). Automatic speech recognition in adverse environments. *Human Factors,* **38** (1), 142–155.

Baber, C., & Parker, A. (1994). Buying a ticket on the Underground. In S.A. Robertson (Ed.), *Contemporary Ergonomics 1994*. London: Taylor and Francis, pp. 64–69.

Baber, C., & Stammers, R.B. (1989). Is it natural to talk to computers: an experiment using the Wizard of Oz technique. In E.D. Megaw, (Ed.), *Contemporary Ergonomics 1989*. London: Taylor and Francis.

Baber, C., & Stanton, N.A. (1994). Task analysis for error identification: a methodology for designing error-tolerant products. *Ergonomics*, **37**, 1923–1941.

Baber, C., Hoyes, T., & Stanton, N.A. (1993). Comparison of GUIs and CUIs: appropriate ranges of actions and ease of use. *Displays*, **14**, 207–215.

Baber, C., Saini, M., & Stubbins, P. (1995). Tacit skills in craft work: implications for automation. *Ergonomics Society Conference 1995*, Canterbury.

Baber, C., Stammers, R.B., & Taylor, R.G. (1991). An experimental assessment of automatic speech recognition in high cognitive workload situations in control room systems. In Y. Quéinnec and F. Daniellou (Eds), *Designing for Everyone*. London: Taylor and Francis, pp. 833–835.

Baber, C., & Stanton, N.A. (1996). Human error identification techniques applied to public technology: predictions compared with observed use. *Applied Ergonomics*, **27**, 119–131.

Baber, C., Usher, D.M., Stammers, R.B., & Taylor, R.G. (1992). Feedback requirements for ASR in the process control room. *International Journal of Man Machine Studies*, **37**, 703–719.

Baddeley, A.D. (1986). *Working Memory*. Oxford: Oxford University Press.

Baddeley, A.D., & Lieberman, K. (1980). Spatial working memory. In R. Nickerson (Ed.), *Attention and Performance VIII*. Hillsdale, NJ: Lawrence Erlbaum Associates.

Ball, R.G., Newton, R.S., & Whitefield, D. (1980). Development of an off-display, high resolution direct touch input device: the RSRE touchpad. *Displays*, **1**, 203–207.

Bannon, L., & Bødker, S. (1991). Beyond the interface: encountering artifacts in use. In J. Carroll (Ed.), *Designing Interaction: psychology at the human–computer interface*. Cambridge: Cambridge University Press.

Barfield, W., Sandford, J., & Foley, J. (1988). The mental rotation and perceived realism of computer-generated three-dimensional images. *International Journal of Man–Machine Studies*, **29**, 669–684.

Barker, D., Carey, M.S., & Taylor, R.G. (1990). Factors underlying mouse pointing performance. In E.J. Lovesey (Ed.), *Contemporary Ergonomics 1990*. London: Taylor and Francis, pp. 359–364.

Barmack, J.E., & Sinaiko, H. (1966). *Human factors problems in computer-generated graphic displays*. Washington, DC: Institute for Defence Analysis Report SD-50-AD36170.

Barnard, P.J., & Hammond, N.V. (1983). *Cognitive Contexts and Interactive Communication*. Hursley: IBM Human Factors Laboratory Report.

Beeching, W.A. (1974). *Century of the Typewriter*. London: Heineman.

Beggs, W.D.A., & Howarth, C.I. (1970). Movement control in a repetitive motor task. *Nature*, **225**, 752–753.

Bekker, M.M., van Nes, F.L., & Juola, J.F. (1994). A comparison of mouse and speech input control of a text-annotation system. *Behaviour and Information Technology*, **14**, 14–22.

Bellik, Y., Ferrari, S., Néel, F., & Teil, D. (1995). Requirements for multimodal dialogue including vocal interaction. *Proceedings of the ECSA Workshop on Spoken Dialogue Systems*. Lisbon: ECSA, pp. 161–164.

Berkun, M.M. (1964). Performance decrement under psychological stress. *Human Factors*, **6**, 21–30.

Bernstein, N. (1967). *The Co-ordination and Regulation of Movements*. New York: Pergamon Press.

Biermann, A.W., Fineman, L., & Heidlage, J.F. (1992). A voice-and touch-driven natural language editor and its performance. *International Journal of Man–Machine Studies*, **37**, 1–21.

Blattner, M., Sumikawa, D., & Greenberg, R. (1989). Earcons and icons: their structure and common design principles. *Human–Computer Interaction*, **4**, 11–44.

Bodensher, H. (1970). A console keyboard for improved man–machine interaction. *Man–Machine Interaction Conference*. London: IEE publication no. 68, pp. 196–200.

Bødker, S. (1989). A human activity approach to user interfaces. *Human Computer Interaction*, **4**, 171–195.

Bolt, R.A. (1980). Put-that-there: voice and gesture at the graphics interface. *Computer Graphics*, **14**, 262–270.

Bolt, R.A. (1984). *The Human Interface: where people and computers meet*. Boston: Lifetime Learning Publications.

Booth, P. (1989). *An Introduction to HCI*. Hillsdale, NJ: LEA.

Bovair, S., Kieras, D.E., & Polson, P.G. (1990). The acquisition and performance of text-editing skill: a cognitive complexity analysis. *Human–Computer Interaction*, **5**, 1–48.

Bowen, H.M., & Guinness, G.V. (1965). Preliminary experiments on keyboard design for semi-automatic mail sorting. *Journal of Applied Psychology*, **49**, 194–198.

Bradley, J.W. (1969). Glove characteristics influencing control manipulability. *Human Factors*, **11**, 21–36.

Brandeau, R.J. (1982). Performance interactions with voice interactive systems: implementation of task complexity. In D.S. Pallett (Ed.), *Proceedings of the Workshop on Standardisation of Speech I/O Technology*. Gaithersberg, MD: National Bureau of Standards.

Bridwell, L., Johnson, P., & Brehe, S. (1984). Composing and computers: case studies of experienced writers. In A. Matsuhashi, (Ed.), *Writing in Real-Time: Modelling Production Processes*. New York: Longman.

Briggs, G.E., Fitts, P.M., & Bahrick, H.P. (1957). Effects of force and amplitude cues on learning and performance in a complex tracking task. *Journal of Experimental Psychology*, **54**, 262–268.

Broadbent, D.E. (1971). *Decision and Stress*. London: Academic Press.

Brown, C.M. (1988). *Human–computer interface design guidelines*. Norwood, NJ: Ablex.

Brown, N.R., & Vosburgh, A.M. (1989). Evaluating the accuracy of a large vocabulary speech recognition system. *Proceedings of the 33rd. Annual Meeting of the Human Factors Society*. Santa Monica, CA: Human Factors Society, pp. 296–300.

Brunner, H., & Richardson, R. (1984). Effects of keyboard design and typing skill on user keyboard preferences and throughout performance. In D. Attwood and C. McCann, (Eds), *Proceedings of the 1984 International Conference on Occupational Ergonomics*. Rexdale, Ontario: Human Factors Association of Canada, pp. 267–271.

Buck, L. (1980). Motor performance in relation to control display gain and target width. *Ergonomics*, **23**, 579–589.

Bühler, K. (1934). *Sprachtheorie*. Stuttgart: Fisher.

Bunt, H.C., Leopold, F.F., Müller, H.F., & van Katwijk, A.F.V. (1978). In search of pragmatic principles in man–machine dialogues. *IPO Annual Progress Report*, **13**, 94–98.

Butsch, R.L.C. (1932). Eye movements and the eye–hand span in typewriting. *Journal of Educational Psychology*, **23**, 104–121.

Button, G. (1990). Going up a blind alley: conflating conversation analysis and computational modelling. In P. Luff, N. Gilbert and D. Frohlich (Eds), *Computers and Conversation*. London: Academic Press, pp. 67–90.

Buxton, W. (1983). Lexical and pragmatic considerations of input structures. *Computer Graphics*, **17**, 31–37.

Buxton, W. (1986). There's more to interaction than meets the eye: some issues in manual input. In D.A. Norman and S.W. Draper (Eds), *User Centred System Design*. Hillsdale, NJ: LEA.

Buxton, W. (1988). *Input: thinking about the first two letters in interaction*. Notes from a tutorial given at HCI '88 Manchester: UMIST 1988.

Buxton, W. (1990a). *The Pragmatics of Haptic Input*. Notes from a tutorial given at Interact '90 Cambridge: University of Cambridge 1990.

Buxton, W. (1990b). A three-state model of graphical input. *Interact '90*. Amsterdam: North Holland, pp. 449–456.

Cakir, A., Hart, D.J., & Stewart, T.F.M. (1980). *Video Display Terminals*. New York: Wiley.

Card, S.K., English, W., & Burr, B. (1978). Evaluation of mouse, rate-controlled isometric joystick, step keys and text keys for text selection on a CRT. *Ergonomics*, **21**, 601–613.

Card, S.K., Moran, T., & Newell, A. (1980). The keystroke level model for user performance time with interactive systems. *Communications of the ACM*, **23**, 396–410.

Card, S.K., Moran, T.P., & Newell, A. (1983). *The Psychology of Human–Computer Interaction*. Hillsdale, NJ: LEA.

Card, S.K., MacKinlay, J.D., & Robertson, G.G. (1991). A morphological analysis of the design space of input devices. *ACM Transactions on Information Systems*, **9**, 99–122.

Card, S.K., MacKinlay, J.D., & Robertson, G.G. (1992). The design space of input devices. In M. M. Blattner and R.B. Danneberg (Eds), *Multimedia Interface Design*. New York: ACM Press.

Carey, M.S. (1985). *Selection Criteria for Computer Input Devices*. Birmingham: Aston University, Applied Psychology Department.

Carlton, M.J. (1983). Amending movements: the relationship between degree of mechanical disturbance and outcome accuracy. *Journal of Motor Behaviour*, **15**, 39–62.

Carroll, J.M. (1991). *Designing Interaction: psychology at the human–computer interface*. Cambridge: Cambridge University Press.

Carroll, J.M., Kellog, W.A., & Rosson, M.B. (1991). The task–artifact cycle. In J. Carroll (Ed.), *Designing Interaction: psychology at the human–computer interface*. Cambridge: Cambridge University Press.

Carter, J.B., & Banister, E.W. (1994). Musculoskeletal problems in VDT work: a review. *Ergonomics*, **37**, 1623–1648.

Carter, K.E.P., Newell, A., & Arnott, J.L. (1988). Studies using a simulated listening typewriter. *Proceedings of Speech '88*. Edinburgh: Institute of Acoustics, pp. 1289–1296.

Chapanis, A. (1975). Interactive human communication. *Scientific American*, **232**, 36–42.

Chapanis, A. (1988) Should you believe what the new ANSI/HFS standard says about numeric keypad layouts? No. *Human Factors Society Bulletin*, **31**, 6–9.

Chapanis, A., & Kinkade, R. (1972). Design of controls. In H. van Cott and R.

Kinkade (Eds), *Engineering Guide to Equipment Design*. Washington, DC: US Government Printing Office.

Clark, H.H., & Clark, E.V. (1977). *Psychology and Language: an introduction to psycholinguistics*. New York: Harcourt Brace, Jovanovich.

Cockburn, C. (1983). The nature of skill: the case of the printers. In C.R. Littler (Ed.), *The Experience of Work*. Aldershot: Ashgate.

Cohen, P.R., Dalrymple, M., Moran, D.B., Pereira, F.C.N., Sullivan, J.W., Gargan, R.A., Schlossberg, J.L., & Sherman, W.T. (1989). Synergistic use of direct manipulation and natural language. *CHI '89*. New York: ACM, pp. 227–233.

Colquhoun, W.P., & Goldman, R.F. (1972). Vigilance under induced hyperthermia. *Ergonomics*, **15**, 621–632.

Conrad, R. (1967). Performance with push-button arrangements. *Het PTT-Bedrijfdeel*, **15**, 110–113.

Conrad, R., & Hull, A.J. (1968). The preferred layout for numeral data-entry keysets Ergonomics, **11**, 165–173.

Conrad, R., & Longman, D.J.A. (1965). Standard typewriter versus chord keyboard: an experimental comaprison. *Ergonomics*, **8**, 77–88.

Cooley, M. (1981). The social implications of CAD. In J. Mermet (Ed.), *CAD in medium sized and small industries*. Amsterdam: North-Holland.

Cooper, W.E. (1983). Introduction. In W.E. Cooper (Ed.), *Cognitive Aspects of Skilled Typewriting*. New York: Springer Verlag.

Crane, P.M. (1984). Human factors of touch screen and voice command data entry on a C3 System. *Proceedings of SID International Symposium*. New York: Palisades Institute of Research Services, pp. 231–234.

Crossman, E.F.R.W. (1956). The information capacity of the human operator in symbolic and non-symbolic control processes. In *Information Theory and the Human Operator*. London: Ministry of Supply Report WR/D2/56.

Crossman, E.F.R.W., & Goodeve, P.T. (1963). Feedback and control of hand movement and Fitts law. *Quarterly Journal of Experimental Psychology 35A*, pp. 153–166.

Crozier, R. (1994). *Manufactured Pleasures: psychological responses to design*. Manchester: Manchester University Press.

Dainoff, M.J. (1982). Occupational stress factors in visual display terminal (VDT) operation: a review of empirical research. *Behaviour and Information Technology*, **1**, 141–176.

Dainoff, M.J., & Mark, L.S. (1987). Task and the adjustment of ergonomic chairs. In B. Knave and P.G. Wideback (Eds), *Work with Visual Display Units '86*. Amsterdam: North-Holland.

Damos, D.L. (1986). The effect of using voice generation and recognition systems on the performance of dual tasks. *Ergonomics*, **29**, 1359–1370.

Damper, R.I. (1984). Voice input aids for the physically disabled. *International Journal of Man–Machine Studies*, **21**, 542–553.

Damper, R.I. (1988). Practical experiences with speech data entry. In E.D. Megaw (Ed.), *Contemporary Ergonomics 1988*. London: Taylor and Francis, pp. 92–97.

Damper, R.I. (1993). Speech as an interface medium: how can it best be used? In C. Baber & J.M. Noyes (Eds), *Interactive Speech Technology*, London: Taylor and Francis.

Daniellou, F., & Garigou, A. (1992). Human factors in design: sociotechnics or ergonomics? In M. Helander and Nagamachi (Eds), *Design for Manufacturability*. London: Taylor and Francis.

Darragh, J.J., & Witten, I.H. (1993). *The Reactive Keyboard*. Cambridge: Cambridge University Press.

Davies, B.L., Robotham, A.J., & Yarwood, A. (1986). *Computer–aided Drawing and Design*. London: Chapman and Hall.

Davies, C., Katifi, H., Ridley, A., & Swash, M. (1991). Mouse trap or personal computer palsy. *Lancet*, **338**, 832.

Davies, D.R., & Parasuraman, R. (1982). *The Psychology of Vigilance*. London: Academic Press.

Deininger, R.L. (1960). Human factors engineering studies of the design and use of pushbutton telephone sets. *The Bell System Technical Journal*, **39**, 995–1012.

Dell, G.S. (1986). A spreading activation theory of retrieval in sentence production. *Psychological Review*, **93**, 283–321.

Denier van der Goon, J.J., & Thuring, J.P. (1965). The guiding of human handwriting movements. *Biological Cybernetics*, **2**, 145–148.

Devoe, D.B. (1967). Alternative to handprinting in the manual entry of data. *IEEE Transactions on Human Factors*, **8**, 21–31.

Diaper, D. (1989). *Task Analysis for Human–Computer Interaction*. Chichester: Ellis Horwood.

Dillon, A., & Sweeney, M. (1988). The application of cognitive psychology to CAD. In D.M. Jones and R. Winder (Eds), *People and Computer IV*. Cambridge: Cambridge University Press, pp. 477–488.

Dillon, R.F., Edey, J.D., & Tombaugh, J.W. (1990) Measuring the true cost of command selection: techniques and results. *CHI'90*. New York: ACM 19–25.

Dix, A., Finlay, J., Abowd, G., & Beale, R. (1993). *Human–Computer Interaction*. New York: Prentice-Hall.

Donders, F.C. (1868) Die schnelligkeit psychischer processe. *Archiv. Anatomie und Physiologie*, pp. 657–681.

Draper, S.W. (1984). The nature of expertise in UNIX. *Interact '84*. Amsterdam: North-Holland.

Driskell, J.E., & Salas, E. (1991). Overcoming the effects of stress on military performance: human factors, training and selection strategies. In R. Gal and A.D. Mangelsdorf (Eds), *Handbook of Military Psychology*. New York: Wiley.

Duncan, J. (1979). Divided attention: the whole is more than the sum of its parts. *Journal of Experimental Psychology: Human Perception and Performance*, **5**, 216–228.

Duncan, J., & Ferguson, D. (1974). Keyboard operating posture and symptoms in operating. *Ergonomics*, **17**, 651–662.

Duncan, S. (1972). Some signals and rules for taking turns in conversation. *Journal of Personality and Social Psychology*, **23**, 282–292.

Duncan, S. (1973). Towards a grammar for dyadic conversation. *Semiotica*, **9**, 29–47.

Duncan, S. (1974). On the structure of speaker–auditor interaction during speaking turns. *Language in Society*, **2**, 161–180.

Dunn, A.G. (1971). Engineering the typing keyboard from the human factors viewpoint. *Computers and Automation February*, pp. 32–33.

Dvorak, A. (1943). There is a better keyboard. *National Business Education Quarterly*, **12**, pp. 51–88.

Eason, K.D. (1984). Towards the experimental study of usability. *Behaviour and Information Technology*, **3**, 133–134.

Eason, K.D. (1987). *Information Technology and Organisational Change*. London: Taylor and Francis.

Eason, K.D. (1989) Designing systems to match organisation reality. In A. Sutcliffe and L. Macauley (eds), *People and Computers V*, pp. 57–69. Cambridge: Cambridge University Press.

Eberts, R.E. (1994). *User Interface Design*. Englewood Cliffs, NJ: Prentice-Hall.

Edwards, E. & Lees, F.P. (1974). *The Human Operator in Process Control*. London: Taylor and Francis.

Eglowstein, H. (1990). Reach out and touch your data. *BYTE July* 23–29.

Ellis, A.W. (1979). Slips of the pen. *Visible Language VIII*, pp. 265–282.

Ellis, A.W. (1982). Spelling and writing (and reading and speaking). In A.W. Ellis (Ed.), *Normality and Pathology in Cognitive Functions*. London: Academic Press.

Ellis, W.E., & Young, A.W. (1988). *Human Cognitive Neuropsychology*. London: LEA.

Ellozy, H.A. (1990). The paper-like interface: an overview. *1990 SID International Symposium Digest of Technical Papers*. Playa del Rey, CA: Society for Information Display, pp. 168–171.

Embrey, D.E. (1986). SHERPA: a systematic human error reduction and prediction approach. *Proceedings of the International Topical Meeting on Advances in Human Factors in Nuclear Power Systems*. Knoxville, Tennessee.

Emery, F.E. (1959). *The Characteristics of a Sociotechnical System*. London: Tavistock Institute Document 527.

Emmons, W.H. (1984). A comparison of cursor key arrangements (box versus cross) for VDUs. In E. Grandjean (Ed.), *Ergonomics and Health in Modern Offices*. London: Taylor and Francis.

Emmons, W.H., & Hirsch, R. (1982). Thirty millimetre keyboards: how good are they? *Proceedings of the 36th. Annual Meeting of the Human Factors Society*. Santa Monica, CA: Human Factors Society, pp. 425–429.

Endo, Y., Akimichi, S., & Milne, M. (1993). The context-based graphic input system: a T-board. In G. Salvendy and M.J. Smith (Eds), *Human–Computer Interaction: Software and Hardware Interfaces*. Amsterdam: North-Holland.

Enfield, C. (1978). A typewriter in your pocket. *Computer Weekly*, **11** (May), 4.

English, W.K., Englebart, D.C., & Berman, M.L. (1967). Display selection techniques for text manipulation. *IEEE Transactions on Human Factors*, **8**, 5–15.

Epps, B.W. (1986). Comparison of six cursor control devices based on Fitts' law models. *Proceedings of the 30th Annual Meeting of the Human Factors Society*. Santa Monica, CA: Human Factors Society, pp. 327–331.

Ericsson, K.A., & Polson, P.G. (1988). An experimental analysis of a memory skill for dinner-orders. *Journal of Experimental Psychology: Learning, Memory and Cognition*, **14**, 305–316.

Ericsson, K.A., & Smith, J. (1991). *Toward a Theory of Expertise*. Cambridge: Cambridge University Press.

Erlich, S.F., & Akiba, E.A. (1985). Successful implementation of voice store and forward technology: a case study. *SIGOA Bulletin*, **6**, 19–26.

Evans, J. St. B.T. (1989). *Bias and Human Reasoning*. Hillsdale, NJ: LEA.

Fairchild, K.M. (1992). *Information Management using Virtual Reality-based Visualisations*. London: Taylor and Francis.

Falzon, P. (1984). The analysis of an operative language. *Interact'84*. Amsterdam: North-Holland.

Fant, G. (1960). *Acoustic Theory of Speech Production*. The Hague, Mouton.

Fendrick, P. (1937). Hierarchical skills in typewriting. *Journal of Educational Psychology*, **28**, 609–620.

Fisher, M. (1986). Voice control for the disabled. In G. Bristow (Ed.), *Electronic Speech Recognition*. London: Collins.

Fitts, P.M. (1954). The information capacity of the human motor system in controlling the amplitude of movement. *Journal of Experimental Psychology*, **47**, 381–391.

Fitts, P.M., & Peterson, J.R. (1964). Information capacity of discrete motor responses. *Journal of Experimental Psychology*, **67**, 103–112.

Fitts, P.M., & Seeger, C.M. (1953). S-R compatibility: spatial characteristics of stimulus and response codes. *Journal of Experimental Psychology*, **46**, 199–210.

Fleischer, A.G., & Becker, G. (1986). Free hand-movements during the performance of a complex task. *Ergonomics*, **29**, 49–63.

Floyd, S.J.H. (1979). *Standard QWERTY versus Maltron-QWERTY: an experimental comparison*. Loughborough: Loughborough Department of Human Sciences.

Foley, J.D., & van Dam, A. (1982). *Fundamentals of Interactive Computer Graphics*. Reading, Mass: Addison-Wesley.

Foley, J.D., & Wallace, V.L. (1974). The art of graphic man–machine conversation. *Proceedings of the IEEE*, **62**, 462–464.

Foley, J.D., van Dam, A., Feiner, S.K., & Hughes, J.F. (1990). *Computer Graphics: principles and practice*. Reading, MA: Addison-Wesley [2nd. edition].

Forester, T. (1989). *Computers in the Human Context*. Oxford: Basil Blackwell.

Fortune, D., Oritz, J.E., & Barline, R. (1991). Adaption of the tongue-touch keypad and zofcom system to educational applications. *Proceedings of the 6th. CUSN Conference*, pp. 249–252.

Foster, J.C., Dutton, R., Love, S., Nairn, I.A., & Vergeynst, N. (1993). Intelligent dialogues in automated telephone services. In C. Baber and J.M. Noyes (Eds), *Interactive Speech Technology*. London: Taylor and Francis.

Foster, L.W., & Flynn, D.M. (1984). Management information technology: its effects on organisational form and function. *MIS Quarterly*, **8**, 229–236.

Franco, G., Castelli, C., & Gatti, C. (1992). Tenosinovite posturale da usa incongruo di un dispositivo di puntamento (mouse) di un elaboratore. *Medicina del Lavoro*, **83**, 352–355.

Frankish, C.F., & Noyes, J.M. (1990). Sources of human error in data entry tasks using speech input. *Human Factors*, **32**, 697–716.

Frankish, C.F., Hull, R., & Morgan, P. (1995). Recognition accuracy and user aceptance of pen interfaces. *CHI'95*. New York: ACM, pp. 503–510.

Frese, M., & Sabini, J. (1985). Action theory: an introduction. In M. Frese and J. Sabini (Eds), *Goal Directed Behaviour*. Hillsdale, NJ: Lawrence Erlbaum Associates.

Frieling, E., Pfitzmann, J., & Derisari-Fard, F. (1987). Optimising input devices of computer-aided design systems. In M. Frese, E. Ulich and W. Dzida (Eds), *Psychological Issues of Human–Computer Interaction in the Workplace*. Amsterdam: North-Holland.

Frolich, D.M. (1993). The history and future of direct manipulation. *Behaviour and Information Technology*, **12**, 315–329.

Frohlich, D., & Luff, P. (1990). Applying the technology of conversation to the technology for conversation. In P. Luff, N., Gilbert and D. Frohlich (Eds), *Computers and Conversation*. London: Academic Press.

Fromkin, V.A. (1980). *Errors in Linguistic Performance: slips of the tongue, ear, pen and hand*. New York: Academic Press.

Furnass, T.A., & Lewis, C.H. (1978). Helmet-mounted display reading performance under whole body vibration. *Proceedings of the UK Informal Group on Human Response to Vibration*. Silsoe: NIAE.

Gaertner, K-P., & Holzhausen, K. (1980). Controlling air traffic with a touch sensitive screen. *Applied Ergonomics*, **11**, 17–22.

Galitz, W.O. (1989). *Handbook of Screen Format Design*. Wellesey, MA: QED Information Sciences [3rd. edition].

Garnham, A. (1985). *Psycholinguistics*. New York: Methuen.

Garrett, J.W. (1971). The human adult hand: some anthropometric and biomechanical considerations. *Human Factors*, **13**, 117–131.

Garrett, M.F. (1984). The organisation of processing structures for language production: application to aphasic speech. In D. Caplan (Ed.), *Biological Perspectives on Language*. Cambridge, MA: MIT Press.

Gaver, W.W. (1986). Auditory icons: using sound in computer interfaces. *Human–Computer Interaction*, **2**, 167–177.

Gaver, W.W. (1989). The sonicfinder: an interface that uses auditory icons. *Human–Computer Interaction*, **4**, 67–94.

Getner, D.R. (1983). Keystroke timing in transcription typing. In W.C. Cooper (Ed.), *Cognitive Aspects of Skilled Typewriting*. Berlin: Springer-Verlag.

Gentner, D.R., & Norman, D.A. (1984). The typist's touch. *Psychology Today*, **8**, 66–72.

Gerard, M.J., Jones, S.K., Smith, L.A., Thomas, R.E., & Wang, T. (1994). An ergonomic assessment of the Kinesis Ergonomic Computer Keyboard. *Ergonomics*, **37**, 1661–1669.

Gescheider, G.A., Caparo, A.J., Frisina, R.D., Hamer, R.D., & Verillo, R.T. (1978). The effects of a surround on vibrotactile thresholds. *Sensory Processes*, **2**, 99–115.

Gibbs, C.B. (1954). The continuous regulation of skilled response by kinesthetic feedback. *British Journal of Psychology*, **45**, 24–39.

Giles, H., & Powisland, P.F. (1975). *Speech Styles and Social Evaluation*. London: Academic Press.

Gill, R., Gordon, S., Dean, S., & McGhee, D. (1993). Integrating cursor control into the computer keyboard. *Proceedings of the 35th. Annual Meeting of the Human Factors Society*. Santa Monica: CA: Human Factors Society, pp. 256–260.

Gillan, D.J., Holden, K., Adams, S., Rudisill, M., & Magee, L. (1990). How does Fitts law fit pointing and dragging? *CHI'90*. New York: ACM, pp. 227–234.

Glencross, D.J., & Barrett, N. (1989). Discrete movements. In D.H. Holding (Ed.), *Human Skills*. Chichester: Wiley.

Göbel, M., Springer, J., & Luzak, H. (1994). Effects of tactile feedback in process control, exemplary in mouse-driven interfaces. In P.T. Kidd and W. Karwowski (Eds), *Advances in Agile Manufacturing*. Amsterdam: IOS Press. 285–288.

Goodnow, J.L., & Levine, R. (1973). The grammar of action: sequence and syntax in children's copying. *Cognitive Psychology*, **4**, 82–98.

Goodwin, N.C. (1975). Cursor positioning on an electronic display using lightpen, lightgun or keyboard for three basic tasks. *Human Factors*, **17**, 289–295.

Gopher, D., Karis, D., & Koenig, W. (1985). The representation of movement schemata in long-term memory: lessons from the acquisition of a transcription skill. *Acta Psychologica*, **60**, 105–134.

Gould, J.D., & Alfaro, L. (1984). Revising documents with text editors, handwriting recognition systems and speech recognition systems. *Human Factors*, **26**, 391–406.

Gould, J.D., & Salaun, J. (1987). Behavioural experiments on handmarking. *ACM Transactions on Office Information Systems*, **5**, 358–377.

Graham, R., & Baber, C. (1993). User stress in ASR. In E.J. Lovesey (Ed.), *Contemporary Ergonomics 1993*. London: Taylor and Francis, pp. 463–469.

Grandjean, E. (1987). *Ergonomics in Computerised Offices*. London: Taylor and Francis.

Greenberg, S. (1993). *The Computer User as Toolsmith*. Cambridge: Cambridge University Press.

Greenstein, J.S., & Muto, W.H. (1988). Keyboards. In A. Sherr (Ed.), *Input Devices*. Boston: Academic Press.

Greer, K.L., & Green, D.W. (1983). Context and motor control in handwriting. *Acta Psychologica*, **54**, 205–215.

Greif, S., & Gediga, G. (1987). A critique and empirical investigation of the "one-best-way" models human–computer interaction. In M. Frese, E. Ulich and W. Dzida (Eds), *Psychological Issues of Human–Computer Interaction in the Workplace*. Amsterdam: North-Holland.

Grice, H.P. (1975). Logic and communication. In P. Cole and J.L. Morgan (Eds), *Syntax and Semantics III: Speech Acts*. New York: Academic Press.

Griffin, M.J. (1990). *Handbook of Human Vibration*. London: Academic Press.

Griffith, R.T. (1949). The Minimotion typewriter keyboard. *Journal of the Franklin Institute*, **248**, 399–436.

Grossberg, S. (1987). Cortical dynamics of thee-dimensional form, colour and brightness perception II: binocular theory. In S. Grossberg (Ed.), *Neural Networks and Natural Intelligence*. Cambridge, MA: MIT Press.

Grudin, J.G. (1983). Errors in patterns in novice and skilled typists. In W.E. Cooper (Ed.), *Cognitive Aspects of Skilled Typewriting*. New York: Springer Verlag.

Gunkel, M. (1962). Uber relative Koordination bei willkurlichen menschlichen Gliederbewegungen. *Plugers Archiv für gesmate Physiologie*, **275**, 472–477.

Hackman, J.R., & Oldham, G.R. (1980). *Work Redesign*. Reading, MA: Addison Wesley.

Hackmeister, R. (1979). Focus on keyboards. *Electronic Design*, **11**, 169–175.

Haigh, R., & Clark, A.K. (1988). Evaluation of a voice recognition system for use by disabled people. In E.D. Megaw (Ed.), *Contemporary Ergonomics 1988*. London: Taylor and Francis, pp. 87–91.

Haley, V.L. (1991). Design for computer accessibility. *Interface '91*, pp. 380–384.

Haller, R., Mutschler, H., & Voss, M. (1984). Comparison of input devices for correction of typing errors in office systems. *Interact '84*. Amsterdam: North-Holland, pp. 218–223.

Hamman, G.E., Shein, F., & Treviranus, J. (1991). Access to MS-Windows 3.0 with the long range wand. *Proceedings of the 6th. Annual CUSN Conference*, pp. 335–344.

Hammerton, M. (1962). An investigation into the optimal gain of a velocity control system. *Ergonomics*, **5**, 539–543.

Hand, C., Sexton, I., & Mullan, M. (1994). A linguistic approach to the recognition of hand gestures. *Proceedings of Designing Future Interaction*. Loughborough: Ergonomics Society.

Hapeshi, K., & Jones, D.M. (1989). The ergonomics of automatic speech recognition interfaces. In D. Oborne (Ed.), *International Review of Ergonomics*. London: Taylor and Francis, pp. 251–290.

Harel, D. (1988). On visual formalisms. *Communications of the ACM*, **31**, 514–530.

Hargreaves, W., Rempel, D., Halpern, N., Markison, R., Kroemer, K., & Litekwa, J. (1992). Towards a more humane keyboard. *CHI'92*. Reading, MA: Addison-Wesley. 365–368.

Harris, S.D., North, R.A., & Owens, J.M. (1978). A system for the assessment of human performance in concurrent verbal and manual control tasks. *Behaviour Research Methods and Instrumentation*, **10**, 329–333.

Hauptmann, A.G., & McAvinney, P. (1993). Gestures with speech for graphic manipulation. *International Journal of Man–Machine Studies*, **38**, 231–249.

Hayes, P.J. (1988). Using a knowledge base to drive an expert system interface with a natural language component. In J.A. Hendler (Ed.), *Expert Systems: the user interface*. Norwood, NJ: Ablex.

Hayes-Roth, B., & Hayes-Roth, F. (1979). A cognitive model of planning. *Cognitive Science*, **3**, 275–310.

Herndon, K.P., van Dam, A., & Gleicher, M. (1994). The challenges of 3D interaction. *SIGCHI Bulletin October*, pp. 312–317.

Hesse, F.W., & Hahn, C. (1994). The impact of interface-induced handling requirements on action generation in technical system control. *Behaviour and Information Technology*, **13**, 228–238.

Heuvelmans, A.M.F., Melotte, H.E.M., & Neve, J.J. (1990). A typewriter system operated by head movements. *Applied Ergonomics*, **21**, 115–120.

Hick, W.E. (1952). On the rate of gain of information. *Quarterly Journal of Experimental Psychology*, **4**, 11–26.

Hirsch, R.S. (1970). Effects of standard versus alphabetic keyboard formats on typing performance. *Journal of Applied Psychology*, **54**, 484–490.

Hoc, J-M. (1988). *The Psychology of Planning*. London: Academic Press.

Hockey, G.R.J. (1979). Stress and cognitive components of skilled performance. In V. Hamilton and D.M. Warburton (Eds), *Human Stress and Cognition: an information processing approach*. Chichester: Wiley.

Holding, D.H. (1989). *Human Skills*. Chichester: Wiley.

Hollingum, J., & Cassford, G. (1987). *Speech Technology at Work*. Berlin: Springer Verlag.

Hone, K.S., & Baber, C. (1995). Optimisation of feedback position in the entry of digits strings by voice. In S.A. Robertson (Ed.), *Contemporary Ergonomics 1995*. London: Taylor and Francis, pp. 181–186.

Hornick, R.J. (1962). Effects of whole body vibration in three directions upon human performance. *Journal of Engineering Psychology*, **1**, 93–101.

Hulstijn, W., & van Galen, G.P. (1983). Programming in writing: reaction time and movement time as a function of sequence length. *Acta Psychologica*, **54**, 23–49.

Hünting, W., Läubli, Th., and Grandjean, E. (1981). Postural and visual loads at VDT workplaces I. Constrained postures. *Ergonomics*, **24**, 917–931.

Hyman, R. (1953). Stimulus information as a determinant of reaction time. *Journal of Experimental Psychology*, **45**, 188–196.

Ibbotson, N.R., & Morton, J. (1981). Rhythm and dominance. *Cognition*, **9**, 125–138.

Ilg, R. (1987). Ergonomic keyboard design. *Behaviour and Information Technology*, **6**, 303–309.

ILO (1982). *Introduction to Work Study*. Geneva: International Labour Organisation.

Iosifescu, M. (1986). *Finite Markov Processes and their Applications*. Chichester: Wiley.

Ivanevich, J.M. (1979). High and low stimulation jobs: a causal analysis of performance-satisfaction relationships. *Academy of Management Journal*, **22**, 206–222.

Ivergard, T. (1989). *Handbook of Control Room Design and Ergonomics*. London: Taylor and Francis.

Jackson, A. (1982). Some problems in the specification of rolling-ball operating characteristics. *Proceedings of IEE Symposium on Man–Machine Systems*. London: IEE Digest no. 212, pp. 103–106.

Jacob, R.J.K. (1990). What you look at is what you get: eye-movement based interaction techniques. *CHI '90*. New York: ACM, pp. 11–18.

Jacob, R.J.K., Leggett, J.J., Myers, B.A., & Pausch, R. (1993). Interaction styles and input/output devices. *Behaviour and Information Technology*, **12**, 69–79.

Jagacinski, R.J., Repperger, D.W., Moran, M.S., Ward, S.L., & Glass, B. (1980). Fitts law and the microstructure of rapid discrete movements. *Journal of Experimental Psychology: Human Perception and Performance*, **6**, 309–320.

Jellinek, H.D., & Card, S.K. (1990). Powermice and user performance. *CHI'90*. New York: ACM, pp. 213–220.

Jensen, S. (1989). Positioning under vibration: performance with indirect input. In E.D. Megaw (Ed.), *Contemporary Ergonomics 1989*. London: Taylor and Francis, pp. 290–295.

Jeyeratnam, J., Ong, C.N., Kee, W.C., Lee, J., & Koh, D. (1989). Musculoskeletal symptoms among VDU operators. In M.J. Smith and G. Salvendy (Eds), *Work with Computers: Organisational, Stress and Health Aspects*. Amsterdam: Elsevier.

John, B.E., & Newell, A. (1987). Predicting the time to recall computer command abbreviations. *CHI'87*. New York: ACM, pp. 33–40.

John, B.E., & Newell, A. (1989). Cumulating the science of HCI: from S-R compatibility to transcription typing. *CHI'89*. New York: ACM, pp. 109–114.

John, B.E., Vera, A.H., & Newell, A. (1994). Towards real-time GOMS: a model of expert behaviour in a highly interactive task. *Behaviour and Information Technology*, **13**, 225–267.

Johnson, E.A. (1967). Touch displays: a programmed man–machine interface. *Ergonomics*, **10**, 271–277.

Junqua, J.C. (1995). The influence of acoustics on speech production: a noise-induced stress phenomenon known as the Lombard reflex. *Proceedings of the ESCA/NATO Workshop on Speech under Stress*. Lisbon: INESC, pp. 83–90.

Kameyama, K., & Ohtomi, K. (1993). A shape modelling system with a volume scanning display and multisensory input device. *Presence*, **2**, 104–111.

Kammersgard, J. (1990). Four different perspectives on human–computer interaction. In J. Preece, and L. Keller (Eds), *Human–Computer Interaction*. Hemel Hempstead: Prentice-Hall.

Kantowitz, B.H., & Elvers, G.C. (1988). Fitts law with an isometric controller: effects of order of control and control-display gain. *Journal of Motor Behaviour*, **20**, 53–66.

Kao, H. (1979). Differential effects of writing instruments on handwriting performance. *Acta Psychologica Taiwanica*, **21**, 9–13.

Karat, J., McDonald, J.E., & Anderson, M. (1984). A comparison of selection techniques: touch panel, mouse and keyboard. *Interact '84*. Amsterdam: North-Holland, pp. 149–153.

Karl, L.R., Pettey, M., & Shneiderman, B. (1993). Speech versus mouse for commands for word processing: an empirical evaluation. *International Journal of Man–Machine Studies*, **39**, 667–687.

Keele, S.W. (1968). Movement control in skilled motor performance. *Psychological Bulletin*, **70**, 387–403.

Kelley, D.F. (1984). Skylink self-service ticketing terminal: design and ergonomics. *Behaviour and Information Technology*, **3**, 391–397.

Kellog, R. (1969). *Analysing Children's Art*. Palo Alto, CA: National Press Books.

Kenney, F. (1985). Electronic mail is both effective and efficient. *The Office*, **101**, 26–31.

Kerr, E.B., & Hiltz, S.R. (1982). *Computer-mediated Communication: status and evaluation*. New York: Academic Press.

Kieras, D., & Polson, P.G. (1986). An approach to the formal analysis of user complexity. *International Journal of Man–Machine Studies*, **22**, 365–394.

Kilbom, A. (1987). Short- and long-term effects of extreme physical inactivity: a review. In B. Knave and P.G. Wideback (Eds), *Work with Visual Display Units '86*. Amsterdam: North-Holland.

Kinkade, R. (1975). Typing speed, keying rate and optimal keyboard layouts. *Proceedings of the 19th. Annual Meeting of the Human Factors Society*. Santa Monica, CA: Human Factors Society, pp. 159–161.

Kirwan, B. (1992a). Human error identification in human reliability assessment. Part 1: Overview of approaches. *Applied Ergonomics*, **23**, 299–318.

Kirwan, B. (1992b). Human error identification in human reliability assessment. Part 2: Detailed comparison of techniques. *Applied Ergonomics*, **23**, 371–381.

Klapp, S.T. (1981a). Motor programming is not the only process which can influence RT: some thoughts on the Marteniuk and MacKenzie analysis. *Journal of Motor Behaviour*, **13**, 320–328.

Klapp, S.T. (1981b). Temporal compatibility in dual motor tasks II: simultaneous articulation and hand movements. *Memory and Cognition*, **9**, 398–401.

Klockenberg, E.A. (1926). *Rationalisierung der Schreibmaschine und ihrer Bedienung.* Berlin: Springer Verlag.

Knapp, R.B., & Lusted, H.S. (1992). Biocontrollers for the physicaly disabled: a direct link from the nervous system to the computer. *Proceedings of the CUSN Technology Conference*, pp. 25–30.

Knowles, C. (1988). Can CCT produce a measure of system usability? In D.M. Jones and R. Winder (Eds), *People and Computers IV.* Cambridge: Cambridge University Press.

Kobrick, J., & Fine, B. (1983). Climate and human performance. In D. Oborne and M. Gruneberg (Eds), *The Physical Environment at Work*. Chichester: Wiley.

Koons, D.B., Sparrell, C.J., & Thorisson, K.R. (1993). Integrating simultaneous input from speech, gaze and hand gestures. In M.T. Maybury (Ed.), *Integrated Multimodal Interfaces*. New York: Academic Press.

Krauss, R.M., & Glucksberg, S. (1977). Social and nonsocial speech. *Scientific American*, **236**, 100–105.

Kroemer, K.H.E. (1972). Human engineering the keyboard. *Human Factors*, **14**, 51–63.

Kroemer, K.H.E. (1986). Coupling the hand with the handle: an improved notation of touch, grip and grasp. *Human Factors*, **28**, 337–339.

Kryter, K.D. (1994). *The Handbook of Hearing and the Effects of Noise*. San Diego: Academic Press.

Kurpa, K., Waris, P., & Rokkanen, P. (1980). Peretendinitis and tenosynivitis: a review. *Scandanavian Journal of Work, Environment and Health*, **5**, 19–24.

Lacquaniti, F., Terzuolo, C., & Viviani, P. (1983). The law relating the kinematic and figural aspects of drawing movements. *Acta Psychologica*, **54**, 115–130.

Lam, S-T., & Greenstein, J.S. (1984). The effects of input medium and task allocation strategy the performance of a human computer system. *Interact '84*. Amsterdam: North-Holland, pp. 458–463.

Landauer, T.K. (1995). *The Trouble with Computers*. Cambridge: MA: MIT Press.

Larochelle, S. (1983). A comparison of skilled and novice performance in discontinuous typing. In W.E. Cooper (Ed.), *Cognitive Aspects of Skilled Typewriting*. Berlin: Springer Verlag.

Lave, J. (1988). *Cognition in Practice*. Cambridge: Cambridge University Press.

Lea, W.A. (1980). *Trends in Speech Recognition*. New York: Prentice Hall.

Lederman, S.J. (1983). Tactual roughness perception: spatial and temporas determinants. *Canadian Journal of Psychology*, **37**, 498–511.

Lederman, S.J., & Klatzky, R.L. (1993). Exploring object properties through haptic exploration. *Acta Psychologica*, **84**, 29–40.

Leedham, C.G., & Downton, A.C. (1986). On-line recognition of Pitman's handwritten shorthand: an evaluation of potential. *International Journal of Man–Machine Studies*, **24**, 375–393.

Leedham, C.G., Downton, A., Brooks, C., & Newell, A. (1984). On-line acquisition of Pitman's handwritten shorthand as a means of rapid data entry. *Interact '84*. Amsterdam: North-Holland, pp. 86–91.

Leiser, R.G. (1989a). Exploiting convergence to improve language understanding. *Interacting with Computers*, **1**, 284–298.

Leiser, R.G. (1989b). Improving natural language speech interfaces by the use of metalinguistic phenomena. *Applied Ergonomics*, **20**, 168–173.

Leonard, J.A. (1959). Tactual choice reactions. *Quarterly Journal of Experimental Psychology*, **11**, 76–83.

Lessenberry, D.D. (1928). *Analysis of Errors.* Syracuse, NY: L.C. Smith and Corona Typewriters.

Levelt, W.J.M. (1989). *Speaking: from intention to articulation.* Cambridge, MA: MIT Press.

Levy, J., & Reid, M.L. (1976). Variations in writing posture and cerebral organisation. *Science*, **194**, 337–339.

Lévy-Leboyer, C. (1989). Noise effects on two industrial tasks. *Work and Stress*, **3**, 315–322.

Lewis, C.H., & Griffin, M.J. (1980). Predicting the effects of vibration frequency and axis and seating conditions on the reading of numeric displays. *Ergonomics*, **23**, 485–501.

Life, M., & Pheasant, S. (1984). An integrated approach to the study of posture in keyboard operation. *Applied Ergonomics*, **15**, 83–90.

Linggard, R. (1990). Beyond speech recognition: language processing. In C. Wheddon and R. Linggard (Eds), *Speech and Language Processing.* London: Chapman and Hall.

Loeb, K. (1983). Membrane keyboards and human performance. *The Bell System Technical Journal*, **6**, 1733–1749.

Long, J. (1976). Visual feedback and skilled typewriting: differential effects of masking the printed copy and the keyboard. *Ergonomics*, **19**, 19–110.

Longacre, R.E. (1983). *The Grammar of Discourse.* New York: Plenum Press.

Loricchio, D.F. (1992). A comparison of three pointing devices: mouse, cursor keys and a keyboard-integrated pushbutton. *Proceedings of the 36th. Annual Meeting of the Human Factors Society.* Santa Monica, CA; Human Factors Society, pp. 303–305.

Loricchio, D.F. (1993). A comparison of keyboard-integrated pointing devices. In G. Salvendy and M.J. Smith (Eds), *Human–Computer Interaction: Software and Hardware Interfaces.* Amsterdam: Elsevier.

Lovesey, E.J. (1989). The pilot-cockpit-weapons interface for close air combat. In E.D. Megaw (Ed.), *Contemporary Ergonomics 1989.* London: Taylor and Francis, pp. 444–449.

Löwstedt, J. (1988). Prejudices and wishful thinking about computer-aided design. *New Technology, Work and Employment*, **3**, 30–37.

Luff, P., Gilbert, N., & Frohlich, D. (1990). *Computers and Conversation.* London: Academic Press.

Lutz, M.C., & Chapanis, A. (1955). Expected locations of digits and letters on ten-button keysets. *Journal of Applied Psychology*, **39**, 314–317.

McAvinney, P. (1990). Tell-tale gestures. *BYTE July* 18–25.

McCauley, R., & Parkinson, R. (1971). The new popularity of the Dvorak simplified keyboard. *Computers and Automation February*, pp. 31–32.

McCormick, E.J. (1976). *Human Factors in Engineering and Design.* New Jersey: McGraw-Hill.

McFarland, K., Ashton, R., & Heath, G. (1989). Tactile perceptual asymmetry: the influence of motor activity and imagery instructions. *British Journal of Psychology*, **80**, 517–526.

Mack, R., & Lang, R. (1989). A benchmark comparison of touch interface techniques for an intelligent work-station windowing environment. *Proceedings of the 33rd. Annual Meeting of the Human Factors Society.* Santa Monica, CA: Human Factors Society, pp. 16–20.

Mack, R., & Montaniz, F. (1991). A comparison of touch and mouse interaction techniques for a graphical windowing software environment. *Proceedings of the 35th. Annual Meeting of the Human Factors Society.* Santa Monica, CA: Human Factors Society, pp. 286–289.

Mackay, D.G. (1982). A theory of the representation and enactment of intentions. In R.A. Magill (Ed.), *Memory and Control of Action*. Amsterdam: North-Holland.

MacKenzie, I.S. (1989). A note on the information-theoretic basis for Fitts law. *Journal of Motor Behaviour*, **21**, 323–330.

MacKenzie, I.S. (1992). Fitts' law as a research and design tool in human–computer interaction. *Human–Computer Interaction*, **7**, 91–139.

MacKenzie, I.S., Sellen, A., & Buxton, W. (1991). A comparison of input devices in elemental pointing and dragging tasks. *CHI'91*. New York: ACM, pp. 161–166.

McLoughlin, I. (1989). CAD-the Taylorisation of drawing office work. *New Technology, Work and Employment*, **4**, 29–41.

McLoughlin, I., & Clark, J. (1988). *Technological Change at Work*. Milton Keynes: Open University Press.

Malone, T.W. (1987). Computer support for organisations: toward an organisational science. In J.M. Carroll (Ed.), *Interfacing Thought: cognitive aspects of human–computer interaction*. Cambridge, MA: MIT Press.

Malt, L.G. (1977). Keyboard design in the electronics era. *Proceedings of the PIRA Symposium on Developments in Data Capture and Photocomposition*. London: PIRA.

Mandal, A.C. (1981). The seated work position: theory and practice. *Applied Ergonomics*, **12**, 19–26.

Marks, L.E. (1975). On coloured-hearing synesthesia: cross-modal translations of sensory dimensions. *Psychological Bulletin*, **82**, 303–331.

Marmaras, M., & Lyritzis, K. (1990). Keyboard layout for occasional users. *Interact'90*. Amsterdam: North-Holland, pp. 707–712.

Marshall, S.L.A. (1947). *Men Against Fire*. New York: Willim Morrow.

Martin, A. (1972). A new keyboard layout. *Applied Ergonomics*, **3**, 48–51.

Martin, G.L. (1989). The utility of speech input in user computer interfaces. *International Journal of Man–Machine Studies*, **30**, 355–375.

Martin, M.G. (1993). Of mice and pens: low risk healthy postures for modern computing. In M.J. Smith and G. Salvendy (Eds), *Human–Computer Interaction: applications and case studies*. Amsterdam: Elsevier.

Marton, F.I., & Sandqvist, G. (1972). Learning while typing. *Quarterly Journal of Experimental Psychology*, **24**, 287–290.

Massaki, F., & Yasuhito, S. (1994). FingeRing: a full-time wearable interface. *CHI'94*. New York: ACM, pp. 81–82.

Matthei, E., & Roeper, T. (1983). *Understanding and Producing Speech*. London: Fontana.

Mayes, J.T., Draper, S.W., McGregor, A.M., & Oatley, K. (1988). Information flow in a user interface: the effect of experience and context on the recall of Macwrite screens. In D.M. Jones and R. Winder (Eds), *People and Computers IV*. Cambridge: Cambridge University Press, pp. 275–290.

Meese, G.B., Kok, R., Lewis, M.I., Schiefer, R.E., & Kustner, P.M. (1989). Performances of a five choice serial reaction time task and an associated vigilance task in the cold. *Ergonomics SA*, **1**, 56–67.

Megaw, E.D. (1972). Direction and extent uncertainty in step-input tracking. *Journal of Motor Behaviour*, **4**, 171–186.

Megaw, E.D. (1975). Fitts tapping revisited. *Journal of Human Movement Studies*, **1**, 163–171.

Mehr, M.H., & Mehr, E. (1972). Manual digital positioning in two axes: a comparison of joystick and trackball controls. *Proceedings of the 16th. Annual Meeting of the Human Factors Society*. Santa Monica, CA: Human Factors Society, pp. 110–116.

Meisel, W.S. (1986). Towards the "Talkwriter". In G. Bristow (Ed.), *Electronic Speech Recognition*. London: Collins.

Meister, D. (1990). Simulation and modelling. In J.R. Wilson and E.N. Corlett (Eds), *Evaluation of Human Work*. London: Taylor and Francis.

Meulenbroek, R.G.J., Rosenbaum, D.A., Thomassen, A.J.W.M., & Schomaker, L.R.B. (1993). Limb-segment selection in drawing behaviour. *The Quarterly Journal of Experimental Psychology*, **46A**, 273–299.

Meyer, D.E., Smith, J.E.K., & Wright, C.E. (1982). Models for the speed and accuracy of aimed movements. *Psychological Review*, **89**, 449–482.

Michaels, S.E. (1971). QWERTY versus alphabetic keyboards as a function of typing skill. *Human Factors*, **13**, 419–426.

Miller, G., Galanter, E., & Pribram, K. (1960). *Plans and the Structure of Behaviour*. New York: Holt, Rinehart and Winston.

Milner, N.P. (1988). A review of human performance and preferences with different input devices to computer systems. In D.M. Jones and R. Winder (Eds), *People and Computers IV*. Cambridge: Cambridge University Press, pp. 341–362.

Mitchell, C.M., & Forren, J.F. (1987). Multimodal user input to supervisory control systems: voice augmented keyboard. *IEEE Transactions of Systems, Man and Cybernetics*, **17**, 594–607.

Montaniz, F., & Mack, R. (1991). A comparison of touch interface techniques for a graphical windowing software environment. *Proceedings of the 35th. Annual Meeting of the Human Factors Society*. Santa Monica, CA: Human Factors Society, pp. 290–294.

Moore, R.K. (1977). Evaluating speech recognisers. *IEEE Transactions on Acoustics, Speech and Signal Processing ASSP-25*, 178–183.

Moore, T.J. (1989). Speech technology in the cockpit. In R.S. Jensen (Ed.), *Aviation Psychology*. Aldershot: Gower Technical.

Moray, N. (1992). Flexible interfaces can promote operator error. In H. Kragt (Ed.), *Enhancing Industrial Performance*. London: Taylor and Francis.

Morris, D. (1994). *Body Talk*. London: Cape.

Moscovitch, M.,& Smith, L.C. (1979). Differences in neural organisation between individuals with inverted and non-inverted handwriting postures. *Science*, **205**, 710–713.

Müller, J. (1848). *The Physiology of the Senses, Voice and Muscular Motion with the Mental Faculties*. London: Walton and Maberly.

Mumford, E. (1987). *Designing Human Systems*. Manchester: Manchester Business School Publications.

Murakami, K., & Taguchi, H. (1991). Gesture recognition using recurrent neural networks. *CHI'91*. New York: ACM, pp. 301–305.

Murata, A. (1991). An experimental evaluation of mouse, joystick, joycard, lightpen, trackball and touchscreen for pointing: basic study in human interface design. In H-J. Bullinger (Ed.), *Human Aspects in Computing: I. Design and Use of Interactive Systems and Work with Terminals*. Amsterdam: Elsevier, pp. 123–127.

Mutschler, H. (1982). Ergonomic aspects for improving recognition performance of voice input systems. *IFAC Analysis, Design and Evaluation of Man–Machine Systems*, pp. 261–267.

Nakaseko, N., Grandjean, E., Hünting, W., & Gierer, R. (1985). Studies on ergonomically designed alphanumeric keyboards. *Human Factors*, **27**, 175–187.

Navon, D., & Gopher, D. (1979). On the economy of the human processing system. *Psychological Review*, **86**, 214–253.

Negroponte, N. (1989). A personal perspective: an iconoclastic view beyond the desktop metaphor. *International Journal of Human–Computer Interaction*, **1**, 109–113.

Neisser, U. (1976). *Cognition and Reality: implications of cognitive psychology.* New York: W.H. Freeman.

Newell, A.F. (1984). Speech; the natural method of man–machine communication? *Interact'84.* Amsterdam: North-Holland, pp. 231–238.

Newell, A.F. (1986). Communicating via speech: the able bodied and the disabled. *IEE Symposium on Speech Recognition.* London: IEE Digest numer 258.

Newman, W.M. (1990). A graphical technique for numerical input. In E.A. Edmonds (Ed.), *The Separable Interface.* London: Academic Press.

Newsome, C. (1995). Are you sitting comfortably? *The Independent 13/2/95,* 23.

Nilsson, J., Glencross, D., & Geffen, G. (1980). The effects of familial sinistrality and preferred hand on dichaptic and dichotic tasks. *Brain and Language,* **10**, 390–404.

Noble, D.F. (1985). *Forces of Production: a social history of industrial automation.* New York: Alfred Knopf.

Norman, D.A. (1988). *The Psychology of Everyday Things.* New York: Basic Books.

Norman, D.A. (1991). Cognitive artifacts. In J.M. Carroll (Ed.), *Designing Interaction: psychology at the human–computer interface.* Cambridge: Cambridge University Press.

Norman, D.A. (1993). *Things that Make us Smart.* Reading, MA: Addison Wesley.

Norman, D.A., & Draper, S. (1984). *User Centred Design.* Hillsdale, NJ: LEA.

Norman, D.A., & Fisher, A. (1982). Why alphabetic keyboards are not easy to use: keyboard layout doesn't much matter. *Human Factors,* **24**, 509–519.

North, J.D., & Lomnicki, Z.A. (1961). Further experiments on human operators in compensatory tracking tasks. *Ergonomnics,* **4**, 339–353.

Noyes, J. (1983). The QWERTY keyboard: a review. *International Journal of Man–Machine Studies,* **18**, 265–281.

Noyes, J.M., & Frankish, C.F. (1989). A review of speech recognition applications in the office. *Behaviour and Information Technology,* **8**, 475–486.

Noyes, J.M., Haigh R., & Starr, A.F. (1989). Automatic speech recognition for disabled people. *Applied Ergonomics,* **20**, 293–298.

Noyes, J.M., Baber, C., & Frankish, C.R. (1992). Industrial Applications of ASR. *Journal of the American Voice I/O Society,* **12**, 51–68.

Noyes, J., Baber, C., & Steel, A. (1994). Ergonomic surveys of VDTs and Manufacturing Workstations: a case study. *Ergonomics Society and IOSH: Working Together to Meet the Challenge of the New EC Regulations.* Loughborough: Ergonomics Society.

Nunberg, G. (1979). The non-uniqueness of semantic solutions: polysemy. *Linguistics and Philosophy,* **3**, 143–184.

Oborne, D.J. (1988). *Ergonomics at Work.* Chichester: Wiley.

Olson, H.F., & Belar, H. (1956). Phonetic typewriter. *Journal of the Acoustical Society of America,* **28**, 1072–1081.

Olson, J.R., & Nilsen, E. (1988). Analysis of the cognition involved in spreadsheet software interaction. *Human–Computer Interaction,* **3**, 309–350.

Olson, J.R., & Olson, G.M. (1990). The growth in cognitive modelling in human–computer interaction since GOMS. *Human–Computer Interaction,* **5**, 221–265.

Oppenheim, A.N. (1992). *Questionnaire Design, Interviewing and Attitude Measurement.* London: Pinter.

Osborn, J.R., & Agogino, A.M. (1992). An interface for interactive spatial reasoning and visualisation. *Proceedings of the Conference on Human Factors In Computing Systems.* Reading, MA: Addison-Wesley, pp. 75–82.

Oviatt, S.L., & Cohen, P.R. (1989). The effects of interaction in spoken discourse. *Proceedings of the 27th. Annual Meeting of the Association for Computational Linguistics.*

Oviatt, S.L., Cohen, P.R., & Wang, M. (1994). Toward interface design for human language technology: modality and structure as determinants of linguistic complexity. *Speech Communication*, **15**, 283–300.

Paivio, A. (1982). *Mental Representation: a dual coding approach*. Oxford: Oxford University Press.

Palfreyman, J., & Swade, D. (1991). *The Dream Machine*. London: BBC Books.

Parsons, M.B. (1994). Performance of manual controls within armoured fighting vehicles. In S.A. Robertson (Ed.), *Contemporary Ergonomics 1994*. London: Taylor and Francis, pp. 150–154.

Pearson, G., & Weiser, M. (1988). Exploratory evaluation of a planar foot-operated cursor positioning device. *CHI '88*. New York: ACM, pp. 13–18.

Peckham, J. (1986). Human factors in speech recognition. In G. Bristow (Ed.), *Electronic Speech Recognition*. London: Collins.

Petajan, E., Bischoff, B., Bodoff, D., & Brooke, N.M. (1988). An improved automatic lip-reading system to enhance speech recognition. *CHI '88*. New York: ACM, pp. 19–25.

Pew, R.W. (1974). Levels of analysis in motor control. *Brain Research*, **71**, 393–400.

Pfurtscheller, G. (1992). Brain–computer interface – a new communication device for handicapped persons. *Proceedings of the 3rd. International Conference on Computers for Handicapped Persons*, pp. 409–415.

Pheasant, S. (1988). *Bodyspace*. London: Taylor and Francis.

Pheasant, S. (1995). A foreseeable risk of injury. In S.A. Robertson (Ed.), *Contemporary Ergonomics 1995*. London: Taylor and Francis, pp. 2–13.

Phillips, A. (1968). *Computer Peripherals and Typesetting*. London: HMSO.

Pickett, J.M. (1980). *The Speech Sounds of Communication: a primer of acoustic phonetics and speech perception*. Baltimore: Baltimore University Press.

Pinsky, L. (1983). What kind of dialogue is it when working with a computer? In T.R.G. Green, S.J. Morrison and D. Shaw (Eds), *The Psychology of Computer Use*. New York: Academic Press.

Polit, A., & Bizzi, E. (1979). Characteristics of motor programs underlying arm movements in monkeys. *Journal of Neurophysiology*, **42**, 183–194.

Poock, G.K. (1980). *Experiments with Voice Input for Command and Control*. Monterey, CA: Naval Postgraduate School Technical Report NPS-55-80-016.

Potter, R., Berman, M., & Shneiderman, B. (1989). An experimental evaluation of three touchscreen strategies within a HyperCard database. *International Journal of Human–Computer Interaction*, **1**, 41–52.

Poulton, E.C. (1966). Tracking behaviour. In E.A. Bilodeau (Ed.), *Acquisition of Skill*. London: Academic Press.

Poulton, E.C. (1974). *Tracking Skill and Manual Control*. New York: Academic Press.

Price, L.A., & Cordova, C.A. (1983). Use of mouse buttons. *CHI '83*. New York: ACM, pp. 262–266.

Pylyshyn, Z. (1984). *Computation and Cognition*. Cambridge, MA: MIT Press.

Quinlan, P. (1991). *Connectionism and Psychology*. New York: Harvester Wheatsheaf.

Rabbitt, P.M.A. (1978). Detection of errors by skilled typists. *Ergonomics*, **21**, 945–958.

Rabbitt, P.M.A., Fearnley, S., & Vyas, S.M. (1975). Programming sequences of complex responses. In P.M.A. Rabbitt and S. Dornic (Eds), *Attention and Performance V.* London: Academic Press.

Rasmussen (1974). Outline of hybrid model of the process plant operator. In T.B. Sheridan and G. Johannsen (Eds), *Monitoring Behaviour and Supervisory Control*. New York: Plenum Press.

Ratz, H.C., & Ritchie, D.K. (1961). Operator performance on a chord keyboard. *Journal of Applied Psychology*, **45**, 303–308.

Reason, J. (1990). *Human Error.* Cambridge: Cambridge University Press.

Reid, P. (1990). Why usability now? *Usability Now! Newsletter 1.* London: DTI 1.

Reising, I.M., & Curry, D.M. (1987). Comparison of voice with multifunction controls: logic is the key. *Ergonomics,* **30**, 1063–1078.

Rhyne, J.R., & Wolf, C.G. (1992). Recognition-based user interfaces. In R. Hartson and D. Hix (Eds), *Advances in Human–Computer Interaction vol. 4.* New York: Ablex, pp. 191–250.

Richardson-Simon, J., Peterson, K.D., & Wang, J.H. (1988). Some different reaction times to stimuli presented simultaneously to separate cerebral hemispheres. *Ergonomics,* **31**, 1837–1846.

Rijpkema, H., & Girard, M. (1991). Gesture and speech. In R.S. Feldman and B. Sime (Eds), *Fundamentals of Non-verbal Behaviours.* Cambridge: Cambridge University Press.

Ringle, M.D., & Bruce, B. (1982). Conversation failure. In W. Lehnert and M.D. Ringle (Eds), *Strategies for Natural Language Processing.* Hillsdale, NJ: Lawrence Erlbaum Associates.

Ritchie, G.J., & Turner, J.A. (1975). Input devices for interactive graphics. *International Journal of Man–Machine Studies,* **7**, 639–660.

Roberts, T.L., & Moran, T.P. (1983). The evaluation of text editors: methodology and empirical results. *Communications of the ACM,* **26**, 265–283.

Robertson, S.P., & Black, J.B. (1986). Structure and development of plans in computer text editing. *Human–Computer Interaction,* **2**, 201–226.

Roe, C., Muto, W., & Blake, T. (1984). Feedback and key discrimination on membrane keypads. *Proceedings of the Human Factors Society 28th. Annual Meeting.* Santa Monica, CA: Human Factors Society, pp. 277–281.

Rogoff, B. (1984). Introduction: thinking and learning in a social context. In B. Rogoff and J. Lave (Eds), *Everyday Cognition.* Cambridge, MA: Harvard University Press.

Rogoff, B., & Lave, J. (1988). *Everyday Cognition.* Cambridge, MA: Harvard University Press.

Rohmert, W. (1985). Ergonomics and manufacturing industry. *Ergonomics,* **28**, 1115–1134.

Rosenbaum, D.A. (1991). *Human Motor Control.* New York: Academic Press.

Rosenbaum, D.A., Kenny, S., & Derr, M.A. (1983). Hierarchical control of rapid movement sequences. *Journal of Experimental Psychology: Human Perception and Performance,* **9**, 86–102.

Rudnicky, A.I., & Hauptmann, A.G. (1991). Models for evaluating interaction protocols in speech recognition. *CHI '91.* New York: ACM, pp. 285–291.

Rumelhart, D.E., & Norman, D.A. (1982). Simulating a skilled typist: a study of skilled cognitive-motor performance. *Cognitive Science,* **6**, 1–36.

Russell, V. (1986). The ergonomics of the Dvorak keyboard. *Proceedings of the International Conference on Work with Display Units,* pp. 239–242.

Rutledge, J.D., & Selker, T. (1990). Force-to-motion functions for pointing. *Interact '90.* Amsterdam: North-Holland, pp. 701–706.

Sacks, H., Schlegoff, E., & Jefferson, G. (1978). A simplest systematics for the organisation of turn-taking for conversation. In J. Schenkein (Ed.), *Studies in the Organisation of Conversational Interaction.* New York: Academic Press.

Salthouse, T.A. (1984). The skill of typing. *Scientific American,* **250**, 128–135.

Salthouse, T.A. (1986). Perceptual, cognitive and motoric aspects of transcription typing. *Psychological Bulletin,* **99**, 303–319.

Sanders, M.S., & McCormick, E.J. (1992). *Human Factors in Engineering and design.* New York: McGraw-Hill.

Sandford, J., Barfield, W., & Foley, J. (1987). Empirical studies of interactive computer graphics: perceptual and cognitive issues. *Proceedings of the 31st. Annual Meeting of the Human Factors Society.* Santa Monica, CA: Human Factors Society, pp. 519–523.

Sauter, S.L. (1984). Predictions of strain in VDU users and traditional office workers. In E. Grandjean (Ed.), *Ergonomics and Health in Modern Offices.* London: Taylor and Francis.

Scarborough, H., & Corbett, M.J. (1992). *Technology and Organisation.* London: Routledge.

Schenkein, J. (1980). A taxonomy of repeating action sequences in natural conversation. In B. Butterworth (Ed.), *Language Production.* New York: Academic Press.

Schiportst, T., Mah, S., & Crawford, J. (1994). Still Dancing: interacting inside the dance. *CHI '94.* New York: ACM, pp. 61–62.

Schmandt, C., Hindus, D., Ackerman, M.S., & Manandhar, S. (1990). Observatons of using speech input for window navigation. *Interact '90.* Amsterdam: North-Holland, pp. 787–793.

Schmidt, R.A., Zelaznik, H.N., Hawkins, B., Frank, J.S., & Quinn, J.T. (1979). Motor output variability: a theory for the accuracy of rapid motor acts. *Psychological Review,* **86**, 415–451.

Schmidt, W., & Zang, W. (1992). Lingu-control: a new interface for the handicapped, clinical and technical aspects. *Proceedings of the 3rd. Annual Conference on Computers for the Handicapped,* pp. 454–457.

Schoeber, M.F., & Clark, H.H. (1989). Understanding by addressees and overhearers. *Cognitive Psychology,* **21**, 211–232.

Schoenberger, R.W. (1974). An investigation of human information processing during whole body vibration. *Aerospace Medicine,* **45**, 143–153.

Schulze, L.J.H., Beaton, R.J., & Snyder, H.L. (1983). Touch entry devices and human performance. Part II: assessing operator performance. *Society for Information Display 1983 Digest,* 164–165. New York: SID.

Schurick, J.M., McCauley, M.H., Roland, E.F., Ruth, J.C., & Williges, B.H. (1985). System design for speech recognition and generation. *Human Factors,* **27**, 115–143.

Searle, J.R. (1969). *Speech Acts.* Cambridge: Cambridge University Press.

Sears, A., & Shneiderman, B. (1991). High precision touchscreens: design strategies and comparisons with a mouse. *International Journal of Man–Machine Studies,* **34**, 593–613.

Sears, A., & Shneiderman, B. (1993). High precision touchscreens: design strategies and comparisons with a mouse. In B. Shneiderman (Ed.), *Sparks of Innovation in Human–Computer Interaction.* Norwood, NJ.: Ablex Publishing Corp., pp. 171–185.

Segal, L.D. (1990). Effects of aircraft cockpit design onc rew communication. In E.J. Lovesey (Ed.), *Contemporary Ergonomics 1990.* London: Taylor and Francis.

Shackel, B. (1981). The concept of usability. In *Proceedings of the IBM Software and Information Usability Symposium.* New York: IBM, pp. 1–30.

Shaffer, L.H. (1975). Control processes in typing. *Quarterly Journal of Experimental Psychology,* **27**, 419–432.

Shaffer, L.H. (1978). Timing in the motor programming of typing. *Quarterly Journal of Experimental Psychology,* **30**, 333–345.

Shaffer, L.H. (1993). Motor programs and musical performance. In A. Buddeley and L. Weiskrantz (Eds), *Attention; Selection, Awareness and Control.* Oxford: Clarendon Press.

Shannon, C.E., & Weaver, W. (1949). *The Mathematical Theory of Communication.* Urbana-Champaign, IL: University of Illinois Press.

Sharifi, S., & Baber, C. (1992). Integrating ergonomics and job design into the introduction of advanced manufacturing technology. In D.J. Browne (Ed.), *Technology Manufacturing for Europe 1992.* Dublin: University College, pp. 64–73.

Sheehy, N.P. (1987). Nonverbal behaviour in dialogue. In R.G. Reilly (Ed.), *Communication Failure in Dialogue and Discourse.* Amsterdam: Elsevier.

Shein, G.F., Treviranus, J., Brownlow, N.D., Milner, M., & Parnes, P. (1992). An overview of human–computer interaction techniques for people with physical disabilities. *International Journal of Industrial Ergonomics,* **9**, 171–181.

Sherr, S. (1988). *Input Devices.* Boston: Academic Press.

Shneiderman, B. (1980). *Software Psychology: Human Factors in Computer and Information Systems.* Boston, MA: Little Brown.

Shneiderman, B. (1992). *Designing the User Interface.* Reading, MA: Addison-Wesley [2nd edition].

Siebel, R. (1962). Performance on a five-finger chord keyboard. *Journal of Applied Psychology,* **46**, 165–169.

Siebel, R. (1972). Data entry devices and procedures. In H. van Cott and R. Kinkade (eds), *Human Engineering Guide to Equipment Design.* Washington, DC: American Institute for Research.

Simpson, C.A. (1986). Speech variability on recognition accuracy associated with concurrent task performance by pilots. *Ergonomics,* **29**, 1343–1357.

Smith, A. (1989). A review of the effects of noise on performance. *Scandinavian Journal of Psychology,* **30**, 185–206.

Smith, H.T. (1980). Human–computer interaction. In H.T. Smith and T.R.G. Green (Eds), *Human Interaction with Computers.* London: Academic Press.

Smyth, M.M., & Silvers, G. (1987). Functions of vision in the control of handwriting. *Acta Psychologica,* **65**, 47–64.

Smyth, M.M., & Wing, A.M. (1984). Movement, action and skill. In A. Wing and M. Smyth (Eds), *The Psychology of Human Movement.* London: Academic Press.

Smyth, M.M., Morris, P.E., Levey, P., & Elli, A. (1987). *Cognition in Action.* Hillsdale, NJ: Lawrence Erlbaum Associates.

Sperber, D., & Wilson, D. (1986). *Relevance: Communication and Cognition.* Oxford: Basil Blackwell.

Spitz, G., & Drumm, D.E. (1991). The WANG headset orb – a new head mounted cursor and keyboard control technology. *Proceedings of the 6th. Annual Conference on Technology and Persons with Disabilities.* Los Angeles, CA: Office of Disabled Students Services, pp. 837–845.

Sproul, L., & Kiesler, S. (1986). Reducing social context cues: electronic mail in organisational communication. *Management Science,* **32**, 1492–1512.

Stammers, R.B., & Bird, J.M. (1980). Controller evaluation of a touch input air traffic data system: an "indelicate" experiment. *Human Factors,* **22**, 581–589.

Stanton, N.A. (1995). Ecological ergonomics: understanding human action in context. In S.A. Robertson (Ed.), Contemporary Ergonomics 1995. London: Taylor and Francis, pp. 62–67.

Stanton, N.A., & Baber, C. (1992). Usability and the EC Directive 90/270. *Displays,* **13**, 151–160.

Stanton, N.A., & Baber, C. (1994). The myth of navigating in hypertext. *Journal of Educational Multimedia and Hypermedia,* **3**, 235–250.

Starkson, B.C. (1992). Get a grip on keyboard input. *Proceedings of Computers for Disabled Persons 3rd. International Conference,* pp. 495–498.

Stephens, R.M., Cottle, M.J., Creasey, G.H., Geggie, C.S., & Workman, D.S.

(1988). Text composition using speech recognition and other computer input devices for people with spinal cord injuries. *Proceedings of Speech '88 the 7th. FASE Symposium*. Edinburgh: Institute of acoustics, pp. 337–344.

Stetson, R.H., & Bouman, H.D. (1935). The coordination of simple skilled movements. *Archives Neerlander de Physiologie*, **20**, 177–254.

Stokes, A., & Kic, K. (1994). *Flight Stress*. Aldershot: Avebury.

Stolpmann, M., & Roller, D. (1993). Sketching editor for engineering design. In G. Salvendy and M.J. Smith (Eds), *Human Computer Interaction: Software and Hardware Interfaces*. Amsterdam: North-Holland.

Straub, H.R., & Granaas, M.M. (1993). Task-specific preference for numeric keypads. *Applied Ergonomics 24*, pp. 289–290.

Sturman, D.J., & Zeltzer, D. (1994). A survey of glove-based input. *IEEE Computer Graphics & Applications*, **29**.

Suchman, L. (1987). *Plans and Situated Actions*. Cambridge: Cambridge University Press.

Sutherland, I. (1963). Sketchpad: a man–machine graphical communication system. *Proceedings of the Spring Joint Computer Conference*, pp. 329–346. Washington, DC: Spartan.

Tatham, M. (1992). Voice output for human–machine interaction. In C. Baber and J.M. Noyes (Eds), *Interactive Speech Technology*. London: London: Taylor and Francis.

Taylor, R.G., & Hinson, N. (1988). Individual differences in the use of a pointing device. In E.D. Megaw (Ed.), *Contemporary Ergonomics 1988*. Taylor and Francis, pp. 521–525.

Taylor, R.M. (1989). Integrating voice, visual and manual transactions: some practical issues from aircrew station design. In M.M. Taylor, F. Neél and D.G. Bouwhuis (Eds), *The Structure of Multimodal Dialogue*. Amsterdam: North-Holland.

Teasdale, N., Forget, R., Bard, C., Paillard, J., Fleury, M., & Lamarre, Y. (1993). The role of proprioceptive information for the production of isometric forces and for handwriting tasks. *Acta Psychologica*, **82**, 179–211.

Teichner, W.H., & Krebs, M.J. (1972). Laws of simple visual reaction time. *Psychological Review*, **79**, 344–358.

Tepper, A. (1993). Future assessment by metaphors. *Behaviour and Information Technology*, **12** 336–345.

Teulings, H-L., Thomassen, A.J., & van Galen, G.P. (1983). Preparation of partly cued handwriting units: the size of movement units in handwriting. *Acta Psychologica*, **54**, 165–177.

Thomas, C.M., & Milan, S. (1987). Which input device should be used with interactive video. *Interact '87*. Amsterdam: North-Holland, pp. 587–592.

Thomassen, A.J.W.M., & Schomaker, L.R.B. (1986). Between-letter context effects in handwriting trajectories. In H.S.R. Kao, G.P. van Galen and R. Hoosain (Eds), *Graphonomics: contemporary research in handwriting*. Amsterdam: North-Holland.

Thorisson, K.R., Koons, D.R., & Bolt, R.A. (1992). Multimodal natural dialogue. *CHI '92*. New York: ACM, pp. 653–654.

Tränkle, U., & Deutschmann, D. (1991). Factors influencing speed and precision of cursor positioning using a mouse. *Ergonomics*, **34**, 161–174.

Trist, E.L., & Bamforth, K.W. (1951). Some social and psychological consequences of the Longwall method of coal getting. *Human Relations*, **4**, 6–24.

Underwood, M.J. (1980). What engineers would like to know from psychologists. In J.C. Simon (Ed.), *Spoken Language Generation and Understanding*. Dordrecht: Reidel.

Usher, D.M. (1983). Comparison of a touch-sensitive VDU and computer-aided keypad for plant control. *Displays (July)*, pp. 157–161.

Usher, D.M. (1993). Automatic speech recognition and mobile radio. In C. Baber and J.M. Noyes (Eds), *Interactive Speech Technology*. London: Taylor and France, pp. 73–84.

Usher, D.M., & Baber, C. (1989). *Automatic Speech Recognition in Grid Control Rooms: Part 2. Development and Assessment of a Telecommand Demonstrator*. Bristol: National Power Report TD/STM/89/10081/N.

van Doorn, R.R.A., & Keuss, P.J.G. (1993). Does the production of letter strokes in handwriting benefit from vision? *Acta Psychologica*, **82**, 275–290.

van Galen, G.P. (1990). Phonological and motoric demands in handwriting: evidence for discrete transmissions of information. *Acta Psychologica*, **74**, 259–275.

van Sommers, P. (1984). *Drawing and Cognition: descriptive and experimental studies of graphic production processes*. Cambridge: Cambridge University Press.

Verwey, W.B. (1993). Effects of extended practice in a one-finger keypressing task. *Acta Psychologica*, **84**, 179–197.

Verwey, W.B. (1994). Evidence for the development of concurrent processing in a sequential keypressing task. *Acta Psychologica*, **85**, 245–262.

Vidulich, M.A. (1986). Speech responses and dual task performance: better time sharing or asymmetric transfer? *Human Factors*, **30**, 517–529.

von Gierke, H.E., McCloskey, K., & Albery, W.B. (1991). Military performance in sustained acceleration and vibration environments. In R. Gal and A.D. Mangelsdorf (Eds), *Handbook of Military Psychology*. New York: Wiley.

Vygotsky, L.S. (1978). *Mind in Society: the development of higher psychological processes*. Cambridge: MA: Harvard University Press.

Waddell, G. (1987). A new clinical model for the treatment of low back pain. *Spine*, **12**, 632–644.

Wagner, E. (1988). *The Computer Display Designer's Handbook*. Bromley: Chartwell Brant.

Walker, N., Meyer, D.E., & Smelcer, J.B. (1993). Spatial and temporal characteristics of rapid cursor-positioning movements with electromechanical mice in human–computer interaction. *Human Factors*, **35**, 431–458.

Wallace, V.L. (1976). The semantics of graphical input devices. *Proceedings of SIGGRAPH/SIGPLAN Symposium on Graphical Languages*. New York: ACM, pp. 61–65.

Wann, J., Nimmo-Smith, I., & Wing, A. (1988). Relation between velocity and curvature in movement: equivalence and divergence between a power law and minimum-jerk model. *Journal of Experimental Psychology: Human Perception and Performance*, **14**, 622–637.

Ward, J.L. (1936). A study of typewriter keyboards. *Educational Research Bulletin*, **15**, 243–246.

Wasserman, A.I. (1985). Extending state transition diagrams for the specification of human–computer interaction. *IEEE Transactions on Software Engineering SE-11*, 699–713.

Waterworth, J.A. (1984). Interaction with machines by voice: a telecommunications perspective. *Behaviour and Information Technology*, **3**, 163–177.

Weber, A., Fassler, C., O'Hanlon, J.F., & Grandjean, E. (1980). Psychophysiological effects of repetitive tasks. *Ergonomics*, **23**, 1033–1046.

Weiner, D., & Ganapathy, S.K. (1989). A synthetic visual environment with hand gesturing and voice input. *CHI '89*. New York: ACM, pp. 235–240.

Welch, J.R. (1977). *Automatic Data Entry Analysis*. Rome, NY: Rome Air Development Centre report RADC-TR-77-306.

Welford, A.T. (1968). *Fundamentals of Skill*. London: Methuen.

West, L.J., & Sabban, Y. (1982). Hierarchy of stroking habits at the typewriter. *Journal of Applied Psychology*, **67**, 370–376.

Whitefield, A. (1983). Pointing as an input technique for human–computer interaction. *IEE Colloquium on Future Input Techniques for Man–Machine Interaction*. London: IEE, pp. 1–5.

Whitefield, A. (1986). Human factors aspects of pointing as an input technique in interactive computer systems. *Applied Ergonomics*, **17**, 97–104.

Whitefield, D., Ball, R.G., & Bird, J.M. (1983). Some comparisons of on-display and off-display touch input devices for interaction with computer generated displays. *Ergonomics*, **26**, 1033–1053.

Whiteside, J., Jones, S., Levy, P.S., & Wixon, D. (1985). User performance with command, menu and iconic interfaces. *CHI '85*. New York: ACM, pp. 185–191.

Wickens, C.D. (1980). The structure of attentional resources. In R. Nickerson (Ed.), *Attention and Performance VIII*. Hillsdale, NJ: LEA.

Wickens, C.D. (1992). *Engineering Psychology and Human Performance*. New York: Harper Collins.

Wickens, C.D., & Liu, Y. (1988). Codes and modalities for multiple resources: a success and some qualifications. *Human Factors*, **30**, 599–616.

Wickens, C.D., Sandry, D.L., & Vidulich, M. (1983). Compatibility and resource competition between modalities of input, central processing and output. *Human Factors*, **235**, 227–240.

Wickens, C.D., Vidulich, M., & Sandry-Garza, D. (1984). Principles of S-C-R-compatibility with spatial and verbal tasks: the role of display location and voice interactive display control interfacing. *Human Factors*, **26**, 533–542.

Wickens, C.D., Stokes, A.F., Barnett, B., & Hyman, F. (1991). The effects of stress on pilot judgment in a MIDIS simulator. In O. Svenson and J. Maule (Eds), *Time Pressure and Stress in Human Judgment and Decision Making*. Cambridge: Cambridge University Press.

Wilensky, R.G. (1978). Why John married Mary: understanding stories with recurring goals. *Cognitive Science*, **2**, 235–266.

Wing, A.M., Nimmo-Smith, I., & Eldridge, M.A. (1983). The consistency of cursive letter formation as a function of position in the word. *Acta Psychologica*, **54**, 197–204.

Witelson, S.F. (1974). Hemispheric specialisation for linguistic and nonlinguistic tactual perception using a dichotomous stimulation technique. *Cortex*, **10**, 3–17.

Wolf, C.G. (1990). Understanding handwriting recognition from the user's perspective. *Proceedings of the Human Factors Society 34th. Annual Meeting*. Santa Monica, CA: Human Factors Society, pp. 249–253.

Wolf, C.G. (1992). A comparative study of gestural, keyboard and mouse interfaces. *Behaviour and Information Technology*, **11**, 13–23.

Woodworth, R.S. (1899). The accuracy of voluntary movement. *Psychological Review*, **23**, 1–114.

Woodworth, R.S., & Schlosberg, H. (1954). *Experimental Psychology*. New York: Holt.

Wright, C.E. (1993). Evaluating the special role of time in the control of handwriting. *Acta Psychologica*, **82**, 5–52.

Wyon, D.P. (1974). The effects of moderate heat stress on typewriting performance. *Ergonomics*, **17**, 309–318.

Young, R.P., & Zelaznick, H.N. (1992). The visual control of aiming hand movements to stationary and moving targets. *Acta Psychologica*, **79**, 59–78.

Zhao, R. (1992). Incremental recognition of hand sketched diagrams graphics in gesture interface. In R. Beale and J. Finlay (Eds), *Neural Networks and Pattern Recognition in HCI*. Chichester: Ellis Horwood.

Zhong, Y.Z., Wah, L.E., Gay, R.,, Ye, W.J., & Yuan, L.D. (1990). Elecpaper: an integrated and intelligent user interface system for CAD. In M.J. Smith and G. Salvendy (Eds), *Human–Computer Interaction: Applications and Case Studies*. Amsterdam: Elsevier.

Zimmerman, T.G., Lanier, J., Blanchard, C., Bryson, S., & Harvill, Y. (1987). A hand gesture interface device. *CHI '87*. New York: ACM, pp. 189–192.

Zipp, P., Haider, E., Halpern, N., & Rohmert, W. (1983). Keyboard design through physiological strain measurements. *Applied Ergonomics*, **14**, 117–122.

Zoltan-Ford, E. (1984). Reducing the variability in natural language interactions with computers. *Proceedings of the 28th. Annual Meeting of the Human Factors Society*. Santa Monica, CA: Human Factors Society, pp. 768–772.

Standards referred to in text

BS 5959 (1980). *Specifications for Key Numbering System and Layout Charts for Keyboards on Office Machines*. London: British Standards Institute.

BS 1909 (1963). *Specifications for Key Layout for Numerical Keypads*. London: British Standards Institute.

ISO 4169 (1979). *Office Machines–Keyboards–Keynumbering System and Layout Charts*. Geneva: International Standards Organisation.

ISO 9241 (in draft). *Ergonomic Requirements for Office Work with Visual Display Terminals Part 4: Keyboard Requirements*. Geneva: International Standards Organisation.

ISO/DP 7942 (1983). *Information Processing Graphics Kernel System (GKS) Functional Description*. Geneva: International Standards Organisation.

Index

A

Acceleration 226, 227
Accuracy 59, 60
Adaption 3, 14, 28, 29
Aircraft 48, 68, 215, 220, 227, 262, 265
    271, 274, 275
Air Traffic Control 80
Alphabetic keyboard 28, 33, 44, 151
Alphametric keyboard 32
Auditory feedback 36, 79, 80, 194
Automobiles 7, 227, 265, 274, 275

B

Breaks (rest) 44, 228, 247

C

C:D ratio 97, 98, 189, 195
Chord keyboards 41–43, 45, 149, 218, 219
Classification, of devices 6, 8, 83–104
Cognitive Complexity Theory (CCT)
    130, 131
Command entry 45, 76, 268–271
Command languages 47
Compatibility 98–102, 139, 193, 230
    conceptual *see* Conceptual
        compatibility
    movement *see* Movement
    modality *see* Modality
    operational *see* Operational
    spatial *see* Spatial
Computer-Aided Design (CAD) 87, 131,
    154, 164, 165–168, 257–259, 263,
    274
Concept keyboard 41

Conceptual compatibility 99, 101
Controls 2, 56, 68
Cooperative principle 202
Cursor Keys 38–40, 57, 65
Cursor positioning 64, 65

D

Data entry 57, 75, 80, 83, 150, 227, 265
Data glove 68
Desk space 2, 3, 58, 103, 195
Desktop, metaphor 7, 16
Device characteristics 6, 92, 93
Device use 3, 4, 6, 8, 11, 62
Dialogue 201, 202, 205, 210
Direct manipulation 5, 171, 172, 175,
    266, 269, 276
Direct pointing device 47, 52, 53, 59, 60,
    84, 85, 99, 110
Disability 101, 216–219
Displacement joystick 48, 50, 59, 97–99,
    192, 194, 246
Dragging 53, 61, 87, 88, 111, 114, 177,
    182, 188, 191
Drawing 11, 53, 58, 75, 83, 87, 114, 115,
    153, 155, 156, 161–163, 169, 172
Dvorak keyboard 31–33, 44, 147, 242

E

Ecological validity 10
EEG (electroencephalogram) 70
Electronic mail (email) 260, 261
Electronic paper 73
Environment 10, 11, 16, 55, 69, 79, 96,
    101, 102, 163, 177, 195, 215–231,
    233, 249, 275

Ergonomics 2, 25, 28, 31, 98, 136
Error, device 75, 77–79, 82, 206, 207
Error, human 1, 5, 40, 43, 45, 59, 100, 108,
    119, 129, 132–134, 141–143, 146,
    158, 159, 176, 190, 197, 208, 216
Excursion envelope 155
Eye tracking devices 8, 69, 70

F

Fatigue 32, 245
Feedback 11, 36, 79, 101, 137, 177, 202,
    209, 231
  auditory *see* Auditory feedback
  kinesthetic *see* Kinesthetic feedback
  tactile *see* Tactile feedback
  visual *see* Visual feedback
Fitts' law 108, 112, 115, 118, 178–183,
    191, 192, 195
Force, keying 36, 44
Frustration 3, 246
Function keys 33, 37
Function keyboard 40, 41, 45, 55, 58, 80,
    81

G

Generic actions 73, 84–91, 104, 109, 113,
    129, 134, 188, 252, 265, 275
Gesture 42, 43, 66–68, 69, 76, 98, 119,
    173, 175, 262
  cursive 74, 75
Gesture recognition 8, 66–70, 269, 270
Gloves 68, 72, 219, 220
Goals 10, 11, 16, 75, 110, 128, 157, 172,
    200, 249, 252, 255
Goals-Operators-Methods-Selection
    (GOMS) 126–130, 134
Graphical user interface (GUI) 47, 115

H

Handwriting *see* Writing
Handwriting recognition 2, 76, 77, 157,
    163
Haptic interaction 70, 71

Harpsichords 25, 26
Head movement 68
Hcat 226
Helicopter 7
Hick-Hyman law 138
Hospitals 3, 7
Human communication 6, 66, 77, 202,
    204, 205, 270
Human factors 2, 28, 37, 41, 45, 55, 62,
    71, 81, 119, 195, 219, 220
Human use (of devices) 2, 3, 107, 113,
'Hunt and peck' (typing) 27, 30, 32, 115,
    145

I

Indirect pointing device 47, 52, 59, 60,
    84, 85, 99, 111, 245
Isometric joystick 48, 50, 59, 97–99, 192,
    194, 246

J

Joystick 3, 47–50, 60, 62, 65, 88, 99, 111,
    180, 245
  displacement *see* Displacement
    joystick
  isometric *see* Isometric joystick
  rate-controlled *see* Rate-controlled
    joystick
  spring-loaded *see* Spring-loaded
    joystick

K

Keyboard 16, 25, 46–48, 53, 60, 61, 65,
    66, 72–74, 90, 115, 117, 136, 172,
    215, 233, 262, 266
  alphabetic *see* Alphabetic keyboard
  alphametric *see* Alphametric keyboard
  chord *see* Chord keyboard
  Dvorak *see* Dvorak keyboard
  Kinesis *see* Kinesis keyboard
  Maltron *see* Maltron keyboard
  QWERTY *see* QWERTY keyboard
  Split *see* Split keyboard

Wearable *see* Wearable keyboard
Keystroke Level Model (KLM) 33,
    114–119, 124, 125, 126, 134, 148,
    182
Kinesis keyboard 34, 241, 242
Kinesthetic feedback 9, 36, 48, 155, 157,
    158, 186, 190, 192, 193, 194, 220,
    274
Knowledge 1, 4, 8, 11, 37, 104, 108, 115,
    128, 129, 130, 151, 166, 167,
    175–177, 200, 201, 253, 270

L

Lightpen 3, 4, 49, 53, 55, 59, 60, 91, 97,
    177, 245
'Light handle' 56, 91

M

Maltron keyboard 34
Markov models 120–122, 134
Mediation 9, 12, 15, 254
MIT MediaLab 7, 71, 269
Modality compatibility 99, 273
Models, of user 6, 11, 12, 15, 98,
    107–135, 145–149, 159, 160, 200
Mole 69
Mouse 3, 4, 15, 16, 47, 51, 52, 59, 60, 65,
    66, 70, 74–76, 93, 95, 99, 100,
    111–113, 115, 117, 170, 177, 180,
    188–192, 195, 215, 243–245, 247,
    255, 262, 266, 268, 269
Movement compatibility 99
Multimodal HCI 168, 175, 265–277
Multiple resource theory 271–275, 276
Muscle grouping 3
Musculoskeletal loading 30, 31, 34, 136,
    151, 232, 251

N

Natural HCI 5, 44, 64, 73, 77
Noise 223–225
Numeric keypad 33, 38, 44, 89, 149, 150,
    151, 217

O

Organisational factors 13, 249–264
Operational compatibility 99, 100, 101,
    150

P

Parallax 55, 60, 74
Pen 52, 55, 72–77, 89, 91, 110, 153–169,
    222, 262
Performance Shaping Factors (PSF)
    94–103, 130, 134
Personal Digital Assistant (PDA) 76, 153
Planning 10, 11, 38, 137, 140, 150,
    158–162, 185, 187, 188, 190, 197,
    200, 255
Pointing 170–196, 218, 227
Pointing device 52, 66, 219, 267
    direct *see* Direct pointing device
    indirect *see* Indirect pointing device
Portable computers 7, 16, 48, 53, 65, 97,
    98, 102, 222, 265
Posture 3, 6, 32, 33, 44, 154, 233, 235,
    240, 243, 245, 251
Praxis 13
Public information system 33, 263
Puck 52, 53
'Put that there' 67, 269, 270

Q

QWERTY keyboard 3, 4, 26, 27–31, 48,
    136, 141–143, 218, 222, 242, 247

R

Rate-controlled joystick 48, 50, 65
Reach envelope 220, 243
Remote control handset 67
Roll bar 65

S

Selection (of objects) 37, 65, 68, 59, 86,
    88, 109, 113, 174, 192, 195, 268
Signalling 66, 67, 74

Sign language 68
Signing 66, 68, 74
Sketching 111, 154, 164, 167, 168, 169, 262
Sociotechnical systems 256, 257
Spatial compatibility 39, 99, 100, 139
Speaking 11, 64, 77, 157, 177, 197–211, 224, 265
Speech recognition 3, 7, 8, 73, 77–81, 86, 89, 90, 119, 120, 163, 197–211, 217, 222, 225, 230, 262, 268–271
Split keyboard 34, 44, 240, 241
Spreadsheet 74, 75, 129
Spring-loaded joystick 48
Stress 3, 229, 230, 238
Stylus 7, 52, 53, 55, 74, 111, 153, 154

T

Tablet 47, 52, 53, 59, 61, 65, 73, 91, 97, 110, 186
Tactile feedback 36, 53, 70, 79, 155, 157, 158, 192, 193, 194, 274
Talkwriter 81, 218
Tanks 225, 227
Task analysis 116, 119, 250, 251
Task-artifact cycle 13, 15, 28, 255
Task-fit 57, 275
Task network model 122–125, 134
Telephone 38
Test-Operate-Test-Exit (TOTE) 11
Text entry 41, 64, 90, 218
Theremin 66
Three-state description 109–114
Tool 8, 9, 12, 13, 66, 82, 96, 166, 249, 253, 263, 267, 276
Tool use 9, 10, 12, 13, 16, 177, 254
Tongue operated device 68
Touch pad 52, 55
Touchscreen 3, 4, 49, 53, 55, 58–60, 70, 80, 81, 91, 99, 110, 177, 188–192, 245, 270
Touch-typing 26–31, 115, 129, 235
Trackball 2, 3, 11, 47, 49–51, 53–55, 59, 60, 65, 70, 93, 97–99, 111–113, 117, 177, 108, 188–192, 195, 245, 266

Training 9, 28, 29, 32, 44, 61, 130, 242, 250, 255, 259, 268
Transaction time 37, 72, 73, 107–109, 112, 115, 117, 121, 129, 134
Typewriter 25, 26, 27
Typing 4, 11, 27, 30, 32, 34, 37, 48, 81, 84, 136–152, 157, 158, 171, 177, 183, 200, 219, 226, 238, 240, 265
Typing speed 27, 30, 31–34, 44, 115, 137, 143–145

U

Usability 3, 9, 94, 95, 265

V

Vending machines 263
Vibration 225
Video-games 11, 68, 87, 88, 129
Virtual device 56, 57
Visual feedback 2, 36, 79, 157, 158, 182, 186, 190, 192, 193, 194

W

Wearable keyboard 71
Whiteboard 164, 262
Widgets 91, 109
Window-Icon-Menu-Pointing device (WIMP) 5, 88, 90, 171, 176, 254
Word processing 38, 252
Work domain 1, 10, 16, 28, 61, 102, 226, 238, 249, 256, 263
Workload 32, 101, 195, 224, 229, 230, 233, 247. 273
Work-Related Upper Limb Disorder 3, 31, 44, 228, 232–248, 259
Workstation 7, 16, 251, 265, 267
Writing 11, 27, 64, 76, 153, 154, 157–160, 168, 177

Y

Yerkes-Dodson law 223, 224